Better Homes and Gardens®

CHRISTMAS COOKING

FROM THE HEART™

Holiday Cooking—Then and Now

Meredith® Books
Des Moines, Iowa

All of us at Meredith® Books are dedicated to providing you with information and ideas to enhance your home. We welcome your comments and suggestions. Write to us at: Meredith Books Editorial Department, 1716 Locust St., Des Moines, IA 50309-3023.

Christmas Cooking from the Heart 2006 is available by mail. To order editions from past years, call 800/627-5490.

Cover Photograph:
Blaine Moats
Pictured: Mocha and Cherry Cake, page 88; Sugar Cookie Star Cutouts, page 96; Cherry-Nut Rum Balls, page 102; White Christmas Cherry-Almond Fudge, page 116; and Buttery Cashew Brittle, page 118.

Back Cover Photograph:
Apple-Cranberry Deep-Dish Pie, page 80

Better Homes and Gardens®
CHRISTMAS COOKING
FROM THE HEART™

Editor: Jessica Saari
Contributing Editor: Winifred Moranville
Contributing Recipe Developers: Tami Leonard, Shelli McConnell, Jennifer Peterson
Assistant Art Director: Todd Emerson Hanson
Copy Chief: Terri Fredrickson
Publishing Operations Manager: Karen Schirm
Senior Editor, Asset and Information Manager: Phillip Morgan
Edit and Design Production Coordinator: Mary Lee Gavin
Editorial Assistant: Cheryl Eckert
Book Production Managers: Pam Kvitne, Marjorie J. Schenkelberg, Rick von Holdt, Mark Weaver
Contributing Copy Editor: Carol DeMasters
Contributing Proofreaders: Judy Friedman, Gretchen Kauffman, Susan J. Kling
Contributing Indexer: Elizabeth Parson
Test Kitchen Director: Lynn Blanchard
Test Kitchen Product Supervisors: Juli Hale, Jill Moberly

Meredith® Books
Executive Director, Editorial: Gregory H. Kayko
Executive Director, Design: Matt Strelecki
Managing Editor: Amy Tincher-Durik
Senior Editor/Group Manager: Jan Miller
Senior Associate Design Director: Ken Carlson
Marketing Product Manager: Gina Rickert

Publisher and Editor in Chief: James D. Blume
Editorial Director: Linda Raglan Cunningham
Executive Director, Marketing: Steve Malone
Executive Director, New Business Development: Todd M. Davis
Executive Director, Sales: Ken Zagor
Director, Operations: George A. Susral
Director, Production: Douglas M. Johnston
Director, Marketing: Amy Nichols
Business Director: Jim Leonard

Vice President and General Manager: Douglas J. Guendel

Better Homes and Gardens® Magazine
Deputy Editor, Food and Entertaining: Nancy Wall Hopkins

Meredith Publishing Group
President: Jack Griffin
Executive Vice President: Bob Mate
Vice President, Corporate Solutions: Michael Brownstein
Vice President, Creative Services: Ellen de Lathouder
Vice President, Manufacturing: Bruce Heston
Vice President, Finance and Administration: Karla Jeffries
Consumer Product Associate Marketing Director: Steve Swanson
Consumer Product Marketing Manager: Wendy Merical
Business Manager: Darren Tollefson
Database Project Director: Chuck Howell

Meredith Corporation
Chairman and Chief Executive Officer: William T. Kerr
President and Chief Operating Officer: Steve Lacy

In Memoriam: E. T. Meredith III (1933–2003)

Table of Contents

Introduction 4

Favorite Holiday Feasts 6

Greatest Appetizer Hits 32

Brightest and Best
  Breakfasts and Brunches 52

Enduring and Endearing
  Holiday Breads 66

Unforgettable Desserts 78

80 Years of Amazing Cookies 92

Gifts for the Season 112

Favorite Fireside Suppers 124

New Year's Eve—
  Then and Now 134

Chalet Cookie Church 144

Terrific Party and
  Potluck Dishes 148

Chalet Cookie
  Church Patterns 156

Index 157

Buttery Cider Glazed Turkey, page 12

The holiday season has always been about food, family, and friends—both yesterday and today.

*Christmas Cooking from the Heart*ℳ takes a loving look back—through 80 years of books and magazines in the Better Homes and Gardens® family of publications—to find the very best holiday recipes throughout the decades. Here, these all-time favorites are presented alongside some of the most exciting recipes from recent years. Chosen from over 60,000 recipes in the files of the Better Homes and Gardens® publications, this collection includes all the holiday favorites—from yesterday and today; they're the dishes the Test Kitchen pros and food editors serve for their own families when it's time to turn off the office computers, cool down the Test Kitchen stoves, and head home for the holidays.

When you think about the dishes you bring to your table for your most memorable holiday gatherings, aren't they usually a mix of recipes old and new? This is the season you pull out that tattered and yellowed, batter-stained recipe card—written in your grandmother's graceful penmanship—for that homespun dessert your family has cherished for decades. It's also the time of year when you flip through glossy magazines, browse the Internet, and catch a few cooking shows to find all-new ideas that feature today's most exciting trends in ingredients and cooking techniques.

Look for dozens of time-honored classics, including heirloom recipes that your grandmother may have made. Scalloped Spinach, Turnips au Gratin, Creamed Onions, Peanut Waffles with Butterscotch Sauce, Feather Rolls, Apple-Cranberry Deep-Dish Pie, Cherry Winks, Pecan Crispies—so many great recipes span the decades as oldies but goodies that have stood the test of time. The selection even includes Best-Ever Chocolate Cake, the dessert that has been deemed the most luscious and chocolaty cake in the history of Test Kitchen cakes.

When you're in the mood for some fascinating new flavors from today, keep browsing. Orange-Fennel Autumn Salad, Crab and Poblano Soup, Curried Chutney and Cheddar Cheese Logs, Twice-Baked Jarlsberg Potatoes, French Pistachio Buttercreams, Very Berry Martinis, Calypso Shrimp Skewers—many of these new recipes call on fascinating global ingredients that have become more widely available than in your grandmothers' day. Or they simply call on new ideas and combinations that help you bring a world of bold, rich flavors to your holiday table.

Also look for the "Then" and "Now" icons in every chapter (see examples, below). Here, one cherished recipe is spotlighted alongside a brand-new takeoff, inspired by the original but tweaked in tempting new ways. For example, cooks always have enjoyed the way Harvard Beets add color and sparkle to the holiday table—what a classic! But if you're looking for a new way to approach beets, try Sweet Glazed Beets with Crème Fraîche. Diners may have swooned over your grandmother's Baked Apples—and they'll swoon for yours too! But if you want to amp up the flavors a notch, go for Molasses-Fig Baked Apples—a sensational twist on the original favorite.

You'll enjoy seeing how cooks from yesterday inspire cooks from today and how what goes around comes around—in delicious, all-new ways.

Whether you choose a recipe from 1936 or 2006, rest assured that it will be something you'll be proud to share. That's because every one of these all-time favorites has gone through the same testing process that all new recipes do. While some of yesterday's favorites may have been updated slightly for today's cooking techniques and tastes, you can be equally sure that each retains the personality and flavor of its era. Enjoy this journey through the years and let these best-of-the-best recipes become your holiday favorites, now and for years to come.

The "Then" icon symbolizes that a recipe is a cherished favorite from years past. The "Now" icon symbolizes that a dish is an updated takeoff of the "Then" recipe, which has been tastefully tweaked and given a modern twist.

Chocolate-Mousse Torte, page 88; Sugar Cookie Star Cutouts, page 96; and Cherry-Nut Rum Balls, page 102

Favorite Holiday Feasts

For eight decades, the pages in the Better Homes and Gardens® family of publications have helped readers bring their very best to the holiday table. The salad, main dish, and side dish recipes here span the generations—from the simple and creamy Turnips au Gratin that your grandmother might have made in the 1930s to some terrific roasts from the '60s. Yet this chapter is not all about nostalgia! Look for a poached-egg-topped salad (a current darling in trendy bistros), a poblano-flecked crab bisque, a zesty ribeye roast, and other wonderfully contemporary recipes too.

Cherry Glazed Pork, page 14

Orange-Fennel Autumn Salad

The ingredients in this salad travel well beyond the usual salad greens, and the creamy citrus dressing brings four intense flavors together in perfect harmony.

Start to Finish: 30 minutes
Makes: 8 side-dish servings

- 1 large fennel bulb
- 4 ounces fresh baby spinach, stems removed (about 3 cups lightly packed spinach)
- 3 cups torn radicchio
- 3 seedless oranges or clementines, peeled and thinly sliced
- 1 recipe Citrus-Yogurt Dressing

1. If desired, snip some of the fennel leaves for a garnish; set aside. Core and thinly slice fennel bulb (to yield about 2½ cups sliced fennel).

2. In a large bowl combine sliced fennel, spinach, radicchio, and orange. Drizzle with Citrus-Orange Dressing; toss gently. If desired, garnish with snipped fennel leaves.

Orange-Fennel Autumn Salad

Citrus-Yogurt Dressing: In a small bowl whisk together ⅓ cup mayonnaise, light mayonnaise, or salad dressing; ⅓ cup plain yogurt; 2 tablespoons frozen orange juice concentrate; and, if desired, 1 tablespoon Pernod (licorice-flavor) liqueur.

Per serving: 118 cal., 8 g total fat (1 g sat. fat), 4 mg chol., 85 mg sodium, 11 g carbo., 2 g fiber, 2 g pro.

Then Wilted Spinach Salad

In earlier decades spinach salads tossed with hot dressings were a popular dish often prepared tableside in formal restaurants. The Better Homes and Gardens® Test Kitchen was quick to adapt the concept to a dish that could easily be made at home.

Start to Finish: 25 minutes
Makes: 8 side-dish servings

- 12 cups torn fresh spinach
- 2 cups sliced fresh mushrooms
- ½ cup thinly sliced green onion
- 6 slices bacon
- ½ cup vinegar
- 4 teaspoons sugar
- 1 teaspoon dry mustard
- 2 hard-cooked eggs (see note, page 24), peeled and chopped

1. In a very large bowl combine spinach, mushrooms, and green onion. If desired, sprinkle with *ground black pepper*; set aside.

2. For dressing, in a 12-inch skillet cook bacon until crisp. Remove bacon, reserving ¼ cup drippings in skillet (add *salad oil*, if necessary). (Or, if desired, substitute ¼ cup salad oil for bacon drippings.) Drain bacon on paper towels. Crumble bacon; set aside. Stir vinegar, sugar, and dry mustard into drippings in skillet. Bring to boiling; remove from heat. Add the spinach mixture. Toss mixture in skillet for 30 to 60 seconds or until spinach wilts.

3. Transfer mixture to a serving dish. Add crumbled bacon and chopped egg; toss to combine. Serve salad immediately.

Per serving: 128 cal., 11 g total fat (4 g sat. fat), 63 mg chol., 150 mg sodium, 4 g carbo., 4 g fiber, 5 g pro.

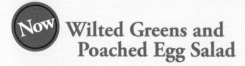

Wilted Greens and Poached Egg Salad

A green salad topped with a poached egg is a classic French bistro dish that is a hot trend in casual American bistros. Choose this irresistible starter when you want to kick off dinner with a dazzler.

Prep: 25 minutes **Cook:** 30 minutes
Makes: 8 servings

<table>
<tr><td>8</td><td>ounces pancetta or 6 slices bacon, cut into small pieces</td></tr>
<tr><td>2</td><td>tablespoons cooking oil</td></tr>
<tr><td>8</td><td>ounces fresh asparagus, trimmed and bias-sliced into 1-inch pieces</td></tr>
<tr><td>¼</td><td>cup sliced green onion</td></tr>
<tr><td>2</td><td>cloves garlic, minced</td></tr>
<tr><td>½</td><td>cup bottled mango chutney</td></tr>
<tr><td>¼</td><td>cup white wine vinegar or cider vinegar</td></tr>
<tr><td>½</td><td>teaspoon dry mustard</td></tr>
<tr><td>8</td><td>eggs</td></tr>
<tr><td>2</td><td>cups shredded radicchio</td></tr>
<tr><td>12</td><td>cups torn butter lettuce, green or red leaf lettuce, and/or romaine
Sliced almonds, toasted (optional)</td></tr>
</table>

1. In a 12-inch skillet cook pancetta over medium heat until crisp. Using a slotted spoon, transfer pancetta to paper towels, reserving 2 tablespoons drippings in skillet. Add oil to skillet. Cook asparagus, green onion, and garlic in hot oil just until asparagus is crisp-tender; remove from heat. Stir in chutney, vinegar, and dry mustard.

2. Lightly grease a medium skillet. Half fill the skillet with water. Bring water to boiling; reduce heat to simmering (bubbles should begin to break the surface of the water). Break one of the eggs into a measuring cup. Carefully slide egg into simmering water, holding the lip of the cup as close to the water as possible. Repeat with three more of the eggs, allowing each egg an equal amount of space. Simmer eggs, uncovered, for 3 to 5 minutes or until the whites are completely set and yolks begin to thicken but are not hard. Remove eggs with a slotted spoon; keep warm. Repeat with remaining 4 eggs.

3. When ready to serve, return asparagus mixture to the heat and bring to boiling. Add radicchio to skillet and cook for 1 to 2 minutes or until it begins to wilt. Add remaining greens in batches, tossing for

Wilted Greens and Poached Egg Salad

30 to 60 seconds or just until wilted. Add pancetta; toss to combine. Divide greens mixture among eight salad plates; top with warm poached eggs. If desired, sprinkle individual servings with toasted sliced almonds. Serve immediately.

Per serving: 252 cal., 18 g total fat (5 g sat. fat), 232 mg chol., 641 mg sodium, 10 g carbo., 2 g fiber, 12 g pro.

Pancetta

A little pancetta (pan-CHEH-tuh) goes a long way to add flavor to recipes. It is just one of the many terrific products from Italy—foods that are more widely available than ever before.

Pancetta is an Italian-style bacon that's made from the belly (or pancia) of a hog. Unlike bacon, pancetta is not smoked but seasoned with pepper and other spices and cured with salt. Pancetta often is sold packaged in a sausagelike roll. Look for pancetta in well-stocked supermarkets, Italian grocery stores, and specialty food shops. In a pinch, substitute regular bacon.

Crab and Poblano Soup, page 11

 **Crab Bisque**

Many great shortcut recipes start by opening a can of soup. Here two different soups combine for an elegant bisque that takes only 20 minutes to make—a perfect dish to start off the holiday feast.

Start to Finish: 20 minutes **Makes:** 6 servings

- 1 10¾-ounce can condensed cream of asparagus soup
- 1 10¾-ounce can condensed cream of mushroom soup
- 2¾ cups milk
- 1 cup half-and-half or light cream
- 1 6½-ounce can crabmeat, drained, flaked, and cartilage removed, or one 6-ounce package frozen crabmeat, thawed
- 3 tablespoons dry sherry or milk

1. In a large saucepan combine cream of asparagus soup, cream of mushroom soup, milk, and half-and-half. Cook over medium heat until boiling, stirring frequently.

2. Stir in crabmeat and sherry; heat through.

Per serving: 227 cal., 12 g total fat (6 g sat. fat), 63 mg chol., 921 mg sodium, 16 g carbo., 1 g fiber, 12 g pro.

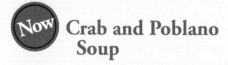

Crab and Poblano Soup

Once hard to find, authentic Mexican ingredients are now more widely available than ever before. Mexican cheese and poblano chile peppers come together to enliven this starter soup.

Start to Finish: 30 minutes
Makes: 8 appetizer servings

- 2 fresh poblano chile peppers, seeded and chopped*
- 1 medium red sweet pepper, seeded and chopped
- ½ cup chopped onion
- 2 cloves garlic, minced
- ¼ cup butter or margarine
- ¼ cup all-purpose flour
- ¼ teaspoon salt
- ¼ teaspoon ground black pepper
- 1 14-ounce can chicken broth
- 2 cups milk
- 6 ounces asadero cheese or quesadilla queso, shredded (1½ cups)
- 1 6½-ounce can lump crabmeat, drained, or 8 ounces fresh lump crabmeat, picked over and cut into bite-size pieces
- 1 recipe Fresh Tomato Salsa
- 1 recipe Crisp Tortilla Strips (optional)

1. In a large saucepan cook chile pepper, sweet pepper, onion, and garlic in hot butter until tender, stirring occasionally. Stir in flour, salt, and black pepper. Add broth all at once, stirring to combine. Cook and stir until thickened and bubbly; cook and stir for 1 minute more.

2. Reduce heat to medium-low. Stir in milk and cheese. Cook and stir for 3 to 5 minutes more or until cheese melts. Stir in crabmeat; heat through.

3. To serve, ladle soup into warm bowls. Top with Fresh Tomato Salsa. If desired, serve with Crisp Tortilla Strips.

Fresh Tomato Salsa: In a small bowl stir together 3 roma tomatoes, seeded and chopped; 1 green onion, thinly sliced; 1 tablespoon snipped fresh cilantro; 2 teaspoons lime juice; and 1 teaspoon fresh jalapeño chile pepper, seeded and finely chopped.* Season to taste with salt and ground black pepper.

*Note: Because chile peppers contain volatile oils that can burn your skin and eyes, avoid direct contact with them as much as possible. When working with chile peppers, wear plastic or rubber gloves. If your bare hands do touch the peppers, wash your hands and nails well with soap and warm water.

Per serving: 204 cal., 12 g total fat (8 g sat. fat), 60 mg chol., 665 mg sodium, 11 g carbo., 1 g fiber, 14 g pro.

Crisp Tortilla Strips: Preheat oven to 350°F. Roll up each of 3 flour tortillas; slice crosswise, which will result in long thin strips. Lightly coat tortilla strips with nonstick cooking spray and spread on a baking sheet. Bake about 5 minutes or until golden. Cool completely.

Potluck Christmas

When friends and family offer to bring food to the holiday table, don't be afraid to let them! This way you'll get a wide assortment of textures and flavors without the added cost and work. It's important to be specific when suggesting foods guests can bring, ensuring dishes are totable and complement other dishes. Here are some suggestions for a foolproof potluck celebration:

• Suggest a theme for the dinner party, such as traditional holiday foods (Figgy Pudding, anyone?), Christmas foods from around the world, or memorable holiday favorites from each guest's childhood.

• Instead of being vague by asking guests to bring some sort of side dish or dessert, request specific foods, such as stuffing or apple pie. This will prevent an all-green-bean-casserole buffet but still allow for some creative freedom.

• Whenever possible, suggest guests bring recipes that require little or no last-minute preparation once they arrive. Ask guests if they need refrigerator or oven space and then prepare accordingly. If utensils or equipment accompany the dish, make sure guests label them with their names.

Buttery Cider Glazed Turkey

Buttery Cider Glazed Turkey

Get ready for some "ooohs" and "aaahs" as you bring this golden-brown beauty to your holiday table. And wait until your guests taste it! They'll love the way turkey and apples combine to create a double dose of moist, well-seasoned taste.

Prep: 45 minutes **Roast:** 3¼ hours
Stand: 15 minutes **Oven:** 325°F
Makes: 16 servings

1 12- to 14-pound turkey
4 cloves garlic, peeled and halved
1 small onion, peeled and cut into wedges
7 medium or 9 small baking apples, cored
    and each cut into 8 wedges (such as
    Golden Delicious, Granny Smith,
    Winesap, or Braeburn)
2 tablespoons butter, melted
2 tablespoons lemon juice
2 cups apple cider or apple juice
5 sticks cinnamon (each about
    3 inches long), broken
⅓ cup butter

⅓ cup packed brown sugar
1 teaspoon dried thyme, crushed
⅓ cup all-purpose flour
    Chicken broth
    Fresh fruit (optional)

1. Preheat oven to 325°F. Season the inside of the turkey cavity generously with *salt* and *ground black pepper*. Rub one of the cut garlic cloves on inside cavity. Place remaining garlic, the onion, and wedges from one of the apples in cavity.

2. Pull turkey skin to back; fasten with skewer. If a band of skin crosses the tail, tuck drumsticks under band. If no band, tie drumsticks securely to tail with 100%-cotton string. Twist wing tips under back. Brush turkey with the 2 tablespoons melted butter. Season with salt and pepper.

3. Place bird, breast side up, on a rack in a shallow roasting pan. Insert an oven-safe meat thermometer into the center of one of the inside thigh muscles, making sure the bulb does not touch bone. Cover bird loosely with foil. Roast for 2½ to 3½ hours or until thermometer registers 160°F. (Cut band of skin or string between drumsticks after 2½ hours.) Toss remaining apple wedges with the lemon juice. Place apples around turkey. Continue to roast, covered with foil, for 30 minutes more.

4. Meanwhile, in a small saucepan combine apple cider and stick cinnamon. Bring to boiling; reduce heat. Boil steadily about 30 minutes or until cider is reduced to ⅔ cup. Add the ⅓ cup butter, the brown sugar, and thyme. Heat and stir until sugar is dissolved. Remove and discard stick cinnamon.

5. Remove foil from turkey; brush turkey and drizzle apples with the cider mixture. Continue roasting, uncovered, 15 to 20 minutes more or until meat thermometer registers 180°F, brushing bird and drizzling cider mixture over fruit every 10 minutes. Remove turkey from oven; discard garlic, onion, and apple from cavity. Transfer turkey to a large serving platter. Surround with apple wedges from roasting pan. Cover with foil; let stand for 15 to 20 minutes.

6. Meanwhile, pour pan drippings into a large measuring cup. Scrape the browned bits from the pan into the measuring cup. Skim and reserve fat from the drippings. Pour ¼ cup of the reserved fat into a medium saucepan (discard remaining fat). Stir in flour. Add enough broth to remaining drippings to measure 2½ cups liquid; add broth mixture all at once to flour mixture. Cook and stir over medium heat until thickened and bubbly. Cook and stir for 1 minute. Season with salt and pepper.

7. Carve turkey. If desired, garnish platter with fresh fruit. Serve turkey with gravy on the side.

Per serving: 544 cal., 26 g total fat (9 g sat. fat), 196 mg chol., 359 mg sodium, 18 g carbo., 2 g fiber, 55 g pro.

Berry-Burgundy Glazed Ham

This recipe took top prize in a 1969 Prize Tested Recipes contest from Better Homes and Gardens® *magazine. Almost four decades later, it is still a flavor-packed way to embellish ham for the holidays.*

Prep: 20 minutes **Bake:** 2¼ hours
Oven: 325°F **Makes:** 32 servings

    1 10- to 14-pound bone-in cooked ham
    1 teaspoon whole cloves
    1 16-ounce can whole cranberry sauce
    ½ cup packed brown sugar
    ½ cup burgundy or other dry red wine
    1 tablespoon yellow mustard

1. Preheat oven to 325°F. Score ham in a diamond pattern by making shallow diagonal cuts at 1-inch intervals; stud with whole cloves. Place ham, fat side up, on rack in a shallow roasting pan. Insert an oven-safe meat thermometer into the center of the ham, making sure the bulb does not touch bone. Bake for 2¼ to 2¾ hours or until thermometer registers 140°F.

2. In a medium saucepan combine cranberry sauce, brown sugar, wine, and mustard. Bring to boiling; reduce heat. Simmer, uncovered, for 15 minutes. Cover; keep warm. Brush ½ cup of the sauce over ham for the last 15 minutes of roasting. Serve ham with remaining sauce on the side.

Per serving: 224 cal., 10 g total fat (3 g sat. fat), 65 mg chol., 1,488 mg sodium, 13 g carbo., 2 g fiber, 19 g pro.

Cranberry-Ginger Relish

Freshen the relish at your next holiday gathering by making it from scratch (it's a cinch!) with fresh cranberries and fresh ginger for extra zest. This is a succulent addition to poultry or pork.

Prep: 10 minutes **Cook:** 15 minutes
Makes: about 3 cups

    1 12-ounce bag fresh cranberries (3 cups)
    1½ cups orange juice
    1 cup sugar
    2 tablespoons grated fresh ginger

1. In a small saucepan combine cranberries, orange juice, sugar, and ginger. Bring mixture boiling, stirring to dissolve sugar; reduce heat. Simmer, uncovered, for 15 minutes. Serve warm or chilled.

Per ¼-cup serving: 90 cal., 0 g total fat (0 g sat. fat), 0 mg chol., 1 mg sodium, 23 g carbo., 1 g fiber, 0 g pro.

Berry-Burgundy Glazed Ham

 **Pork Roast with Harvest Fruits**

Flavorful pork shoulder is braised in balsamic vinegar and red wine, a combo that balances the sweetness of the fruit. One of the ingredients, quince, is a yellow-skinned fruit that resembles both a pear and an apple in flavor and appearance. This fruit can be found in supermarkets from October to December.

Prep: 30 minutes **Roast:** 3 hours **Oven:** 325°F
Makes: 8 to 10 servings

- 1 5- to 6-pound boneless pork shoulder roast, trimmed and tied to retain its shape
- 3 tablespoons olive oil
- 1 large yellow onion, finely chopped
- 1½ cups pitted dried plums (prunes) and/or dried apricots
- 1½ cups dried figs, halved
- 1 quince, peeled, cored, and coarsely chopped (optional)
- 1 cup balsamic vinegar
- 1 cup dry red wine
- 3 bay leaves
- 2 tablespoons snipped fresh rosemary or 2 teaspoons dried rosemary, crushed
- 4 medium apples (such as Granny Smith), peeled, cored, and quartered

In Praise of Pork Shoulder

In decades past, pork shoulder has been ignored in favor of leaner cuts such as pork loin. Taking the lead from bistro chefs, who favor the hearty, fork-tender appeal of this rich, bold meat, home cooks now enjoy this inexpensive cut.

The trick to coaxing the tough cut into a tender beauty is in braising it. Braising is a method of slow cooking food in a small amount of liquid in a covered pan. It can be done either on the stovetop or in the oven. The moist-heat treatment loosens the fibers and makes the fat melt into the meat, creating tender cuts that yield to a butter knife.

1. Preheat oven to 325°F. In a 6- to 8-quart oval roasting pan brown meat on all sides in hot oil. Remove the meat from the pan and pour off all but 2 tablespoons of the drippings. Sprinkle meat lightly with *salt* and freshly ground *black pepper;* set aside. Reduce the heat to medium.

2. Add the onion to hot drippings; cook about 5 minutes or until tender. Add dried plums, figs, quince (if desired), vinegar, wine, bay leaves, and rosemary. Bring to boiling; cook for 1 minute. Remove pan from heat.

3. Return the meat to the pan; cover. Roast for 2¾ hours. Add apple. Cover and roast about 15 minutes more or until meat and apple are tender. Using a slotted spoon, remove the meat and the fruit from the pan; cover meat and fruit loosely with foil and keep warm. Discard bay leaves.

4. For sauce, place pan on stovetop and cook, uncovered, over medium-high heat about 15 minutes or until the liquid is reduced to 1¼ cups, stirring and scraping up any browned bits.

5. To serve, slice pork and arrange it on a platter with the fruit. Spoon some of the sauce over the pork. Pass remaining sauce.

Per serving: 724 cal., 22 g total fat (7 g sat. fat), 183 mg chol., 394 mg sodium, 67 g carbo., 8 g fiber, 59 g pro.

 Cherry Glazed Pork

This recipe hails from the 1960s and will make a lovely holiday entrée if you prefer not to serve the traditional turkey. Present it with Turnips au Gratin (page 22), circa 1932, and the modern Orange-Fennel Autumn Salad (page 8) for a menu that spans the decades.

Prep: 25 minutes **Roast:** 1½ hours
Stand: 15 minutes **Oven:** 325°F
Makes: 8 servings

- 1 3-pound boneless pork loin roast (single loin)
  Salt
  Ground black pepper
- 1 12-ounce jar cherry preserves
- ¼ cup red wine vinegar

Cherry Glazed Pork

2 tablespoons light-colored corn syrup
¼ teaspoon ground cinnamon
¼ teaspoon ground nutmeg
¼ teaspoon ground cloves
¼ teaspoon salt
¼ cup slivered almonds, toasted

1. Preheat oven to 325°F. Rub roast with salt and pepper. Place the roast on a rack in a shallow roasting pan. Roast, uncovered, for 1½ to 1¾ hours or until an instant-read thermometer inserted in the center of the roast registers 155°F.

2. Meanwhile, for glaze, in a small saucepan combine cherry preserves, red wine vinegar, corn syrup, cinnamon, nutmeg, cloves, and the ¼ teaspoon salt. Cook and stir until mixture boils; reduce heat. Simmer, uncovered, for 3 to 5 minutes or until sauce is slightly thickened. Stir in almonds. Keep the sauce warm.

3. Spoon some of the glaze over the roast for the last 5 minutes of roasting. Cover meat with foil; let stand for 15 minutes. The temperature of the meat after standing should be 160°F. Reheat remaining glaze. Spoon some of the warm glaze over the meat; pass remaining glaze with meat.

Per serving: 395 cal., 10 g total fat (3 g sat. fat), 107 mg chol., 254 mg sodium, 34 g carbo., 1 g fiber, 39 g pro.

Celebration Roast

Savory, succulent—and very, very special—a beef ribeye roast is a sensational way to indulge family and friends at the holidays. A horseradish, garlic, and pepper rub adds a zesty coating.

Prep: 25 minutes **Roast:** 1¾ hours
Stand: 15 minutes **Oven:** 350°F
Makes: 12 to 16 servings

    2 tablespoons cream-style
       prepared horseradish
    4 cloves garlic, minced
    4 to 5 teaspoons cracked black pepper
    ½ teaspoon salt
    1 4- to 6-pound boneless beef ribeye roast
    8 medium onions
    6 small red and/or white onions (optional)
    1 tablespoon olive oil
    1 recipe Horseradish-Peppercorn Cream
       (optional)

1. Preheat oven to 350°F. In a small bowl stir together horseradish, garlic, 3 teaspoons of the cracked peppercorns, and the salt. Rub horseradish mixture onto roast. Place roast, fat side up, on a rack in a shallow roasting pan. Insert an oven-safe meat thermometer into the center of the roast. Roast, uncovered, until desired doneness. For medium-rare doneness, allow 1¾ to 2 hours or until thermometer registers 135°F. For medium doneness, allow 2 to 2½ hours or until thermometer registers 150°F. Remove roast from oven. Cover with foil; let stand for 15 minutes. The temperature of the meat after standing should be 145°F for medium-rare doneness or 160°F for medium doneness.

2. Meanwhile, slice root ends off onions (if using; so onions will stand upright). Brush onions with olive oil. Sprinkle with remaining 1 to 2 teaspoons cracked peppercorns. For the last 1¼ hours of the roasting time, arrange onions upright around roast.

3. To serve, slice meat. If desired, serve Horseradish-Peppercorn Cream and onions with roast.

Per serving: 294 cal., 16 g total fat (7 g sat. fat), 89 mg chol., 199 mg sodium, 5 g carbo., 1 g fiber, 31 g pro.

Horseradish-Peppercorn Cream: In a medium mixing bowl beat ½ cup whipping cream with an electric mixer on medium speed just until soft peaks form (tips curl). Fold in 2 tablespoons cream-style prepared horseradish and 1 teaspoon Dijon-style mustard. If not using immediately, cover and store horseradish mixture in the refrigerator for up to 6 hours. To serve, sprinkle with 1 to 2 tablespoons cracked pink and black peppercorns. Makes about 1 cup sauce.

Goldilocks Potatoes

Yukon gold potatoes and a sprinkle of cheese give these luscious potatoes their appealing color and cute name. The irresistible richness of these potatoes is worthy of the holiday season.

Prep: 15 minutes **Bake:** 20 minutes
Oven: 350°F **Makes:** 4 servings

    2 pounds Yukon gold or other potatoes,
       peeled and cut up
    ½ teaspoon salt
    ⅛ teaspoon ground black pepper
       Milk (optional)
    ½ cup whipping cream
    ⅓ cup shredded American or cheddar cheese

1. Preheat oven to 350°F. In a large covered saucepan cook potato in enough boiling water to cover for 15 to 20 minutes or until tender; drain. Mash with a potato masher or beat with an electric mixer on low speed. Season with the salt and pepper. If necessary, add a small amount of milk to reach desired consistency.

2. Grease four 10- to 12-ounce individual casseroles or a 1- to 1½-quart casserole. Spoon potato mixture into prepared casserole(s). In a chilled mixing bowl beat whipping cream with chilled beaters of an electric mixer on medium speed until soft peaks form (tips curl); fold in cheese. Spoon cheese mixture over potato. Place casserole(s) on a baking sheet. Bake about 20 minutes or until light brown and heated through.

Per serving: 281 cal., 15 g total fat (9 g sat. fat), 52 mg chol., 484 mg sodium, 32 g carbo., 3 g fiber, 7 g pro.

Goldilocks Potatoes

Candied Mashed Sweet Potatoes

Classic candied sweet potato bake gains a sophisticated update with a splash of liqueur in this recipe. Try orange liqueur for a nice flavor contrast; praline liqueur will intensify the nutty sweetness of the other ingredients.

Prep: 30 minutes **Bake:** 1¾ hours
Cool: 20 minutes **Oven:** 350°F
Makes: 12 side-dish servings

  5 **pounds sweet potatoes**
  ½ **cup chopped pecans**
  ¼ **cup granulated sugar**
  1 **tablespoon butter or margarine**
  2 **tablespoons milk**
  2 **tablespoons orange liqueur, praline liqueur, or milk**
  2 **tablespoons butter or margarine, softened**
  2 **tablespoons packed brown sugar**
  1 **teaspoon salt**
  ¾ **teaspoon pumpkin pie spice**

1. Preheat oven to 350°F. Wash sweet potatoes and pierce several times with a fork. Place sweet potatoes into a foil-lined 15×10×1-inch baking pan. Bake for 1¼ to 1½ hours or until tender. Cool about 20 minutes.

2. Meanwhile, butter a sheet of foil and lightly grease a 2-quart rectangular baking dish; set aside. For candied pecans, in a heavy small skillet combine pecans, granulated sugar, and the 1 tablespoon butter; cook and stir over medium heat for 4 to 6 minutes or until sugar melts and turns golden brown. (Do not overcook.) Immediately remove from heat and spread nut mixture onto prepared foil. Cool completely; break into small pieces. Set aside.

3. Remove peel from sweet potatoes; discard peel. Place sweet potato pulp into a very large bowl; mash pulp by hand or beat with an electric mixer on medium speed until nearly smooth. Stir in milk, liqueur, the 2 tablespoons butter, the brown sugar, salt, and pumpkin pie spice. Beat until fluffy. Spread mixture into prepared baking dish.

4. Bake for 30 to 40 minutes or until heated through. Sprinkle with candied pecans before serving.

Make-Ahead Tip: Prepare as directed through step 3. Wrap candied pecans in plastic wrap; store at room temperature for up to 3 days. Cover unbaked casserole with foil. Store in the refrigerator for up to 3 days. Preheat oven to 350°F. Bake covered dish for 20 minutes. Uncover and bake for 30 to 40 minutes more or until heated through. Sprinkle with candied pecans before serving.

Per serving: 206 cal., 6 g total fat (2 g sat. fat), 8 mg chol., 287 mg sodium, 35 g carbo., 5 g fiber, 3 g pro.

Make-Ahead Mashed Potatoes

Sometimes a recipe garners "favorite" status not only because it tastes great, but also because it makes life easier. With this recipe, you can forget last-minute potato mashing and gravy making. This is a simple make-ahead dish so rich you don't need gravy.

Prep: 50 minutes **Chill:** 6 hours
Bake: 1⅓ hours **Oven:** 350°F
Makes: about 12 side-dish servings

  5 **pounds baking potatoes**
  1 **8-ounce package cream cheese, softened**
  1 **8-ounce carton dairy sour cream**
  1 **teaspoon salt**
  1 **teaspoon dried parsley flakes**
  ½ **teaspoon garlic powder**
  ¼ **teaspoon ground black pepper**
  2 **tablespoons butter or margarine, cut up**

1. Grease a 3-quart casserole; set aside. Peel and quarter potatoes. In a covered large saucepan cook potatoes in a large amount of boiling water for 20 to 25 minutes or until tender. Drain and mash.

2. Add cream cheese to hot potatoes and stir until combined. Stir in sour cream, salt, parsley flakes, garlic powder, and pepper. Spread mashed potatoes in prepared casserole. Dot with butter. Cover and chill in the refrigerator for 6 to 24 hours.

3. Preheat oven to 350°F. Bake, covered, about 1⅓ hours or until an instant-read thermometer inserted in the center registers 165°F.

Per serving: 236 cal., 13 g total fat (8 g sat. fat), 34 mg chol., 282 mg sodium, 27 g carbo., 2 g fiber, 5 g pro.

Belgian Creamed Potatoes

This 1950s recipe is similar to au gratin potatoes but easier because it doesn't call for a white sauce. This is the perfect treat for dinner-parties.

Prep: 15 minutes **Bake:** 1 hour
Oven: 350°F **Makes:** 6 side-dish servings

    4 cups thinly sliced potato
    1 cup sliced leek
    ½ teaspoon salt
    ¾ cup whipping cream
    2 tablespoons butter or margarine
    ¾ cup shredded Swiss cheese (3 ounces)

1. Preheat oven to 350°F. In a 1½-quart casserole combine potato, leek, and salt. Add whipping cream; dot potato mixture with butter. Bake, covered, for 30 minutes.

2. Uncover and gently stir. Bake, uncovered, for 25 to 30 minutes more or until potato is tender. Sprinkle with cheese; bake about 5 minutes more or until cheese is melted.

Per serving: 274 cal., 19 g total fat (12 g sat. fat), 64 mg chol., 269 mg sodium, 20 g carbo., 2 g fiber, 7 g pro.

Three-Cheese Scalloped Potatoes

Three sensational cheeses—Gouda, cheddar, and Parmesan—team up to create the perfect potato dish. This is more than a special-occasion treat!

Prep: 30 minutes **Bake:** 1 hour 10 minutes
Stand: 15 minutes **Oven:** 350°F
Makes: 6 side-dish servings

    1 large onion, thinly sliced and separated
       into rings
    2 cloves garlic, minced
    2 tablespoons butter or margarine
    2 tablespoons all-purpose flour
 1¾ cups milk
    1 cup diced ham
 1½ pounds potatoes, such as long white,
       round white, round red, or yellow, peeled
       and thinly sliced (4 cups)

    ¾ cup shredded smoked Gouda cheese
       (3 ounces)
    ¾ cup shredded cheddar cheese (3 ounces)
    ¼ cup grated Parmesan cheese

1. Preheat oven to 325°F. For sauce, in saucepan cook onion and garlic in hot butter until tender. Stir in flour, ½ teaspoon *salt*, and ¼ teaspoon *black pepper*. Add milk all at once. Cook and stir until thickened and bubbly. Stir in ham. Remove from heat.

2. Place half of the sliced potato into greased 1½-quart oval, round, or square baking dish. Top with half of the sauce. Sprinkle with Gouda and cheddar cheeses. Add remaining potato and sauce.

3. Cover and bake for 35 minutes. Uncover and bake for 30 to 35 minutes more or until potatoes are tender and golden. Sprinkle with Parmesan cheese. Bake, uncovered, 5 minutes more or until cheese is golden. Let stand for 15 minutes before serving.

Per serving: 312 cal., 17 g total fat (10 g sat. fat), 58 mg chol., 926 mg sodium, 16 g carbo., 2 g fiber, 15 g pro.

Horseradish Mashed Potatoes

These quick-as-a-wink mashed potatoes get a kick from spicy horseradish and are a delicious accompaniment to roast beef.

Prep: 15 minutes **Cook:** 20 minutes
Makes: 8 servings

    8 medium russet potatoes (about
       2½ pounds), peeled and chopped
    6 tablespoons butter or margarine
    ¾ cup dairy sour cream
    2 to 3 tablespoons prepared horseradish

1. In a saucepan cook potato in a large amount of boiling lightly salted water for 20 minutes or until tender; drain. Return potato to pan. Mash potato (or press through a ricer). Add butter, ½ teaspoon *salt*, sour cream, and horseradish; stir until smooth. If necessary, add *milk* to reach desired consistency.

Per serving: 233 cal., 13 g total fat (8 g sat. fat), 33 mg chol., 260 mg sodium, 27 g carbo., 2 g fiber, 4 g pro.

 **Lemon-Dill Potatoes**

Cheese on twice-baked potatoes may seem like a given, but this recipe substitutes lemon and dill for a healthful flair.

Prep: 15 minutes **Bake:** 1 hour **Oven:** 425°F
Makes: 8 side-dish servings

- 4 large baking potatoes
- ⅓ cup dairy sour cream
- ¼ cup butter or margarine, melted
- 2 tablespoons finely snipped fresh dill or
  1½ teaspoons dried dill
- 1 tablespoon lemon juice
- ½ teaspoon garlic salt
- ⅛ teaspoon ground black pepper

1. Preheat oven to 425°F. Scrub potatoes thoroughly with a brush. Pat dry with paper towels. Prick potatoes with a fork. Bake for 40 to 60 minutes or until tender.

2. Cut potatoes in half lengthwise. Scoop pulp out of each potato half, leaving a thin shell. Place potato pulp into a large mixing bowl. Add sour cream, 3 tablespoons of the butter, the dill, lemon juice, garlic salt, and pepper. Beat with an electric mixer on low speed until smooth. Mound the mixture into potato shells.

3. Place into a 3-quart rectangular baking dish. Brush potatoes with remaining butter. Bake about 20 minutes or until light brown.

Per serving: 131 cal., 8 g total fat (5 g sat. fat), 19 mg chol., 111 mg sodium, 14 g carbo., 1 g fiber, 2 g pro.

 **Twice-Baked Jarlsberg Potatoes**

Cheesy twice-baked potatoes became popular in the mid-20th century and featured American or cheddar cheese. This winner showcases Jarlsberg, a type of Swiss cheese.

Prep: 30 minutes **Bake:** 1 hour 5 minutes
Stand: 10 minutes **Oven:** 425°F/400°F
Makes: 8 servings

- 8 baking potatoes (about 3 pounds total)
- ¼ cup butter
- ½ cup chopped leek (white and tender green parts only)
- ¼ cup chopped shallot
- 4 cloves garlic, minced
- 1 tablespoon snipped fresh flat-leaf parsley
- 1 cup dairy sour cream or plain yogurt
- 3 ounces Jarlsberg cheese, finely shredded (¾ cup)

1. Preheat oven to 425°F. Scrub potatoes with a brush; pat dry. Prick potatoes with a fork. Bake potatoes for 40 to 60 minutes or until tender. Let baked potatoes stand about 10 minutes. Cut a lengthwise slice from the top of each potato; discard skin from slice and place pulp into a medium bowl. Scoop pulp out of each potato. Add the pulp to the bowl. Reduce oven temperate to 400°F.

2. In a medium skillet melt butter over medium heat. Add leek, shallot, and garlic; cook and stir for 5 to 7 minutes or until tender. Add parsley; cook and stir for 30 seconds. Set aside.

3. Mash the potato pulp with a potato masher or an electric mixer on low speed. Add sour cream and butter-leek mixture; beat until almost smooth. (If necessary, stir in 1 to 2 tablespoons *milk* to reach desired consistency.) Season to taste with *salt* and *black pepper*. Stir in the Jarlsberg cheese. Spoon the mashed potato mixture into the potato shells.

4. Place stuffed potatoes in a 3-quart baking dish. Bake for 25 minutes.

Per serving: 273 cal., 14 g total fat (8 g sat. fat), 32 mg chol., 153 mg sodium, 32 g carbo., 3 g fiber, 8 g pro.

Twice-Baked Jarlsberg Potatoes

Oysters au Gratin

For some, oyster stew is a Christmas Eve tradition. If you want to serve a flavorful main course, try this elegant recipe. Serve with a crisp, tart salad to contrast with the casserole's rich flavors.

Prep: 30 minutes **Bake:** 10 minutes
Oven: 400°F **Makes:** 4 servings

  2 **pints shucked fresh or frozen oysters**
  ¼ **cup butter or margarine**
  1 **cup sliced fresh mushrooms**
  1 **clove garlic, minced**
  2 **tablespoons all-purpose flour**
  ¾ **cup milk**
  ¼ **cup dry white wine**
  2 **tablespoons snipped fresh parsley**
  ½ **teaspoon Worcestershire sauce**
  ¾ **cup soft bread crumbs**
  ¼ **cup grated Parmesan cheese**

1. Preheat oven to 400°F. Thaw oysters, if frozen. Rinse oysters; pat dry with paper towels. In a large skillet melt 1 tablespoon of the butter over medium heat. Add oysters; cook for 3 to 4 minutes or until oyster edges curl. Drain oysters. Divide oysters among four 8- to 10-ounce casseroles or four 10-ounce custard cups.

2. For sauce, in the same skillet melt 2 tablespoons of the butter over medium heat. Add mushrooms and garlic; cook until tender. Stir in flour. Add milk all at once. Cook and stir until thickened and bubbly. Stir in wine, parsley, and Worcestershire sauce. Spoon over oysters.

3. In a small saucepan melt the remaining butter; stir in the bread crumbs and Parmesan cheese. Sprinkle bread crumb mixture over casseroles. Bake about 10 minutes or until crumbs are brown.

Per serving: 345 cal., 19 g total fat (10 g sat. fat), 98 mg chol., 722 mg sodium, 23 g carbo., 1 g fiber, 18 g pro.

Turnips au Gratin

Turnips arguably receive the award for being the most under-appreciated root vegetable of all time! Yet someone in 1932 knew that all it took was a luscious cream sauce and a soft, crumbly bread topping to transform the humble root into something really special. Tote this unexpected side dish to a holiday potluck if you want to put something surprising on the table.

Prep: 30 minutes **Bake:** 20 minutes **Oven:** 375°F
Makes: 6 to 8 side-dish servings

  2 **pounds turnips, peeled and cubed**
     (about 6 cups)
  3 **tablespoons butter or margarine**
  3 **tablespoons all-purpose flour**
  ¼ **teaspoon salt**
  ⅛ **teaspoon ground black pepper**
  2 **cups milk**
  ½ **cup shredded American cheese (2 ounces)**
  2 **cups soft bread crumbs (about 2 slices)**
  3 **tablespoons butter or margarine, melted**

1. Preheat oven to 375°F. In a covered large saucepan cook the cubed turnip in boiling water about 6 minutes or until nearly tender. Drain well in a colander. In a medium saucepan melt 3 tablespoons butter over medium heat. Stir in flour, salt, and pepper. Add milk all at once. Cook and stir until thickened and bubbly. Remove from heat; add the cheese, stirring until melted. Stir in turnip. Transfer to a 2-quart square baking dish.

2. In a medium bowl combine bread crumbs and 3 tablespoons melted butter. Sprinkle over turnip mixture. Bake about 20 minutes or until crumb mixture is golden.

Per serving: 265 cal., 17 g total fat (10 g sat. fat), 46 mg chol., 533 mg sodium, 22 g carbo., 3 g fiber, 8 g pro.

Butternut Squash Gratin with Creamed Spinach

This is it—that dazzler you can deliver when your favorite holiday host says, "Please bring a side dish."

Prep: 20 minutes **Bake:** 30 minutes
Oven: 425°F/475°F **Makes:** 8 side-dish servings

1¾	to 2 pound butternut squash
1	tablespoon olive oil
	Salt
	Ground black pepper
16	cups fresh spinach
1	cup half-and-half or light cream
1	tablespoon cornstarch
1	cup finely shredded Parmesan cheese
½	cup purchased crème fraîche

1. Preheat oven to 425°F. Lightly grease a 2-quart baking dish; set aside. Peel squash; cut into ¼-inch slices. Remove seeds from slices; halve large slices. Arrange slices in a 15×10×1-inch baking pan. Brush both sides lightly with olive oil. Season with salt and pepper. Bake for 20 minutes. Remove from oven. Increase oven temperature to 475°F.

2. Meanwhile, in a 4- to 6-quart Dutch oven cook spinach in boiling lightly salted water, half at a time, about 1 minute or until wilted. Drain and cool slightly; squeeze out excess liquid. Coarsely chop spinach; set aside. In a medium saucepan combine half-and-half and cornstarch; cook and stir until thickened and bubbly. Stir in spinach; spread mixture into bottom of the prepared dish. Arrange squash over spinach mixture.

3. In a small bowl stir together Parmesan cheese and crème fraîche. Spread mixture over squash in dish. Bake for 10 to 15 minutes or until squash is tender and Parmesan mixture is light brown. If desired, season to taste with salt and pepper.

Per serving: 187 cal., 14 g total fat (8 g sat. fat), 38 mg chol., 308 mg sodium, 11 g carbo., 2 g fiber, 7 g pro.

Butternut Squash Gratin with Creamed Spinach

Leeks au Gratin

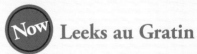 **Leeks au Gratin**

Consider this recipe a grandchild of Creamed Onions, with mellow leeks substituted for pearl onions.

Prep: 40 minutes **Bake:** 10 minutes **Oven:** 450°F
Makes: 8 to 10 side-dish servings

  8 **hard-cooked eggs,* peeled**
10 **medium leeks**
  6 **tablespoons butter**
  2 **tablespoons all-purpose flour**
1½ **cups milk**
  2 **ounces white cheddar cheese, shredded**
      (½ cup)
 ¼ **cup grated Parmesan cheese**
 ¼ **teaspoon cayenne pepper**

1. Preheat oven to 450°F. Quarter eggs lengthwise. Arrange in a single layer in a 1½- to 2-quart au gratin dish or a 10-inch quiche dish; set aside.

2. Remove green portion from leeks. Halve leeks lengthwise. Wash thoroughly; pat dry with paper towels. Remove roots from leeks; cut leeks lengthwise into thin strips (to yield about 5 cups). In a large skillet melt 4 tablespoons of the butter over medium heat. Add leek; cook until tender, stirring occasionally. Spoon leek over eggs in dish.

3. For sauce, in the same skillet melt the remaining 2 tablespoons butter over medium heat; whisk in flour. Add milk all at once; cook until thickened and bubbly, whisking to make smooth. Whisk in half of the white cheddar cheese, the Parmesan cheese, and cayenne pepper. Season to taste with *salt* and *black pepper*. Pour sauce over the leeks and eggs in dish. Top with remaining cheese. Bake about 10 minutes or until edges are bubbly and top is golden brown.

Test Kitchen Tip: If using a broiler-safe dish, broil for 1 to 2 minutes for additional browning.

*Note: To hard cook eggs, place eggs in a single layer in a 2-quart saucepan. Add enough cold water to come 1 inch above the eggs. Bring to a rapid boil over high heat. Remove from heat, cover, and let stand for 15 minutes; drain. Run cold water over the eggs until cool enough to handle; drain.

Per serving: 333 cal., 22 g total fat (11 g sat. fat), 141 mg chol., 200 mg sodium, 32 g carbo., 2 g fiber, 4 g pro.

Creamed Onions

If you're serving baked ham or a beef roast and don't feel like making gravy, this delightfully old-fashioned dish can stand in as the saucy something you need as an accompaniment.

Start to Finish: 25 minutes
Makes: 6 side-dish servings

- 1 16-ounce package frozen small whole onions
- 3 tablespoons butter
- 2 tablespoons all-purpose flour
- ¼ teaspoon salt
    Dash ground white pepper
- 1⅓ cups milk
- 4 ounces Muenster cheese, shredded (1 cup)
    Fresh parsley sprigs (optional)

1. Cook onions according to package directions. Drain. In a small saucepan melt butter; stir in flour, salt, and pepper. Add milk; cook and stir until mixture is thickened and bubbly. Add cheese; stir to melt. Stir in onions; heat through. If desired, garnish with parsley.

Per serving: 183 cal., 13 g total fat (8 g sat. fat), 38 mg chol., 286 mg sodium, 11 g carbo., 1 g fiber, 7 g pro.

Scalloped Spinach

Oven meals—those in which the main course, sides, and dessert are cooked at the same temperature in the oven—were popular during the 1940s because they helped with energy-saving war rationing efforts. This rich, yummy recipe is a great find from that era. Serve it with a simple roast or as part of a buffet.

Prep: 15 minutes **Bake:** 1 hour
Stand: 10 minutes **Oven:** 350°F
Makes: 6 to 8 side-dish servings

- 3 10-ounce packages frozen chopped spinach, thawed and well drained
- 4 eggs, beaten
- 1 cup shredded American cheese (4 ounces)
- ¾ cup milk
- ¼ cup finely chopped onion
- ¾ teaspoon salt
- ¼ teaspoon ground black pepper
- 1 cup soft bread crumbs
- 1 tablespoon butter, melted

1. Preheat oven to 350°F. Grease a 1½-quart straight-sided round baking dish (about 8 inches in diameter*); set aside. In a large bowl combine spinach, eggs, ¾ cup of the cheese, the milk, onion, salt, and pepper. Spoon into prepared baking dish.

2. Bake for 50 minutes. In a small bowl combine the remaining ¼ cup cheese, the bread crumbs, and melted butter; sprinkle around outer edge of spinach mixture. Bake for 10 to 15 minutes more or until a knife inserted 1 inch from center comes out clean. Let stand for 10 minutes before serving.

*Note: You may use an oval casserole. However, if it is larger and more shallow than the 8-inch round baking dish, cover and bake for 30 minutes. Uncover casserole; add crumbs. Bake for 10 to 15 minutes or until a knife inserted in center comes out clean.

Per serving: 209 cal., 12 g total fat (6 g sat. fat), 166 mg chol., 893 mg sodium, 10 g carbo., 4 g fiber, 13 g pro.

Scalloped vs. au Gratin

Scalloped, au gratin, and creamed are terms that describe some of our favorite dishes—especially those served around the holidays. A creamed dish is easily defined—it's simply one in which the food is served in a cream sauce. But what's the difference between a scalloped and au gratin dish? Because of the similarity between the two dishes, sometimes they're used interchangeably, but technically there is a difference.

• **Au Gratin:** Some diners mistakenly think that "au gratin" has something to do with cheese. That's not always the case. In fact, a "gratin" is any dish that's topped with cheese or a bread-crumb/butter mixture, (or a combination of the two) then baked or broiled until the top is brown and crispy.
• **Scalloped:** A scalloped dish is one in which the food is layered—often with a cream sauce—and then baked. As with an au gratin dish, a scalloped dish can be topped with bread crumbs and/or cheese.

Green Beans Parmesan

If you feel you've "bean" there, done that with classic green bean casserole (the one with canned fried onions on the top), try this rich and creamy gourmet version. The "Wow! What is it?" secret is crisp water chestnuts studded throughout.

Prep: 20 minutes **Bake:** 30 minutes **Oven:** 350°F
Makes: 6 to 8 side-dish servings

- 1 16-ounce package frozen French-style green beans
- 2 tablespoons butter or margarine
- ¼ cup chopped onion
- 2 tablespoons all-purpose flour
- ½ teaspoon salt
- 1¼ cups milk
- ¼ cup grated Parmesan cheese
- 1 8-ounce can sliced water chestnuts, drained
- ¾ cup soft bread crumbs
- 2 tablespoons butter or margarine, melted

1. Preheat oven to 350°F. Cook beans according to package directions; drain. In a medium saucepan melt 2 tablespoons butter over medium heat. Add onion; cook until tender. Stir in flour and salt. Stir in milk all at once; cook and stir until thickened and bubbly. Stir in half of the Parmesan cheese. Stir in beans and water chestnuts; transfer to a 1-quart casserole.

2. In a small bowl toss together the remaining cheese, crumbs, and melted butter; sprinkle over bean mixture in casserole. Bake about 30 minutes or until bubbly.

Per serving: 209 cal., 12 g total fat (6 g sat. fat), 27 mg chol., 370 mg sodium, 24 g carbo., 2 g fiber, 6 g pro.

Choosing Parmesan Cheese

The original Parmesan—Parmigiano-Reggiano from Italy—ranks high as one of the world's great cheeses. Imported from Italy, it is expensive, but its buttery, nutty flavor is outstanding. Domestic versions of Parmesan are available; however, they are usually milder than the imported variety, but they're also more economical. When purchasing Parmesan cheese, choose the type that fits your taste and budget. For the freshest flavor, buy chunk cheese and shred or grate only what you need at one time.

While grated Parmesan finds its way into a variety of recipes, it's not for grating only! Serve shards of the cheese (it can't be sliced) alongside olives, nuts, and crusty bread as an appetizer. Or serve chunks of the cheese with fruit after the main course.

Swiss Corn Bake

First published in 1968, this scrumptious casserole is a tasty and easy alternative to scalloped corn.

Prep: 25 minutes **Bake:** 30 minutes
Stand: 10 minutes **Oven:** 350°F
Makes: 6 side-dish servings

- 3½ cups cut fresh corn kernels or one 16-ounce package frozen whole kernel corn
- ¼ cup finely chopped onion
- 2 eggs
- 2 5-ounce cans evaporated milk (1⅓ cups)
- ½ teaspoon garlic salt
- ¼ teaspoon ground black pepper
- 1 cup shredded process Swiss or Gruyère cheese (4 ounces)

1. Preheat oven to 350°F. Grease a 2-quart square baking dish; set aside. In a covered medium saucepan cook fresh corn and onion in a small amount of boiling lightly salted water for 6 minutes. (Or cook frozen corn and onion according to package directions for corn.) Drain well.

2. In a medium bowl beat eggs with a fork. Stir in drained corn and onion, evaporated milk, garlic salt, and pepper. Stir in ¾ cup of the cheese. Pour into prepared dish.

3. Sprinkle remaining ¼ cup cheese over corn mixture. Bake for 30 minutes. Let stand for 10 minutes before serving.

Per serving: 247 cal., 11 g total fat (7 g sat. fat), 104 mg chol., 437 mg sodium, 26 g carbo., 2 g fiber, 13 g pro.

 **Harvard Beets**

To save time on the big day, do some of your shopping beforehand for items that store well. Purchase fresh beets up to a week before cooking and store them, unwashed, in an open plastic bag in the refrigerator.

Start to Finish: 1 hour **Makes:** 4 side-dish servings

- 4 medium beets (1 pound) or one 16-ounce can sliced or diced beets
- 2 tablespoons sugar
- 2 tablespoons vinegar
- 2 teaspoons cornstarch
- 1 tablespoon butter or margarine

1. Cut off all but 1 inch of stem and root of each fresh beet; wash. Do not peel. In a covered large saucepan cook fresh beets in a large amount of boiling water for 40 to 50 minutes or until tender. Drain, reserving ⅓ cup liquid; cool beets slightly. Slip skins off beets and slice or dice. (Or drain canned beets, reserving ⅓ cup liquid.)

2. In a saucepan combine the beet liquid, sugar, vinegar, and cornstarch. Cook and stir until thickened and bubbly. Cook and stir for 2 minutes more. Stir in beets and butter; heat through.

Per serving: 85 cal., 3 g total fat (2 g sat. fat), 8 mg chol., 82 mg sodium, 15 g carbo., 4 g fiber, 1 g pro.

 **Sweet-Glazed Beets With Crème Fraîche**

Roasting beets, rather than boiling them, makes their mellow-sweet flavors shine. You'll love the way the ginger and cider flavors provide a bright, sweet contrast to the deeply flavored root veggie.

Prep: 45 minutes **Roast:** 45 minutes
Oven: 400°F **Makes:** 8 side-dish servings

- 3 pounds medium beets (10 to 12)
- 1 cup cider vinegar
- ½ cup packed brown sugar
- ¼ cup orange marmalade
- ¼ teaspoon ground ginger
- ½ cup purchased crème fraîche*

1. Preheat oven to 400°F. Scrub beets; cut off beet stems to within ½ inch of top. Place 3 or 4 beets on a 12-inch piece of heavy-duty foil; bring up sides of foil around beets. Repeat with remaining beets to make 3 or 4 bundles. Place in a shallow baking pan. Roast for 45 to 60 minutes or until tender. Cool until easy to handle; peel beets** and cut into bite-size pieces. Place in a bowl and keep warm; set aside.

2. Meanwhile, for glaze, in a saucepan combine vinegar and brown sugar. Bring to boiling; reduce heat. Boil gently, uncovered, for 15 to 18 minutes or until reduced to ½ cup. Remove from heat. Stir in orange marmalade and ginger. Cool slightly. Pour glaze over beets. Serve beets warm, using a slotted spoon. Top servings with crème fraîche.

***Note:** If you can't find crème fraîche in your supermarket, substitute by combining ½ cup whipping cream (do not use ultra-pasteurized) and ½ cup dairy sour cream. Cover the mixture and let it stand at room temperature for 2 to 5 hours or until it thickens. Cover and refrigerate for up to 1 week.

****Note:** To easily peel beets, hold under running water and use your fingers to loosen and remove the skins from the beets. You may want to wear rubber gloves to prevent discoloring your hands.

Per serving: 171 cal., 4 g total fat (3 g sat. fat), 13 mg chol., 102 mg sodium, 33 g carbo., 3 g fiber, 2 g pro.

Festive Food Decorations

Lavish table decorations are beautiful, but who has time? Instead, think about how food can serve to beautify your table—for example, the striking garnet color of the beet recipes, left. Here are some other ideas:

• For a centerpiece, arrange in-season fruits in a stemmed bowl, including bright oranges, green-gold pears, and crimson red apples. Invite people to enjoy the fruits while lingering at the table after dinner.
• Showcase that plate of beautifully decorated Christmas cookies a friend delivered. Set them on a stemmed platter to show off their festive shapes—and invite everyone to enjoy them with coffee after dinner. (Also worth stacking high on a pedestal: cupcakes frosted in Christmasy colors and topped with lush piles of coconut.)
• Cranberries can add sparkle and color too. Serve a cake or pie on a stemmed plate that's placed on a large plate. Surround the bottom of the stem with a circle of fresh cranberries.
• Take a tip from earlier generations of cooks and tap into the appeal of a shimmering fruit-studded gelatin mold to add a festive note.

Old-Fashioned Bread Stuffing

 Old-Fashioned
Bread Stuffing

Here's the utterly classic, always-welcome bread stuffing that generations of cooks confidently serve year after year.

Prep: 15 minutes **Bake:** 30 minutes **Oven:** 325°F
Makes: 12 to 14 side-dish servings

1½	**cups sliced celery**
1	**cup chopped onion**
½	**cup butter**
1	**tablespoon snipped fresh sage or**
	1 teaspoon poultry seasoning
¼	**teaspoon ground black pepper**
12	**cups dry bread cubes***
1	**to 1¼ cups chicken broth****

1. Preheat oven to 325°F. In a large skillet cook celery and onion in hot butter until tender. Remove from heat. Stir in sage and pepper. Place dry bread cubes into a large bowl; add onion mixture. Drizzle with enough chicken broth to moisten, tossing lightly to combine.

2. Place stuffing into an ungreased 2½-quart casserole.** Bake, covered, for 30 to 45 minutes or until heated through.

*Note: To make 12 cups dry bread cubes, preheat oven to 300°F. Cut 20 to 21 slices bread into ½-inch cubes (to yield about 14 cups cubed bread). Spread cubes in a single layer in a large, shallow roasting pan. Bake, uncovered, for 10 to 15 minutes or until dry, stirring twice. Cool. (Bread will continue to dry and crisp as it cools.) Or let bread stand, loosely covered, at room temperature for 8 to 12 hours.

**Note: If you want to use the bread mixture to stuff one 10- to 12-pound turkey, use ¾ cup to 1 cup chicken broth to moisten the bread cube mixture. Roast according to turkey roasting directions until an instant-read thermometer inserted in center of stuffing mixture registers 165°F.

Per serving: 181 cal., 10 g total fat (5 g sat. fat), 22 mg chol., 342 mg sodium, 20 g carbo., 1 g fiber, 4 g pro.

Make-Ahead Tip: Prepare as directed through step 1. Place stuffing into a 2½-quart casserole. Cover and chill for up to 24 hours. Preheat oven to 325°F. Bake casserole, covered, for 50 to 60 minutes or until heated through. (For safety reasons, do not make stuffing ahead if planning to use for stuffing a turkey.)

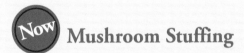 **Mushroom Stuffing**

This up-to-date mushroom stuffing takes advantage of shiitakes, which are now as common as button mushrooms. You'll also appreciate the way this timesaving recipe starts with purchased stuffing mix.

Prep: 25 minutes **Bake:** 50 minutes **Oven:** 325°F
Makes: 10 to 12 side-dish servings

¼	**cup butter or margarine**
6	**cups sliced fresh shiitake and/or**
	button mushrooms
¼	**cup sliced green onion**
2	**teaspoons soy sauce**
2	**teaspoons Worcestershire sauce**
½	**teaspoon dried rosemary, crushed**
¼	**teaspoon ground black pepper**
5	**cups herb-seasoned stuffing mix**
	(about 8 ounces)
3	**cups coarsely shredded carrot**
	(6 medium)
1	**to 1¼ cups water**

1. Preheat oven to 325°F. In a large skillet melt butter over medium heat. Add mushrooms; cook about 5 minutes or just until tender, stirring occasionally. Add green onion for the last 1 minute of cooking. Remove from heat. Stir in soy sauce, Worcestershire sauce, rosemary, and pepper.

2. In a large bowl combine stuffing mix, carrot, and mushroom mixture. Drizzle with enough of the water to moisten.

3. Place in a 3-quart casserole.* Bake, covered, for 50 to 60 minutes or until heated through. (Or bake in a 375°F oven for 35 to 45 minutes or until heated through.)

*Note: If desired, use the mushroom mixture to stuff an 11- to 12-pound turkey. Roast according to turkey roasting directions until an instant-read thermometer inserted in the center of the stuffing mixture registers 165°F.

Per serving: 192 cal., 7 g total fat (3 g sat. fat), 13 mg chol., 541 mg sodium, 28 g carbo., 4 g fiber, 6 g pro.

 **Spicy Chorizo Stuffing**

Sausage is often added to stuffing to enhance its flavors. This recipe increases the appeal of the usual sausage stuffing by using chorizo, a spicy pork sausage enjoyed in Hispanic cooking.

Prep: 40 minutes **Bake:** 40 minutes
Oven: 325°F **Makes:** 10 to 12 servings

> 12 **cups Italian bread cubes**
>   **(about 14 ounces)**
> 8 **ounces bulk chorizo sausage**
> 1 **cup chopped onion**
> ½ **cup butter or margarine**
> ½ **cup chopped bottled roasted**
>   **red sweet peppers**
> ½ **cup pine nuts, toasted**
> ¼ **teaspoon ground black pepper**
> 1½ **to 2 cups chicken broth**
> 1 **tablespoon snipped fresh chives**
>   **or parsley**

1. Preheat oven to 325°F. Place bread cubes in a single layer in two 15×10×1-inch baking pans. Bake about 10 minutes or until golden, stirring once or twice; set aside.

2. In a large skillet cook chorizo until brown. Drain; set aside. In the same skillet cook onion in hot butter until tender; stir in roasted red sweet pepper.

3. In a large bowl toss together bread cubes, chorizo-onion mixture, toasted pine nuts, and black pepper. Drizzle with enough of the broth to moisten, tossing lightly to combine.

4. Place all of the stuffing in a 2-quart baking dish. Bake, covered, for 30 to 45 minutes or until heated through. For a crisper top, uncover baking dish for the last 10 minutes of baking time. Before serving, sprinkle with chives.

Note: If you want to use the bread mixture to stuff one 10- to 12-pound turkey, use the minimum amount of broth. Spoon lightly into the neck and body cavities of turkey. (Place any remaining stuffing in a casserole; drizzle with enough of the remaining chicken broth (¼ to ½ cup) to make a stuffing of desired moistness. Cover and chill casserole until ready to bake.) Pull neck skin to back and fasten with a skewer. Tuck drumsticks under band of skin by tail, if present, or tie drumsticks to tail. Twist wing tips under the back. Place turkey on rack in a large roasting pan; cover with foil, leaving air space between bird and foil. Roast in a 325°F oven for 3 to 3¾ hours or until thermometer inserted in center of inside thigh registers 180°F (thermometer inserted in stuffing should register 165°F). Remove foil for the last 45 minutes of roasting. Bake stuffing in a covered casserole alongside turkey for 40 to 45 minutes or until heated through.

Per serving: 344 cal., 23 g total fat (10 g sat. fat), 45 mg chol., 722 mg sodium, 24 g carbo., 1 g fiber, 11 g pro.

Spicy Chorizo Stuffing

Ginger Marinated Fruit

Imagine the brightest, most refreshing fruit salad possible and you'll have a good idea of what this tangy little number is all about. Ginger is the secret ingredient that brings out the flavor.

Prep: 25 minutes **Marinate:** 1 hour
Makes: 8 to 10 servings

- ½ **cup water**
- 2 **tablespoons frozen orange juice concentrate, thawed**
- 1 **tablespoon grated fresh ginger**
- 1 **teaspoon finely shredded orange peel**
- ¼ **cup honey**
- 2 **tablespoons orange liqueur or orange juice**
- 6 **cups cut-up assorted fresh fruit (such as kiwifruits, apples, oranges, cantaloupe, honeydew melon, pineapple, pears, and/or red seedless grapes)**
  Fresh mint sprigs (optional)

1. In a small saucepan combine the water, orange juice concentrate, ginger, and orange peel. Bring to boiling; reduce heat. Simmer, covered, over low heat for 5 minutes. Remove saucepan from heat. Stir in honey and liqueur. Cool completely.

2. Place fruit in a large bowl; pour cooled ginger mixture over fruit. Toss to coat. Cover and marinate in the refrigerator for 1 to 12 hours, stirring occasionally. If desired, garnish with fresh mint.

Per serving: 107 cal., 0 g total fat (0 g sat. fat), 0 mg chol., 10 mg sodium, 25 g carbo., 2 g fiber, 1 g pro.

Cranberry Fluff

Your grandmother probably made this old-fashioned fruit salad—it's been around a few decades! Then as now, the pretty pink, whipped-cream-laced treat is a tasty way to coax the kids to eat fruit.

Prep: 20 minutes **Stand:** 1 hour
Makes: 10 servings

- 1½ **cups finely chopped fresh cranberries**
- 2¼ **cups tiny marshmallows**
- ½ **cup sugar**
- 1½ **cups chopped tart apple**
- ½ **cup seedless green grapes, halved**
- ⅓ **cup chopped walnuts**
- ¾ **cup whipping cream**

1. In a bowl combine cranberries, marshmallows, and sugar. Cover and let stand at room temperature for 1 hour. Stir in apple, grapes, and walnuts; set aside.

2. In a chilled medium bowl beat whipping cream with chilled beaters of an electric mixer on medium speed until soft peaks form (tips curl). Fold into cranberry mixture.

Make-Ahead Tip: Prepare as directed. Cover and chill for up to 24 hours.

Per serving: 188 cal., 9 g total fat (4 g sat. fat), 25 mg chol., 18 mg sodium, 27 g carbo., 2 g fiber, 1 g pro.

Ginger Marinated Fruit

Fruit Salade Flan

Fruit Salade Flan

Even if you're not a fan of gelatin salads, you might consider trying this refreshing version from 1973. The base has a lusciously creamy texture with a zippy lemon flavor—a perfect contrast to richer holiday foods. The fruit topping adds color and sparkle to your Christmas table.

Prep: 30 minutes **Chill:** 8 hours **Makes:** 8 servings

  2 **3-ounce packages lemon-flavored gelatin**
  3 **cups boiling water**
  ½ **cup mayonnaise or salad dressing**
  1 **3-ounce package cream cheese, cut up**
  ½ **of 6-ounce can frozen lemonade
       concentrate (⅓ cup), thawed**
  2 **cups sliced fresh strawberries**
  1 **small banana, diagonally sliced**

1. In a medium bowl dissolve gelatin in the boiling water. Remove 1 cup of the gelatin mixture and let stand at room temperature. Pour remaining gelatin into blender. Add mayonnaise, cream cheese, and lemonade concentrate to blender; cover and blend just until smooth. Transfer to a large bowl. Chill about 1½ hours or until partially set (consistency of unbeaten egg whites), stirring occasionally.

2. Pour gelatin-mayonnaise mixture into a 9-inch springform pan or 9-inch round cake pan with a removable bottom. Chill for 30 to 45 minutes or until almost firm.

3. Arrange strawberries and banana on top of gelatin-mayonnaise mixture in pan. Chill 1 cup reserved gelatin until slightly thickened. Spoon over fruits. Cover and chill about 6 hours or until set.

Per serving: 264 cal., 15 g total fat (4 g sat. fat), 17 mg chol., 228 mg sodium, 31 g carbo., 1 g fiber, 3 g pro.

Greatest Appetizer Hits

Kick off this holiday season with a revival of the punch bowl—you'll find a bounty of beverages to fill it for one of the most festive and colorful ways to serve a crowd. As for the nibbles, name your pleasure: Choose from an array of traditional and all-new takes on cheese balls, sausage bites, wings, and dips. Or try the best-ever version of baked Brie or a newfangled Hot Reuben Dip that will disappear in a flash. You're sure to find something that will hit the spot; after all, these recipes have jump-started parties with aplomb for decades.

Holiday Shrimp Rounds, page 48

Dublin Eggnog

This superlative cold-weather hot drink brings together two holiday-favorite flavors—Irish coffee and eggnog—in perfect harmony.

Start to Finish: 10 minutes
Makes: 6 (7-ounce) servings

- 3 cups dairy eggnog
- 2 cups double-strength coffee
- 4 to 6 ounces Irish whiskey
- Sugar (optional)
- Whipped cream
- Ground nutmeg

1. In a large saucepan heat eggnog and coffee over low heat until hot, stirring often. Do not boil. Remove from heat. Stir in whiskey. If desired, sweeten with sugar. Pour into six Irish coffee cups or mugs. Top servings with whipped cream and nutmeg.

Per serving: 219 cal., 10 g total fat (6 g sat. fat), 75 mg chol., 70 mg sodium, 17 g carbo., 0 g fiber, 5 g pro.

White Strawberry Sangria

If you have a lot of salty and/or spicy goodies on the menu, count on this sangria to provide a fruity, refreshing contrast.

Prep: 10 minutes **Chill:** 1 hour
Makes: about 5 (8-ounce) servings

- 1 750-milliliter bottle dry white wine (such as Pinot Grigio or Sauvignon Blanc)
- ½ cup strawberry schnapps
- ¼ cup sugar
- 2 cups sliced fresh strawberries
- Ice
- Whole strawberries (optional)

1. In a 2-quart pitcher stir together wine, schnapps, and sugar until sugar dissolves. Add sliced strawberries. Chill for 1 to 4 hours. Serve over ice. If desired, garnish with whole strawberries.

Per serving: 221 cal., 0 g total fat (0 g sat. fat), 0 mg chol., 8 mg sodium, 22 g carbo., 1 g fiber, 1 g pro.

Orange-Eggnog Punch

This creamy, dreamy, orange-spiked punch will remind you of the cream-filled orange ice confections you enjoyed as a kid. If you wish, spike the punch with some orange-flavor liqueur.

Start to Finish: 10 minutes
Makes: about 20 (4-ounce) servings

- 1 quart dairy eggnog, chilled
- 1 6-ounce can frozen orange juice concentrate, thawed
- 1 1-liter bottle lemon-lime carbonated beverage, chilled
- 1 pint vanilla ice cream

1. In a punch bowl combine eggnog and orange juice concentrate. Slowly add carbonated beverage. Top with scoops of vanilla ice cream. If desired, sprinkle with *ground nutmeg*.

Per serving: 139 cal., 6 g total fat (4 g sat. fat), 44 mg chol., 47 mg sodium, 19 g carbo., 0 g fiber, 3 g pro.

Honey Party Punch

This is the sort of crowd-pleasing punch that generations of families have shared. Rekindle this welcoming tradition for your next holiday gathering.

Prep: 15 minutes **Chill:** 4 hours
Makes: 12 (about 7-ounce) servings

- ¼ cup honey
- ¼ cup boiling water
- 3 cups unsweetened pineapple juice
- 2 cups water
- ¾ cup orange juice
- ¼ cup lemon juice
- ¼ cup lightly packed fresh mint leaves
- 1 1-liter bottle ginger ale, chilled
- 1 recipe Fruited Ice Ring (see page 35) (optional)
- Fresh fruit, cut up (optional)

1. In a large bowl combine honey and the ¼ cup boiling water. Stir in pineapple juice, the 2 cups water, the orange juice, lemon juice, and mint. Cover; chill for 4 to 24 hours.

White Strawberry Sangria, page 34

2. To serve, discard mint leaves. Pour punch into punch bowl; stir in ginger ale. Carefully slide Fruited Ice Ring into punch bowl. If desired, garnish servings with fruit on a decorative pick.

Per serving: 94 cal., 0 g total fat (0 g sat. fat), 0 mg chol., 8 mg sodium, 24 g carbo., 0 g fiber, 0 g pro.

Fruited Ice Ring: Pour about ½ inch water into a 3-cup ring mold. Arrange maraschino cherries, halved orange slices, halved lemon slices, and fresh mint leaves on top; freeze until solid. Carefully add water to fill mold; freeze again until solid. To unmold, wrap ring mold in hot towel; invert onto plate and remove mold.

Cheese by Threes

For a simple yet classy appetizer, simply go to a local cheese purveyor or well-stocked supermarket. A selection of three cheeses is perfect—it's just enough for a nice sampling but not overwhelming. Serve with cured meats, gourmet olives, and crackers. Here are a few examples of such trios:

• Manchego (a firm sheep's milk cheese from Spain), Saint-Marcellin (a creamy French cow's milk cheese), and Shropshire Blue (an English blue cheese of cow's milk)

• Ossau-Iraty (a firm sheep's milk cheese from France), Sweet Grass Dairy Green Hill Cheese (a soft, creamy cow's milk cheese from Georgia), and Cabrales (a Spanish blue cheese of goat's, cow's, and sheep's milk)

• Aged Gouda (a Dutch cow's milk cheese), Crottin (a French goat cheese), and Point Reyes Original Blue (a Californian cow's milk blue cheese)

Cranberry-Pineapple Punch

Cranberry-Pineapple Punch

Prep: 10 minutes **Chill:** 1 hour
Makes: 14 (about 8-ounce) servings

½ cup sugar
½ cup water
2 cups cranberry juice, chilled
1 cup orange juice, chilled (about 3 oranges)
1 cup unsweetened pineapple juice, chilled
¾ cup lemon juice, chilled (about 4 lemons)
1 2-liter bottle ginger ale, chilled
1 recipe Citrus Cranberry Ice Ring, broken

1. For syrup, in a small saucepan combine sugar and the water. Cook and stir over medium heat until sugar dissolves. Transfer to a small bowl or 1-cup glass measure. Cover and chill for 1 hour.

2. In a large punch bowl stir together the cranberry juice, orange juice, pineapple juice, lemon juice, and chilled syrup. Stir in ginger ale. Serve immediately. Garnish with pieces of Citrus Cranberry Ice Ring.

Citrus Cranberry Ice Ring: Fill ring mold half full with water. Place lemon peel curls, lime peel curls, fresh cranberries, and fresh mint leaves in water. Freeze until firm. Fill with water; freeze.

Per serving: 118 cal., 0 g total fat (0 g sat. fat), 0 mg chol., 12 mg sodium, 30 g carbo., 0 g fiber, 0 g pro.

Punch Bowl Revival

Your grandmother probably had a punch bowl and perhaps your mother did too. But where's yours? The pleasures of punch fit today's easygoing styles of entertaining. When you're too busy to fully stock a bar (and too fun loving to spend party time replenishing a cola here or a Chardonnay there), rely on the punch bowl.

A good punch served graciously shakes guests out of their "I'll have the usual" routine. More colorful than beer, more stylish than soda, and more refreshing than wine, these snazzy sippers set a festive tone for your party.

A word about setting the stage: Punch time isn't the time for plastic jugs and paper cups. Much of what gives punch its panache is its presentation, and the right vessel is everything. Fortunately, because people in this country have enjoyed punch for ages (Martha Washington was known to tipple a glass or two with guests), vintage punch bowls, cups, pitchers, and glasses are brimming at antiques and collectibles shops.

If vintage isn't your style, look for more contemporary punch ware in home furnishing stores and mail order catalogs.

Spiced Fruit Punch

This 1981 punch started out as an all-purpose base that could be used with wine, liquor, or lemon-lime carbonated beverage. This updated version, uses white wine.

Prep: 10 minutes **Cook:** 10 minutes
Chill: 2 hours **Makes:** 25 (4-ounce) servings

½ cup water
⅓ cup sugar
12 inches stick cinnamon, broken
½ teaspoon whole cloves
4 cups apple juice or apple cider, chilled
1 12-ounce can apricot nectar, chilled

¼ cup lemon juice
2 750-milliliter bottles dry white wine, chilled
  Apricot slices (optional)
  Fresh mint sprigs (optional)

1. In a small saucepan combine the water, sugar, stick cinnamon, and whole cloves. Bring to boiling; reduce heat. Simmer, covered, for 10 minutes. Cover and chill for 2 to 24 hours.

2. Pour the sugar mixture through a fine-mesh sieve; discard spices. In a punch bowl combine the sugar mixture, apple juice, apricot nectar, and lemon juice. Pour in wine. If desired, garnish with apricot slices and fresh mint.

Per serving: 78 cal., 0 g total fat (0 g sat. fat), 0 mg chol., 5 mg sodium, 10 g carbo., 0 g fiber, 0 g pro.

Twinkling Ginger Champagne Punch

This sparkling drink is perfect to serve before or after dinner. For a nonalcoholic version, use the gingered syrup (without the vodka) in sparkling water or sparking cider. Even if the drink is nonalcoholic, it still looks fabulous in a Champagne flute.

Prep: 10 minutes **Cook:** 10 minutes
Chill: 4 hours **Makes:** 8 (about 4-ounce) servings

¼ cup sugar
¼ cup light-colored corn syrup
¼ cup water
3 tablespoons finely snipped
   crystallized ginger
½ cup vodka
1 750-milliliter bottle Champagne, chilled

1. In a small saucepan combine sugar, corn syrup, the water, and crystallized ginger. Bring to boiling; reduce heat. Simmer, uncovered, for 10 minutes. Remove from heat. Stir in vodka; cool to room temperature. Cover and chill for 4 to 24 hours. Strain the vodka mixture to remove the ginger; discard ginger.

Twinkling Ginger Champagne Punch

2. Pour vodka mixture into a large bowl. Slowly pour the Champagne down the side of the bowl; stir gently with an up-and-down motion to mix.

3. To serve, ladle punch mixture into champagne glasses or punch cups. Serve immediately.

Per serving: 150 cal., 0 g total fat (0 g sat. fat), 0 mg chol., 13 mg sodium, 16 g carbo., 0 g fiber, 0 g pro.

Toasted Nuts with Rosemary

A few years ago when cocktails came back into style, these glazed nuts were developed with martinis in mind! Serve them at your next party with your favorite shaken-over-ice party sipper.

Prep: 15 minutes **Bake:** 15 minutes
Oven: 350°F **Makes:** about 3 cups

  Nonstick cooking spray
1 egg white
2 teaspoons snipped fresh rosemary or
  1 teaspoon dried rosemary, crushed
½ teaspoon coarsely ground black pepper
½ teaspoon salt
3 cups walnut pieces, hazelnuts, and/or
  whole almonds
  Fresh rosemary sprigs (optional)

1. Preheat oven to 350°F. Line a 13×9×2-inch baking pan with foil; lightly coat pan with nonstick cooking spray and set aside. In a medium bowl beat the egg white slightly with a fork until frothy. Add rosemary, pepper, and salt, beating until combined. Add nuts; toss to coat.

Toasted Nuts with Rosemary

2. Spread mixture in an even layer in the prepared baking pan. Bake for 15 to 20 minutes or until golden, stirring once.

3. Remove foil with nuts from pan and set aside to cool. Break up any large pieces. If desired, garnish with rosemary sprigs. Store in an airtight container in the freezer for up to 1 month.

Per 2-tablespoon serving: 99 cal., 10 g total fat (1 g sat. fat), 0 mg chol., 51 mg sodium, 2 g carbo., 1 g fiber, 2 g pro.

Spicy Lime Snack Mix

This crunchy snack mix is an inviting party kick-off meant to be casually nibbled over cocktails. With plenty of lively flavors in the mix, this one will really get guests talking!

Prep: 20 minutes **Bake:** 20 minutes
Oven: 300°F **Makes:** about 8 cups (16 servings)

4 cups bite-size shredded wheat biscuits
1½ cups chow mein noodles or pretzel sticks
1 cup peanuts
1 cup cashews
1 cup whole almonds
¼ cup finely chopped shallot
¼ cup butter
1 tablespoon finely shredded lime peel
2 tablespoons lime juice
1 fresh serrano chile pepper, seeded and
  finely chopped (see note, page 11) or
  ½ teaspoon crushed red pepper
1 tablespoon dried cilantro
1 teaspoon garlic salt
½ teaspoon onion salt
½ teaspoon ground ancho chile pepper or
  chili powder

1. Preheat oven to 300°F. Line a 15×10×1-inch baking pan with foil; set aside.

2. In a bowl combine shredded wheat biscuits, chow mein noodles, peanuts, cashews, and almonds.

3. In a small saucepan cook shallot in hot butter until tender. Stir in lime peel, lime juice, serrano chile pepper, dried cilantro, garlic salt, onion salt, and ground ancho chile pepper; cook and stir for 1 minute. Pour over cereal-nut mixture; toss to coat. Pour into prepared pan.

4. Bake for 20 minutes, stirring twice. Remove from oven. Spread mixture onto a large piece of buttered foil to cool. Store in an airtight container for up to 3 days.

Per ½-cup serving: 242 cal., 18 g total fat (4 g sat. fat), 8 mg chol., 229 mg sodium, 16 g carbo., 3 g fiber, 7 g pro.

Green Goddess Dip

When freshly made and brimming with the zippy flavors of anchovies, lemon, garlic, and fresh herbs, Green Goddess may be one of the world's all-time-great dressings. Somewhere along the line the flavors were parlayed into a terrific dip.

Start to Finish: 30 minutes **Makes:** 2¼ cups dip

⅓ **cup refrigerated or frozen egg product, thawed**
3 **tablespoons lemon juice**
2 **teaspoons Dijon-style mustard**
1 **clove garlic, minced**
1 **cup cooking oil**
4 **to 5 anchovy fillets, drained and chopped (1 tablespoon)**
1 **cup loosely packed fresh parsley leaves**
¼ **cup loosely packed fresh tarragon leaves**
¼ **cup snipped fresh chives**
2 **green onions, chopped**
4 **ounces cream cheese, cubed and softened**
¼ **cup tarragon vinegar**
   Salt
   Assorted vegetable dippers (such as Belgian endive, fresh pea pods, yellow and/or red sweet pepper strips, baby carrots, and/or blanched green beans) (crudités; see tip, page 41)

1. In a large food processor or blender combine egg product, lemon juice, mustard, and garlic; cover and process or blend until combined. With the processor running, add oil in a thin, steady stream. (When necessary, stop and scrape down sides of blender.)

Green Goddess Dip

2. Add anchovy, parsley, tarragon, chives, and green onion; pulse until blended. Add the softened cream cheese and vinegar; pulse to incorporate. Season to taste with salt. Serve with vegetable dippers.

Make-Ahead Tip: Prepare as directed through step 2. Cover and chill for up to 1 week. Serve with vegetable dippers.

Per 2 tablespoons dip: 138 cal., 14 g total fat (3 g sat. fat), 8 mg chol., 76 mg sodium, 1 g carbo., 0 g fiber, 2 g pro.

Hot Reuben Dip

Hot Reuben Dip

When you model a hot dip after a beloved sandwich, you have a surefire hit.

Prep: 10 minutes **Bake:** 25 minutes
Oven: 350°F **Makes:** 18 appetizer servings

- 1 14- or 16-ounce can sauerkraut, rinsed and well drained
- 1½ cups shredded cheddar cheese (6 ounces)
- 1½ cups shredded Swiss cheese (6 ounces)
- 6 ounces corned beef, chopped (about 1 cup)
- 1 cup mayonnaise or salad dressing
   Party rye bread, toasted baguette slices, and/or crackers

1. Preheat oven to 350°F. Pat rinsed and drained sauerkraut dry with paper towels. In a large bowl combine sauerkraut, cheeses, corned beef, and mayonnaise. Spread into a 9-inch quiche dish or 1½-quart casserole.

2. Bake about 25 minutes or until hot and bubbly. Serve with rye bread.

Microwave Directions: Spoon mixture into a 1½-quart microwave-safe casserole. Microwave on 100% power (high) for 5 to 6 minutes or until heated through, stirring twice. Serve as directed.

Per serving: 190 cal., 17 g total fat (6 g sat. fat), 32 mg chol., 396 mg sodium, 2 g carbo., 1 g fiber, 7 g pro.

Four-Onion Dip

Four onions combine with a few "secret ingredients"—honey and orange peel—for a headturning update on the ever-popular onion dip.

Prep: 30 minutes **Chill:** 1 hour
Makes: about 2 cups

- 1 cup chopped sweet onion or shallot
- ½ cup thinly sliced leek
- ½ cup thinly sliced green onion with tops
- 2 cloves garlic, minced
- 2 tablespoons butter or margarine
- 1 8-ounce carton dairy sour cream
- ½ cup mayonnaise or salad dressing
- ½ teaspoon honey or packed brown sugar
- ¼ teaspoon salt
- ¼ teaspoon crushed red pepper
   Dash ground black pepper
- 1 teaspoon finely shredded orange peel
   Assorted crackers and/or vegetable dippers (crudités; see tip, below)

1. In a large skillet cook sweet onion, leek, green onion, and garlic in hot butter about 5 minutes or until tender; cool.

2. In a blender or food processor combine cooked onion mixture, sour cream, mayonnaise, honey, salt, crushed red pepper, and black pepper. Cover and blend or process until nearly smooth. Transfer to a serving bowl. Stir in orange peel. Cover and chill for 1 to 24 hours. Serve with assorted crackers and/or vegetable dippers.

Per 2 tablespoons dip: 101 cal., 10 g total fat (4 g sat. fat), 13 mg chol., 93 mg sodium, 3 g carbo., 0 g fiber, 1 g pro.

Classy Crudités

An array of appetizers really benefits from an artfully arranged tray of crudités (raw vegetables, such as carrots, sweet pepper strips, and sugar snap peas). To serve the pick of the crop at its best, remember:

• If you prepare crudités in advance, refresh the cut vegetables in ice water before storing. Drain well, then seal them in resealable plastic bags, each lined with a paper towel to absorb excess moisture. Store in the refrigerator.

• Arrange crudités on a serving platter and cover them with damp paper towels. Refrigerate up to two hours before serving (mist towels occasionally to remoisten).

• If desired, serve crudités with a tasty sauce for dipping, such as Four-Onion Dip (left) or Green Goddess Dip (page 39).

 ## Olive Cheese Ball

Dating from 1959, this recipe stands the test of time. The pleasing combo of cream cheese, blue cheese, ripe olives, and walnuts still makes a terrific appetizer.

Prep: 20 minutes **Stand:** 45 minutes
Chill: 4 hours **Makes:** 3 cups spread

- 1 **8-ounce package cream cheese**
- 8 **ounces blue cheese, crumbled**
- ¼ **cup butter or margarine**
- ⅔ **cup chopped pitted ripe olives, well drained (one 4½-ounce can)**
- 2 **tablespoons snipped fresh chives**
- ⅓ **cup coarsely chopped walnuts or almonds, toasted**
  Assorted crackers or apple slices

1. In a large bowl let cream cheese, blue cheese, and butter stand at room temperature for 30 minutes. Beat cheeses and butter with an electric mixer on low speed until smooth. Stir in olives and chives. Cover and chill for 4 to 24 hours.

2. Shape mixture into a ball; cover and chill until serving time. To serve, roll in nuts. Let stand for 15 minutes before serving. If desired, garnish with *parsley*. Serve with assorted crackers.

Per 2 tablespoons spread: 100 cal., 10 g total fat (5 g sat. fat), 23 mg chol., 220 mg sodium, 1 g carbo., 0 g fiber, 3 g pro.

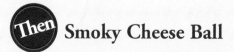 ## Smoky Cheese Ball

This oldie-but-goodie is a favorite of Test Kitchen veteran Maryellyn Krantz, who says, "Christmas wouldn't be Christmas at my house without this delicious cheese ball." Surprisingly, it freezes really well so you can enjoy it later. If you are hosting a small party, divide the mixture into two balls and freeze the extra one.

Prep: 20 minutes **Stand:** 45 minutes
Chill: 4 hours **Makes:** 3½ cups spread

- 2 **8-ounce packages cream cheese**
- 2 **cups finely shredded smoked cheddar, Swiss, or Gouda cheese (8 ounces)**
- ½ **cup butter or margarine**
- 2 **tablespoons milk**
- 2 **teaspoons bottled steak sauce**
- 1 **cup finely chopped mixed nuts**
  Assorted crackers, flatbread, and/or crusty French bread

1. In a large mixing bowl let the cream cheese, shredded cheese, and butter stand at room temperature for 30 minutes. Add milk and steak sauce; beat with an electric mixer on medium speed until fluffy. Cover and chill for 4 to 24 hours.

2. Divide mixture in half. Shape into two balls; roll in nuts. Let stand for 15 minutes before serving. Serve with crackers.

Make-Ahead Tip: Prepare as directed, except do not roll in nuts. Wrap cheese ball in moisture- and vaporproof plastic wrap. Freeze for up to 1 month. To serve, thaw in refrigerator overnight. Roll in nuts. Let stand at room temperature for 30 minutes before serving.

Per tablespoon spread: 73 cal., 7 g total fat (4 g sat. fat), 17 mg chol., 71 mg sodium, 1 g carbo., 0 g fiber, 2 g pro.

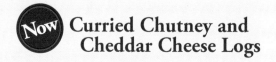 ## Curried Chutney and Cheddar Cheese Logs

Chutney, curry, peanuts, and coconut combine for an all-new, globally inspired version of this ever-favorite party snack. At large gatherings, prepare this recipe with one or two other cheese balls, so there's a cheese spread for every taste. Serve with an assortment of crackers, apple wedges, and pear slices for a complete appetizer spread!

Prep: 25 minutes **Stand:** 45 minutes
Chill: 4 hours **Makes:** about 2 cups spread

- 2 **3-ounce packages cream cheese**
- 6 **ounces aged white cheddar cheese or sharp cheddar cheese, finely shredded (1½ cups)**
- ¼ **cup butter**
- ½ **teaspoon curry powder**
- ¼ **cup bottled mango chutney, snipped**
- 2 **tablespoons thinly sliced green onion**
- 1 **tablespoon snipped fresh mint (optional)**
- ¼ **cup coconut, toasted**

Olive Cheese Ball and Smoky Cheese Ball

¼ cup finely chopped honey-roasted peanuts
  Apple wedges, pear slices, crackers,
    and/or flatbread

1. In a large mixing bowl let cream cheese, shredded cheese, and butter stand at room temperature for 30 minutes. Add curry powder. Beat with an electric mixer on medium speed until light and fluffy. Using a wooden spoon, stir in chutney, green onion, and, if desired, mint. Cover and chill for 4 to 24 hours.

2. Before serving, divide mixture in half. Shape each half into an 8-inch-long log. In a shallow dish combine coconut and peanuts. Roll logs in coconut-peanut mixture.

3. Let stand for 15 minutes before serving. Serve with apples, pears, crackers, or flatbread.

Per 2 tablespoons spread: 131 cal., 12 g total fat (7 g sat. fat), 30 mg chol., 141 mg sodium, 3 g carbo., 0 g fiber, 4 g pro.

Herbed Leek Tart

Believe it or not, this elegant (and outstandingly delicious) tart starts with something as simple as a refrigerated pizza crust.

Prep: 25 minutes **Bake:** 15 minutes
Stand: 5 minutes **Oven:** 425°F
Makes: 24 pieces

- 1   13.8-ounce package refrigerated pizza dough
- 6   medium leeks, thinly sliced (2 cups)
- 3   cloves garlic, minced
- 2   tablespoons olive oil
- 4   teaspoons snipped fresh savory or thyme
- 3   tablespoons creamy Dijon-style mustard blend
- 1   cup shredded Gruyère cheese (4 ounces)
- ¼   cup pine nuts or chopped almonds, toasted

1. Preheat oven to 425°F. Grease a large baking sheet. Unroll pizza dough onto prepared baking sheet; press to form a 13×9-inch rectangle. Cut rectangle in half lengthwise, forming two 13×4½-inch rectangles. Separate rectangles on baking sheet so edges are at least 1 inch apart. Bake for 7 minutes.

2. Meanwhile, in a large skillet cook leek and garlic in hot olive oil about 5 minutes or until tender. Remove from heat. Stir in snipped herb. Spread mustard blend over prebaked crusts. Top each evenly with leek mixture, cheese, and nuts.

3. Bake for 8 to 10 minutes more or until cheese is melted and crust is golden. Let stand for 5 minutes before serving. Cut each rectangle into 12 pieces.

Per pieces: 82 cal., 5 g total fat (1 g sat. fat), 5 mg chol., 96 mg sodium, 8 g carbo., 0 g fiber, 3 g pro.

Gouda Pecan Spread

Gouda Pecan Spread

Gouda is a semifirm Dutch cheese with an assertive, yet mild, flavor that goes well with nuts—especially pecans, as you'll find out once you taste this three-ingredient spread.

Prep: 20 minutes **Stand:** 30 minutes
Chill: 1 hour **Makes:** 1½ cups spread

- 1   cup finely shredded Gouda cheese (4 ounces)
- ¼   cup dairy sour cream
- ¼   cup very finely chopped pecans
     Assorted crackers and/or sweet pepper pieces

1. Place cheese in a medium mixing bowl; let stand at room temperature for 30 minutes. Add sour cream and pecans. Beat with an electric mixer until combined and mixture is creamy. Cover and chill for 1 hour. Serve with crackers.

Note: For easier shredding, chill the Gouda cheese well before preparing.

Per tablespoon spread: 29 cal., 3 g total fat (1 g sat. fat), 6 mg chol., 40 mg sodium, 0 g carbo., 0 g fiber, 1 g pro.

Golden Cheese Wheel

A flavorful Muenster cheese filling nestles inside a thin homemade bread crust for a surefire standout on an appetizer table.

Prep: 30 minutes **Rise:** 1 hour **Bake:** 25 minutes
Oven: 375°F **Makes:** 12 wedges

Golden Cheese Wheel

  1 package active dry yeast
  ⅔ cup warm water (110°F to 115°F)
1¾ to 2 cups all-purpose flour
  2 tablespoons cooking oil
  ½ teaspoon sugar
  ½ teaspoon salt
  1 egg, beaten
  3 cups shredded Muenster cheese
      (12 ounces)
  ½ cup snipped fresh parsley
  ¼ teaspoon garlic powder
  ⅛ teaspoon black pepper
  1 egg, slightly beaten
  1 tablespoon water
1½ teaspoons sesame seeds

1. In a large mixing bowl dissolve yeast in the warm water. Add 1 cup of the flour, the oil, sugar, and salt. Beat with an electric mixer on low to medium speed for 30 seconds, scraping bowl frequently. Beat on high speed for 3 minutes. Using a wooden spoon, stir in as much of the remaining flour as you can.

2. Turn out dough onto a lightly floured surface. Knead in enough of the remaining all-purpose flour to make a moderately stiff dough that is smooth and elastic (6 to 8 minutes total).

3. Shape dough into a ball. Place in a lightly greased bowl, turning once to grease surface of dough. Cover; let rise in a warm place until double in size (about 1 hour).

4. Preheat oven to 375°F. Grease a 12-inch round pizza pan; set aside. Punch dough down. Turn out onto a lightly floured surface; divide into two portions. Cover and let rest for 10 minutes. On a lightly floured surface, roll one dough portion into a 13-inch circle. Place circle on prepared pizza pan (dough will extend past edges of pan).

5. In a medium bowl combine the 1 beaten egg, the cheese, parsley, garlic powder, and pepper. Spread over dough in pan. Roll remaining dough into 13-inch circle. Place over filling. Trim top and bottom layers of dough to ½ inch beyond the edge of the pan; seal and flute edges.

6. In a small bowl combine 1 slightly beaten egg and 1 tablespoon water; brush over top of dough. Sprinkle with sesame seeds. Bake for 25 to 30 minutes or until golden brown. Cut into narrow wedges. Serve hot.

Make-Ahead Tip: Prepare as directed through step 5. Cover and chill for up to 2 hours. Continue as directed in step 6.

Per wedge: 203 cal., 12 g total fat (6 g sat. fat), 62 mg chol., 289 mg sodium, 14 g carbo., 1 g fiber, 10 g pro.

Phyllo-Wrapped Hazelnut And Brie

No matter what you call them—hazelnuts, filberts, or cobnuts—these rich nuts add just the right amount of crunch to the caramelized onions that top this elegant phyllo-wrapped appetizer.

Prep: 40 minutes **Bake:** 20 minutes
Stand: 5 minutes **Oven:** 400°F
Makes: 12 servings

- 2 **tablespoons butter**
- 4 **medium sweet onions (such as Vidalia, Maui, and Walla Walla), cut into thin wedges (about 2 cups)**
- ⅓ **cup chopped hazelnuts (filberts) or walnuts, toasted**
- 8 **sheets frozen phyllo dough (14×9 inches), thawed**
- ¼ **cup butter, melted**
- 2 **4½-ounce rounds Brie or Camembert cheese**
- ¼ **cup apricot spreadable fruit**
  Pear and/or apple wedges and/or assorted crackers

1. In a large skillet melt butter over medium-low heat. Add onion; cover and cook for 13 to 15 minutes or until onion is tender, stirring occasionally. Uncover; cook and stir over medium-high heat for 3 to 5 minutes more or until onion is golden. Stir in nuts. Cool completely.

2. Preheat oven to 400°F. Unfold phyllo dough; remove one sheet of dough. (As you work, cover the remaining phyllo dough with plastic wrap to prevent it from drying out.) Lightly brush dough with some of the ¼ cup melted butter. Place another sheet of the phyllo dough crosswise on top of the first sheet; brush with butter. Repeat with two more sheets of the phyllo dough, brushing each with butter and laying sheets diagonally over the first two sheets to form a large octagon shape.

3. Slice one round of the Brie in half horizontally. Place bottom half in center of phyllo stack. Spread bottom half of cheese round with 1 tablespoon of the apricot spreadable fruit; top with one-fourth of the onion mixture. Top with other half of the Brie, cut side down, 1 tablespoon spreadable fruit, and another one-fourth of the onion mixture.

4. Bring phyllo up and over topping, pleating it as needed to cover and slightly twisting it on top to close. Brush phyllo with butter. Repeat with remaining phyllo, butter, Brie, spreadable fruit, and onion mixture.

5. Place each wrapped Brie round in an 8×8×2-inch baking pan or place both rounds in a 13×9×2-inch baking pan. Bake about 20 minutes or until golden brown. Let stand for 5 to 10 minutes before serving. Serve with fruit wedges and/or crackers.

Per serving: 195 cal., 15 g total fat (8 g sat. fat), 38 mg chol., 234 mg sodium, 11 g carbo., 1 g fiber, 6 g pro.

Party Nachos

Every appetizer spread needs one extra-hearty dish for guests who nibble (rather than dine) their way through an evening. Loaded with satisfying ingredients, these nachos will do the trick.

Prep: 10 minutes **Bake:** 5 minutes per batch
Oven: 400°F **Makes:** 8 to 10 servings

- 8 **ounces tortilla chips (about 10 cups)**
- 2 **cups shredded cheddar cheese (8 ounces)**
- 2 **cups shredded Monterey Jack cheese (8 ounces)**
- 3 **green onions, sliced**
- 1 **cup chopped seeded tomato**
- 1 **4-ounce can diced green chile peppers, drained**

Party Nachos

1　2¼-ounce can sliced pitted ripe olives, drained
1　15-ounce can black beans, rinsed and drained
　　Purchased salsa (optional)
　　Dairy sour cream (optional)
　　Purchased guacamole (optional)

1. Preheat oven to 400°F. Divide tortilla chips between two 12-inch round pizza pans. Top chips with half of the cheddar cheese, half of the Monterey Jack cheese, the green onion, tomato, and chile peppers. Sprinkle with remaining cheeses, the olives, and black beans.

2. Bake, one pan at a time, for 5 to 7 minutes or until cheese melts. Serve immediately. If desired, serve with salsa, sour cream, and/or guacamole.

Per serving: 414 cal., 27 g total fat (13 g sat. fat), 55 mg chol., 720 mg sodium, 28 g carbo., 5 g fiber, 20 g pro.

 **Sweet-and-Sour Glazed Chicken Sausage Bites**

Take advantage of the many fascinating varieties of cooked chicken sausages that are available today. They taste terrific in this updated rendition of the saucy sausage party morsel.

Prep: 20 minutes　**Cook:** 30 minutes
Makes: 18 to 20 servings

1　tablespoon olive oil
½　cup finely chopped onion
⅓　cup finely chopped red sweet pepper
3　cloves garlic, minced
⅔　cup bottled chili sauce
⅔　cup apple jelly
2　tablespoons soy sauce
2　teaspoons cornstarch
2　teaspoons grated fresh ginger or ½ teaspoon ground ginger
¼　teaspoon crushed red pepper
3　12-ounce packages apple chardonnay, sun-dried tomato, spicy jalapeño, and/or other specialty cooked chicken sausage, cut into ¾-inch slices

1. In a large saucepan heat oil over medium heat. Add onion, sweet pepper, and garlic; cook and stir about 3 minutes or until vegetables are tender. Stir in chili sauce, apple jelly, soy sauce, cornstarch, ginger, and crushed red pepper. Cook and stir until bubbly. Stir in sausage slices. Cook, covered, over medium-low heat about 20 minutes or until heated through, stirring occasionally.

Per serving: 125 cal., 3 g total fat (1 g sat. fat), 47 mg chol., 659 mg sodium, 12 g carbo., 1 g fiber, 12 g pro.

 **Sausage Bites**

Various takes on this tried-and-true favorite have peppered the pages of Better Homes and Gardens publications over the years. This one stands out because of its simplicity.

Prep: 10 minutes　**Cook:** 20 minutes
Makes: 16 to 20 servings

1　cup bottled barbecue sauce
½　cup apricot preserves
1　teaspoon dry mustard
1　pound cooked bratwurst, cut into ¾-inch-thick slices
1　pound cooked kielbasa, cut into ¾-inch-thick slices
8　ounces small cooked smoked sausage links

1. In a large saucepan combine barbecue sauce, apricot preserves, and dry mustard. Cook and stir until bubbly. Stir in bratwurst, kielbasa, and smoked sausage links. Cook, covered, over medium-low heat about 20 minutes more or until heated through, stirring occasionally.

Per serving: 272 cal., 21 g total fat (8 g sat. fat), 42 mg chol., 742 mg sodium, 11 g carbo., 0 g fiber, 9 g pro.

Slow Cooker Directions: In a 3½- or 4-quart slow cooker combine barbecue sauce, apricot preserves, and dry mustard. Stir in bratwurst, kielbasa, and smoked sausage links. Cover and cook on low-heat setting for 4 to 5 hours or on high-heat setting for 2½ to 3 hours. Serve immediately, or keep warm on low-heat setting for up to 1 hour.

Calypso Shrimp Skewers

When you want to pull out all the stops for a party, you can't go wrong with shrimp. These flavor-packed appetite pleasers will make guests feel special.

Prep: 30 minutes **Bake:** 4 minutes
Oven: 375°F **Makes:** about 30 appetizers

  1 **pound fresh or frozen large shrimp (about 30)**
  ⅓ **cup honey**
  1 **teaspoon grated fresh ginger**
  ⅔ **cup shredded coconut**
  ⅔ **cup finely chopped peanuts**
  1 **3-ounce package thinly sliced prosciutto, cut into 7×½-inch strips**
  1 **7-ounce container crème fraîche**
  1 **teaspoon finely shredded lime peel**
     Lime juice

1. Thaw shrimp, if frozen. Peel and devein shrimp. Rinse shrimp; pat dry with paper towels. Meanwhile, soak about thirty 6-inch wooden skewers in water for 30 minutes. Line a baking sheet with foil.

2. Preheat oven to 375°F. In a small bowl combine honey and ginger; set aside. In a shallow dish combine coconut and peanuts; set aside. Drain skewers. Beginning at the tail end, thread each shrimp lengthwise on a skewer until it is straight. Brush each shrimp with the honey mixture, coating completely, then roll in coconut mixture. Wrap one strip of prosciutto around each shrimp.

Holiday Shrimp Rounds

3. Arrange skewers of wrapped shrimp on prepared baking sheet. Bake for 4 to 6 minutes or until golden and shrimp are opaque.

4. In a small bowl stir together crème fraîche, lime peel, and enough lime juice to make desired consistency. Serve with shrimp.

Outdoor Grill Directions: For a charcoal grill, arrange medium-hot coals around a drip pan. Test for medium heat above the pan. Place shrimp on grill rack over the drip pan. Cover and grill for 5 to 8 minutes or until shrimp are opaque. (For a gas grill, preheat grill. Reduce heat to medium. Adjust for indirect cooking. Place shrimp on the grill rack. Grill as above.)

Per appetizer: 72 cal., 5 g total fat (2 g sat. fat), 25 mg chol., 111 mg sodium, 4 g carbo., 0 g fiber, 4 g pro.

Holiday Shrimp Rounds

When this enduring party recipe originally appeared in 1976, it called for a tricky from-scratch pastry crust. Now, puff pastry simplifies the prep, making the little gems elegant and easy.

Prep: 25 minutes **Bake:** 12 minutes
Stand: 40 minutes **Oven:** 375°F
Makes: 28 appetizers

  1 **17.3-ounce package frozen puff pastry sheets (2 sheets)**
  ½ **cup shredded cheddar cheese (2 ounces)**
     Milk
  8 **ounces cooked and peeled medium shrimp, thawed if frozen**
  1 **8-ounce package cream cheese, softened**
  ¼ **cup milk**
  1 **teaspoon lemon juice**
  1 **teaspoon Worcestershire sauce**
  1 **teaspoon snipped fresh dill or**
    ¼ **teaspoon dried dill**
     Dash garlic powder

1. Allow puff pastry sheets to stand at room temperature for 40 minutes to thaw. Unfold pastry and place on a lightly floured surface; sprinkle evenly with cheese. Using a lightly floured rolling pin, roll each to a 12-inch square, rolling cheese into dough.

2. Preheat oven to 375°F. Using a 2-inch floured biscuit cutter, cut out rounds from each square (to yield about 56 rounds total). Using a 1-inch round hors d'oeuvre cutter, cut a circle out of the center of half of the dough rounds. Place remaining rounds about 2 inches apart on ungreased baking sheets; brush with milk and top each with 1 of the rounds with center removed. Prick center of stack with a toothpick before baking. (If desired, arrange cutout centers on the baking sheets in between the larger rounds.)

3. Bake about 12 minutes or until puffed and golden. Cool on wire rack.

4. Meanwhile, for the filling, coarsely chop shrimp; set aside. In a medium mixing bowl combine cream cheese, the ¼ cup milk, the lemon juice, Worcestershire sauce, dill, and garlic powder. Beat with an electric mixer on medium speed until smooth; stir in chopped shrimp.

5. Spoon filling onto baked pastry rounds. If desired, top each with a fresh *dill sprig*.

Make-Ahead Tip: Prepare as directed through step 3. Arrange in a single layer in an airtight container or freezer container. Store at room temperature for up to 24 hours or freeze for up to 3 months. Thaw pastry rounds, if frozen. Continue as directed in steps 4 and 5.

Per appetizer: 123 cal., 9 g total fat (2 g sat. fat), 27 mg chol., 124 mg sodium, 7 g carbo., 0 g fiber, 4 g pro.

Sesame-Soy Meatballs

Sesame-Soy Meatballs

No chapter of best appetizer recipes would be complete without a terrific party meatball. In this version, soy sauce and sesame seeds add intrigue.

Prep: 30 minutes **Chill:** 1 hour
Broil: 10 minutes **Makes:** 40 appetizers

- 1 **pound lean ground beef**
- ⅓ **cup finely chopped green onion**
- ¼ **cup finely chopped onion**
- 3 **tablespoons soy sauce**
- 2 **tablespoons sesame seeds, toasted**
- 1 **tablespoon sugar**
- ½ **of a medium fresh pineapple, peeled, cored, and cut into 1-inch pieces**
- 1 **medium papaya, peeled, seeded, and cut into 1-inch pieces**

1. In a medium bowl combine ground beef, green onion, onion, soy sauce, sesame seeds, and sugar. Shape meat mixture into 40 meatballs, each about 1 inch in diameter. Transfer meatballs to a 15×10×1-inch baking pan; cover and chill for 1 hour.

2. Preheat broiler. Place meatballs onto the unheated rack of a broiler pan. Broil 3 to 4 inches from the heat for 10 to 12 minutes or until cooked through turning occasionally. Serve with pineapple and papaya pieces.

Per appetizer: 60 cal., 4 g total fat (1 g sat. fat), 4 mg chol., 167 mg sodium, 1 g carbo., 0 g fiber, 4 g pro.

Spicy Wings with Avocado Salsa

Party wings take on the fresh, vibrant flavors of the Southwest. Serve with tortilla chips—after the wings are gone, guests will be glad to scoop up leftover salsa with a chip.

Prep: 15 minutes **Bake:** 30 minutes
Oven: 425°F **Makes:** about 36 servings

   Nonstick cooking spray
1 3-pound package frozen chicken wing pieces (about 36), thawed
2 tablespoons cooking oil
1 tablespoon ground cumin
2 teaspoons garlic salt
1½ teaspoons paprika
1½ teaspoons lemon-pepper seasoning
¼ to ½ teaspoon cayenne pepper
2 medium ripe avocados, halved, pitted, and peeled
¼ cup chopped red onion
2 tablespoons snipped fresh cilantro
1 to 2 tablespoons lemon juice

1. Preheat oven to 425°F. Lightly coat the rack of an unheated broiler pan with nonstick cooking spray; set aside. Place the chicken pieces in a large bowl. In a small bowl combine oil, cumin, 1½ teaspoons of the garlic salt, the paprika, lemon-pepper seasoning, and cayenne pepper. Pour spice mixture over chicken, tossing to coat. Arrange wing pieces in a single layer on the rack of the prepared broiler pan. Brush with any spice mixture remaining in bowl. Bake about 30 minutes or until wings are browned, tender, and no longer pink.

2. Meanwhile, in a medium bowl mash avocado with a fork until slightly chunky. Stir in red onion, cilantro, lemon juice, and the remaining ½ teaspoon garlic salt. Cover with plastic wrap, pressing it onto surface to prevent browning; chill until serving time or up to 24 hours.

3. Spoon the avocado mixture into a serving bowl. Place onto a serving platter. Surround with the chicken pieces. If desired, garnish with *cilantro* and/or *jalapeño peppers* (see note, page 11).

Per serving: 106 cal., 8 g total fat (2 g sat. fat), 39 mg chol., 134 mg sodium, 1 g carbo., 1 g fiber, 7 g pro.

Soy-Sauced Chicken Wings

Here's a hit from 1978. It combines soy sauce, fresh ginger, and five-spice powder for an intriguing Asian accent to the party wing.

Prep: 25 minutes **Bake:** 25 minutes
Marinate: 2 hours **Oven:** 425°F
Makes: 12 to 18 appetizer servings

12 to 18 chicken wings (2 to 3 pounds)
⅔ cup soy sauce
¼ cup sliced green onion
¼ cup rice vinegar
¼ cup cooking oil
1 tablespoon sugar
1 tablespoon grated fresh ginger
2 cloves garlic, minced
½ teaspoon crushed red pepper
½ teaspoon five-spice powder

1. Cut off and discard tips of chicken wings. Cut wings at joints to form 24 to 36 pieces. Place chicken pieces in a large resealable plastic bag set in a deep bowl. In a medium bowl combine soy sauce, green onion, vinegar, oil, sugar, ginger, garlic, crushed red pepper, and five-spice powder. Pour over chicken in bag. Seal bag; turn to coat chicken pieces. Marinate in the refrigerator for 2 to 24 hours, turning bag occasionally.

2. Preheat oven to 425°F. Drain chicken, discarding marinade. Place chicken pieces onto the unheated rack of a broiler pan. Bake for 25 to 30 minutes or until chicken is tender and no longer pink.

Per serving: 135 cal., 10 g total fat (2 g sat. fat), 38 mg chol., 434 mg sodium, 1 g carbo., 0 g fiber, 10 g pro.

Brightest and Best
Breakfasts
and Brunches

These hall-of-fame recipes have pleased the breakfast and brunch bunch for years! Start the day brightly with Citrus-Mint Kiss in everyone's glass. Then choose Chocolate Chip Pancakes with Raspberry Syrup or Peanut Waffles with Butterscotch Sauce if you have a crowd of kids around the table. For more sophisticated guests, serve Baked Eggs with Cheese and Basil Sauce or Mushroom, Spinach, and Havarti Quiche. Everyone will love Stuffed French Toast or a magical Puffed Oven Pancake. You'll find the right recipe for any morning throughout the holiday season.

Mushroom, Spinach, and Havarti Quiche, page 64

Warm Citrus Fruit with Brown Sugar

Warm Citrus Fruit with Brown Sugar

Grapefruit broiled with brown sugar is a classic. Why not embellish it by adding some oranges and pineapple to the mix? The result is a bright, sweet-tart start to the morning.

Prep: 15 minutes **Broil:** 5 minutes
Makes: 4 servings

- 2 **medium red grapefruit, peeled and sectioned, or 1½ cups drained refrigerated grapefruit sections**
- 2 **medium oranges, peeled and sectioned**
- 1 **cup fresh pineapple chunks or one 8-ounce can pineapple chunks, drained**
- 2 **tablespoons rum (optional)**
- ¼ **cup packed brown sugar**
- 2 **tablespoons butter, softened**

1. Preheat broiler. In a medium bowl combine grapefruit, orange, and pineapple. Transfer to a 1-quart broilerproof au gratin dish or casserole.*

2. If desired, in a small saucepan heat rum until it almost simmers. Carefully pour over fruit. Stir gently to coat.

3. In a small bowl stir together brown sugar and butter until well mixed; sprinkle over fruit. Broil about 4 inches from the heat for 5 to 6 minutes or until sugar is bubbly and fruit is warmed.

*****Note:** For single servings, use four au gratin dishes and omit the rum.

Per serving: 192 cal., 6 g total fat (4 g sat. fat), 16 mg chol., 68 mg sodium, 35 g carbo., 4 g fiber, 2 g pro.

Citrus-Mint Kiss

When you want to offer overnight guests something more eye-opening than the usual fruit juice, this zippy sipper will do the trick. If you're feeling festive, add a splash of Champagne or vodka to the mix.

Prep: 10 minutes **Stand:** 1 hour
Chill: 2 hours **Makes:** 6 servings

- 1 **cup snipped fresh mint leaves**
- 2 **cups water**
- ⅔ **cup sugar**
- 1 **teaspoon finely shredded orange peel**
- 2 **cups orange juice**
- ⅔ **cup lemon juice**
  Cracked ice
  Fresh mint sprigs (optional)

1. Place mint in a medium bowl. In a small saucepan combine the water and sugar; bring to boiling, stirring until sugar dissolves. Remove from heat. Pour sugar mixture over mint leaves. Stir in orange peel, orange juice, and lemon juice. Cover and let stand at room temperature for 1 hour. Strain. Cover and chill for 2 to 24 hours.

2. To serve, transfer chilled mixture to a pitcher. Pour over ice in glasses. If desired, garnish with mint sprigs.

Per serving: 95 cal., 0 g total fat (0 g sat. fat), 0 mg chol., 3 mg sodium, 24 g carbo., 0 g fiber, 0 g pro.

Stuffed French Toast

Eclectic urban cafes popped up in the 1990s, serving gourmet breakfasts and serious coffee. This favorite from 1992 would be right at home in one of those cozy neighborhood spots.

Start to Finish: 35 minutes **Oven:** 300°F
Makes: 10 to 12 slices

- 1 **8-ounce package cream cheese, softened**
- 1 **cup apricot preserves**
- 1 **teaspoon vanilla**
- ½ **cup chopped walnuts**
- 1 **16-ounce loaf French bread**
- 4 **eggs**
- 1 **cup whipping cream**
- ½ **teaspoon ground nutmeg**
- ½ **teaspoon vanilla**
- ¼ **cup orange juice**
  Fresh or frozen raspberries (optional)

1. Preheat oven to 300°F. In a medium mixing bowl combine cream cheese, 2 tablespoons of the apricot preserves, and the 1 teaspoon vanilla; beat with an electric mixer on medium speed until fluffy. Stir in nuts; set aside.

2. Cut bread into ten to twelve 1½-inch slices; cut a pocket about 2 inches deep in the top of each bread slice, being careful not to cut all the way to the sides. Fill each pocket with a rounded tablespoon of the cream cheese mixture.

3. In a medium bowl whisk together eggs, whipping cream, nutmeg, and the ½ teaspoon vanilla. Using tongs, quickly dip the filled bread slices in the egg mixture, allowing excess mixture to drip off (take care not to squeeze out the filling). Cook on a lightly greased griddle over medium heat about 4 minutes or until golden brown, turning once. Keep warm in the oven while cooking remaining slices.

4. Meanwhile, in a small saucepan combine the remaining apricot preserves and the orange juice; heat and stir until mixture is melted. To serve, drizzle the apricot preserves mixture over the hot French toast. If desired, top with raspberries.

Per slice: 449 cal., 24 g total fat (12 g sat. fat), 143 mg chol., 388 mg sodium, 49 g carbo., 2 g fiber, 10 g pro.

Reduced-Fat Stuffed French Toast: Prepare as directed, except use reduced-fat cream cheese (Neufchâtel); substitute 1 cup refrigerated or frozen egg product, thawed, for the whole eggs; and use fat-free milk instead of the whipping cream.

Per slice: 337 cal., 11 g total fat (4 g sat. fat), 18 mg chol., 430 mg sodium, 49 g carbo., 2 g fiber, 11 g pro.

Peanut Waffles with Butterscotch Sauce

There are quicker ways to make waffles, but when you take the time to beat egg whites, you'll obtain the sort of fluffy, dreamy consistency that has made these breakfast treats a favorite since 1938. Try the Butterscotch Sauce over pound cake.

Prep: 25 minutes **Cook:** per waffle maker directions
Makes: 16 to 20 (4-inch) waffles

1¾ cups all-purpose flour
 2 tablespoons sugar
 1 tablespoon baking powder
 ¼ teaspoon salt
 2 egg yolks
1¾ cups milk
 ½ cup cooking oil
 ½ cup finely chopped peanuts
 2 egg whites
 1 recipe Butterscotch Sauce
    Banana slices (optional)
    Chopped peanuts (optional)

1. Lightly grease waffle maker; preheat. In a large bowl stir together flour, sugar, baking powder, and salt. In a medium bowl beat egg yolks with a fork; stir in milk and oil. Add egg mixture to flour mixture all at once, stirring until combined but still slightly lumpy. Stir in the ½ cup peanuts. Set aside.

2. In a small mixing bowl beat egg whites with an electric mixer on medium to high speed until stiff peaks form (tips stand straight). Gently fold egg whites into batter, leaving a few fluffs of egg white. Do not overmix.

3. Pour 1 to 1¼ cups of the batter onto grids of waffle maker. Close lid quickly; do not open during cooking. Cook according to manufacturer's directions. When done, use a fork to lift waffle off grid. Repeat with remaining batter.

4. Serve hot with warm Butterscotch Sauce. If desired, top with banana slices and sprinkle with additional peanuts.

Butterscotch Sauce: In a medium saucepan combine 1¼ cups packed brown sugar, ⅔ cup light-colored corn syrup, ¼ cup milk, and ¼ cup butter. Bring just to boiling; reduce heat. Simmer, uncovered, for 20 minutes, stirring occasionally. Serve warm. (Refrigerate any remaining sauce; reheat in saucepan over low heat.)

Per waffle + 2 tablespoons sauce: 293 cal., 13 g total fat (4 g sat. fat), 36 mg chol., 146 mg sodium, 41 g carbo., 1 g fiber, 4 g pro.

Puffed Oven Pancake

Sometimes called a German pancake or a Dutch baby, this baked pancake is lusciously eggy, yet delightfully airy.

Prep: 10 minutes **Bake:** 20 minutes
Oven: 400°F **Makes:** 6 servings

 2 tablespoons butter or margarine
 3 eggs
 ½ cup all-purpose flour
 ½ cup milk
 ¼ teaspoon salt
 ¼ cup orange marmalade
 3 cups sliced fresh fruit (such as strawberries, nectarines, pears, or peeled peaches)
    Powdered sugar (optional)
    Whipped cream (optional)

Puffed Oven Pancake

56

1. Preheat oven to 400°F. Place butter in a 10-inch ovenproof skillet. Place skillet in oven for 3 to 5 minutes or until butter is melted.

2. Meanwhile, for batter, in a medium bowl beat eggs with a wire whisk or rotary beater. Add flour, milk, and salt; beat until smooth. Immediately pour batter into the hot skillet. Bake for 20 to 25 minutes or until puffed and brown.

3. Meanwhile, in a small saucepan melt the orange marmalade over low heat. To serve, top pancake with fruit; spoon melted marmalade over fruit. If desired, sift powdered sugar on top and serve with whipped cream. Cut into wedges and serve warm.

Per serving: 176 cal., 7 g total fat (4 g sat. fat), 119 mg chol., 188 mg sodium, 23 g carbo., 2 g fiber, 5 g pro.

Chocolate Chip Pancakes With Raspberry Syrup

Sprinkling pancakes with chocolate chips may sound like something that would appeal mostly to kids. But the rich, flaky pancakes themselves, served with raspberry syrup, make this treat plenty sophisticated.

Prep: 25 minutes **Cook:** 2 minutes per batch
Makes: about 12 (4-inch) pancakes

1½ **cups all-purpose flour**
  3 **tablespoons sugar**
  1 **teaspoon baking powder**
 ½ **teaspoon baking soda**
 ¼ **teaspoon salt**
  2 **eggs, slightly beaten**
  1 **8-ounce carton dairy sour cream**
  1 **cup milk**
 ¼ **cup butter, melted**
 ½ **cup miniature or regular semisweet**
     chocolate pieces
  1 **teaspoon cooking oil**
 ½ **cup fresh raspberries**
  1 **12-ounce bottle raspberry-flavored**
     pancake and waffle syrup

1. In a large bowl combine flour, sugar, baking powder, baking soda, and salt. Make a well in center of flour mixture; set aside.

Chocolate Chip Pancakes with Raspberry Syrup

2. In a medium bowl combine eggs and sour cream. Whisk until smooth. Stir in milk and melted butter. Add egg mixture all at once to flour mixture. Stir just until moistened (batter should be lumpy). Gently fold in the ½ cup chocolate pieces.

3. On a griddle or in a large heavy skillet heat oil over medium heat for 3 to 4 minutes. Pour about ⅓ cup batter per pancake onto the hot griddle.

4. Cook for 1 to 2 minutes on the first side or until the pancakes have bubbly surfaces and the edges look slightly dry. Using a wide pancake turner, carefully flip the pancakes. Cook for 1 to 1½ minutes more on the second side or until golden. Repeat with remaining batter. Add additional oil to griddle between batches as necessary.

5. Meanwhile, stir raspberries into raspberry-flavored syrup. Serve pancakes immediately with raspberry syrup mixture. If desired, top with *whipped cream* and additional chocolate pieces.

Per 4-inch pancake: 263 cal., 11 g total fat (6 g sat. fat), 55 mg chol., 202 mg sodium, 38 g carbo., 1 g fiber, 4 g pro.

Cinnamon Breakfast Muffins

In 1972, these cakelike muffins won a prize at a local fair in Vermont. The Better Homes and Gardens® *magazine editors at the time were so taken by the buttery little gems that they published the recipe in the magazine.*

Prep: 15 minutes **Bake:** 20 minutes
Oven: 350°F **Makes:** 12 muffins

1½ cups all-purpose flour
½ cup sugar
1½ teaspoons baking powder
¼ teaspoon ground nutmeg
⅛ teaspoon salt
1 egg
½ cup milk
⅓ cup butter, melted
¼ cup sugar
½ teaspoon ground cinnamon
¼ cup butter, melted

1. Preheat oven to 350°F. Grease twelve 2½-inch muffin cups; set aside.

2. In a medium bowl stir together flour, the ½ cup sugar, the baking powder, nutmeg, and salt. Make a well in the center of the flour mixture. In a small bowl beat egg with a fork; stir in milk and the ⅓ cup melted butter. Add egg mixture to flour mixture; stir just until moistened (the batter may be lumpy).

3. Spoon batter into prepared muffin cups, filling each two-thirds full. Bake for 20 to 25 minutes or until golden.

4. In a small bowl combine the ¼ cup sugar and the cinnamon. Remove muffins from oven; remove from muffin cups. Immediately dip baked muffins into the ¼ cup melted butter, then into sugar-cinnamon mixture. Serve warm.

Per muffin: 189 cal., 10 g total fat (6 g sat. fat), 42 mg chol., 128 mg sodium, 24 g carbo., 0 g fiber, 2 g pro.

Cream Cheese-Raspberry Coffee Cake

This moist, rich coffee cake makes it onto the favorites list again and again. It's sumptuously rich, easy, and it serves a crowd. If you wish, substitute your favorite flavor of preserves for the raspberry.

Prep: 20 minutes **Bake:** 30 minutes
Cool: 30 minutes **Oven:** 350°F
Makes: 24 servings

1 8-ounce package cream cheese or reduced-fat cream cheese (Neufchâtel), softened
1 cup granulated sugar
½ cup butter, softened
1¾ cups all-purpose flour
2 eggs
¼ cup milk
1 teaspoon baking powder
½ teaspoon baking soda
½ teaspoon vanilla
¼ teaspoon salt
½ cup seedless red raspberry jam
Powdered sugar

1. Preheat oven to 350°F. Grease a 13×9×2-inch baking pan. Set aside.

2. In a large mixing bowl combine cream cheese, granulated sugar, and butter; beat with electric mixer on medium speed until smooth. Add ¾ cup

Cinnamon Breakfast Muffins

of the flour, the eggs, milk, baking powder, baking soda, vanilla, and salt. Beat about 1 minute or until combined. Add remaining flour; beat on low speed just until combined. Spread batter evenly in prepared pan. In a small bowl stir jam with a spoon until nearly smooth. Spoon jam in 8 to 10 mounds on top of batter in pan. Using a thin spatula or knife, swirl preserves into batter.

3. Bake for 30 to 35 minutes or until a toothpick inserted into cake portion near center comes out clean. Cool cake in pan on wire rack for 30 minutes. Sift with powdered sugar. Cut into squares; serve warm.

Per serving: 158 cal., 8 g total fat (4 g sat. fat), 39 mg chol., 127 mg sodium, 20 g carbo., 0 g fiber, 2 g pro.

Baked Eggs with Cheese and Basil Sauce

This relatively recent recipe from the 1990s is a variation on the classic French dish "oeufs en cocotte" in which eggs are baked in a sauce in the oven. Served alongside toast and fruit, it makes an enjoyable breakfast for overnight guests.

Prep: 15 minutes **Bake:** 18 minutes
Oven: 350°F **Makes:** 4 servings

  3 tablespoons butter or margarine
  2 tablespoons all-purpose flour
  ¼ teaspoon salt
  ⅛ teaspoon ground black pepper
  3 tablespoons snipped fresh basil or
     ½ teaspoon dried basil, crushed
  1 cup milk
     Nonstick cooking spray
  4 eggs
     Salt
     Ground black pepper
  ¼ cup shredded mozzarella cheese (1 ounce)
     Snipped fresh basil (optional)

1. Preheat oven to 350°F. For basil sauce, in a small saucepan melt butter over medium heat. Stir in the flour, the ¼ teaspoon salt, the ⅛ teaspoon pepper, and, if using, the dried basil. Add milk all at once. Cook and stir until thickened and bubbly. Cook and stir for 1 minute more. Remove from heat. Stir in the 3 tablespoons fresh basil, if using.

2. Lightly coat four 8- to 10-ounce round baking dishes or 6-ounce custard cups with nonstick cooking spray. To assemble, spoon about 2 tablespoons of the basil sauce into each prepared dish. Gently break an egg into the center of each dish; season with salt and pepper. Spoon remaining basil sauce over eggs. Bake for 18 to 20 minutes or until eggs are set. Sprinkle with cheese. Let stand until cheese melts. If desired, garnish with additional snipped basil.

Per serving: 216 cal., 16 g total fat (9 g sat. fat), 245 mg chol., 419 mg sodium, 6 g carbo., 0 g fiber, 10 g pro.

Brunch Egg Casserole

Love bacon and eggs? This recipe from 1970 combines those two breakfast favorites with "toast" (actually, timesaving purchased croutons) in one easy dish. Serve it with a fresh fruit salad and you're set.

Prep: 15 minutes **Bake:** 45 minutes
Stand: 10 minutes **Oven:** 325°F **Makes:** 6 servings

  2 cups seasoned croutons
  1 cup shredded cheddar cheese (4 ounces)
  4 eggs
  2 cups milk
  1 teaspoon yellow mustard
     Dash ground black pepper
  4 slices bacon, crisp-cooked and crumbled
     Crisp-cooked crumbled bacon (optional)

1. Preheat oven to 325°F. Grease a 2-quart square baking dish. In prepared baking dish combine croutons and cheese. Set aside. In a medium bowl combine eggs, milk, mustard, and pepper; beat until combined. Pour egg mixture over croutons. Sprinkle with the crumbled bacon.

2. Bake about 45 minutes or until a knife inserted off center comes out clean. Let stand for 10 minutes before serving. If desired, sprinkle top with additional crumbled bacon.

Per serving: 257 cal., 16 g total fat (7 g sat. fat), 174 mg chol., 495 mg sodium, 13 g carbo., 1 g fiber, 15 g pro.

Turkey Benedict

2 tablespoons water
2 tablespoons lemon juice
1 cup butter, cut up and softened
1 fresh serrano chile pepper, seeded and finely chopped*
8 to 10 ounces roasted turkey breast slices
8 poached eggs**

1. For biscuits, preheat oven to 400°F. In a medium bowl combine the flour, parsley, sugar, baking powder, and salt. Using a pastry blender, cut in the ⅓ cup butter until mixture resembles coarse crumbs. Add the half-and-half, buttermilk, and garlic. Using a fork, gently mix until a slightly sticky dough forms. Do not overmix. Turn out onto a floured surface. Knead a few times until nearly smooth. Roll or pat dough to a 6-inch square. Cut into 4 squares. Place on an ungreased baking sheet. Bake for 18 to 20 minutes or until brown on tops; set aside.

2. While biscuits are baking, for sauce, in the top of a double boiler whisk together egg yolks, the water, and lemon juice. Place over simmering water (the bottom of the pan should not touch the water) and whisk until the mixture thickens and doubles in volume (an instant-read thermometer inserted in the mixture should read 160°F; you may need to tilt the pan to get an accurate reading). Gradually add the softened butter pieces to the egg yolk mixture, whisking constantly after each addition until butter melts. Remove the double boiler from heat. Stir chile pepper into sauce. Keep sauce warm over water.

3. Heat a griddle or large skillet over medium-high heat. Add turkey and cook about 4 minutes or until brown, turning once. To assemble, split the biscuits. Arrange on a serving platter. Divide turkey among biscuit halves. Place poached eggs on turkey. Spoon some of the sauce over eggs. Serve with remaining sauce.

*Note: Because chile peppers contain volatile oils that can burn your skin and eyes, avoid direct contact with them as much as possible. When working with chile peppers, wear plastic or rubber gloves. If your bare hands do touch the peppers, wash your hands and nails well with soap and warm water.

**To poach eggs: Half fill a large saucepan with water. Bring the water to boiling; reduce heat to just simmering. Break 1 egg into a measuring cup or custard cup. Carefully slide the egg into the simmer-

Turkey Benedict

This creative version of eggs Benedict really stands out. The recipe uses feathery baking powder biscuits instead of English muffins, and the savory sauce takes a little spark from serrano chile. What a great way to use leftover turkey at the holidays!

Start to Finish: 1 hour **Oven:** 400°F
Makes: 8 servings

1¾ cups all-purpose flour
2 tablespoons snipped fresh parsley
1 tablespoon sugar
1 tablespoon baking powder
¾ teaspoon kosher salt or ½ teaspoon salt
⅓ cup cold butter
½ cup half-and-half or light cream
¼ cup buttermilk
¼ teaspoon bottled minced roasted garlic
2 egg yolks

ing water, holding the lip of the cup as close to the water as possible. Repeat with 3 more eggs, allowing each egg an equal amount of space. Simmer, uncovered, for 3 to 5 minutes or until yolks and whites are set. Remove eggs with a slotted spoon to an oven-safe shallow dish. Cover and keep warm in a 300°F oven. Repeat with remaining eggs. (Or use an egg poaching pan and follow the manufacturer's directions for preparation.)

Per serving: 535 cal., 41 g total fat (23 g sat. fat), 384 mg chol., 832 mg sodium, 23 g carbo., 1 g fiber, 19 g pro.

Cheese and Mushroom Brunch Eggs

For holiday entertaining, serve slices of fresh in-season citrus fruit to contrast with the earthy flavors in this casserole. Remember the casserole for springtime gatherings too, when roasted asparagus would provide a seasonally perfect accompaniment.

Prep: 30 minutes **Bake:** 15 minutes
Stand: 10 minutes **Oven:** 350°F
Makes: 6 servings

  2 **tablespoons butter or margarine**
  2 **tablespoons all-purpose flour**
1⅓ **cups milk**
  ½ **cup shredded Swiss or Gruyère cheese**
      (2 ounces)
  ¼ **cup grated Parmesan cheese**
  ⅛ **teaspoon salt**
  ⅛ **teaspoon ground nutmeg**
  1 **tablespoon butter**
1½ **cups sliced fresh mushrooms (such as**
      button, shiitake, or cremini)
  ¼ **cup thinly sliced green onion**
 12 **eggs, beaten**
      Tomato slices, cut in half (optional)

1. For sauce, in a medium saucepan melt the 2 tablespoons butter over medium heat. Stir in flour. Cook and stir for 1 minute. Add milk all at once. Cook and stir until thickened and bubbly. Stir in Swiss cheese, Parmesan cheese, salt, and nutmeg. Cook and stir until cheeses melt. Remove from heat; set aside.

2. Preheat oven to 350°F. In a large nonstick skillet melt the 1 tablespoon butter over medium heat. Add mushrooms and green onion; cook until tender. Add eggs. Cook, without stirring, until egg mixture begins to set on the bottom and around the edges. Using a large spatula, lift and fold the partially cooked egg mixture so that the uncooked portion flows underneath. Continue cooking until egg mixture is cooked through but still glossy and moist.

3. Transfer half of the scrambled egg mixture to a 2-quart square baking dish. Drizzle about half of the sauce over egg mixture. Top with the remaining scrambled egg mixture and remaining sauce.

4. Bake for 15 to 20 minutes or until heated through. If desired, top with tomato slices. Let stand for 10 minutes before serving.

Double-Batch Brunch Eggs: Prepare as directed, except double all ingredients and use a 12-inch nonstick skillet. Cook half of the mushrooms and green onion in 1 tablespoon hot butter until tender. Beat 12 eggs together at one time and add the 12 beaten eggs to mushroom mixture in skillet. Cook as in step 3. Transfer scrambled egg mixture to a 3-quart rectangular baking dish. Repeat with remaining butter, mushrooms, green onion, and eggs. Top egg mixture in dish with half of the sauce. Top with remaining egg mixture and remaining sauce. Bake, uncovered, about 25 minutes or until heated through. If desired, top with tomato slices. Let stand for 10 minutes before serving. Makes 12 servings.

Per serving regular and double-batch variation: 292 cal., 21 g total fat (10 g sat. fat), 454 mg chol., 322 mg sodium, 7 g carbo., 0 g fiber, 19 g pro.

Easy Cheese and Mushroom Brunch Eggs: Prepare as directed, except omit the first 7 ingredients and step 1. Substitute one 16-ounce jar purchased light Alfredo sauce for the prepared sauce. Continue as directed.

Per serving: 331 cal., 23 g total fat (11 g sat. fat), 462 mg chol., 833 mg sodium, 12 g carbo., 0 g fiber, 19 g pro.

Christmas Morning Strata

Strata is the ultimate make-ahead holiday brunch dish. This one achieves "favorite" status not only for its terrific flavors but also for the way the pink ham and green broccoli combine for a holiday look.

Prep: 20 minutes **Chill:** 2 hours
Bake: 1 hour **Stand:** 5 minutes
Oven: 325°F **Makes:** 6 servings

    1 cup broccoli florets
    5 cups ½-inch French bread cubes
       (about 8 ounces)
    2 cups shredded cheddar cheese (8 ounces)
    1 cup cubed cooked ham (6 ounces)
    3 eggs, beaten
 1¾ cups milk
    2 tablespoons finely chopped onion
    1 teaspoon dry mustard
       Dash ground black pepper

1. Grease a 2-quart square baking dish; set aside. In a 1-quart microwave-safe casserole dish combine broccoli florets and 1 tablespoon water. Cover with plastic wrap and microwave on 100% power (high) for 2 to 3 minutes or just until tender; drain well. (Or in a covered small saucepan cook broccoli in a small amount of boiling water for 4 to 6 minutes or just until tender; drain well.) Set aside.

2. Layer half of the bread cubes in the prepared baking dish. Top with cheese, ham, and broccoli. Top with the remaining bread cubes. In a medium bowl combine beaten eggs, milk, onion, mustard, and pepper. Pour egg mixture evenly over layers in baking dish. Cover and chill for 2 to 24 hours.

3. Preheat oven to 325°F. Bake about 1 hour or until a knife inserted near the center comes out clean. Let stand for 5 minutes before serving.

Per serving: 377 cal., 20 g total fat (11 g sat. fat), 165 mg chol., 886 mg sodium, 25 g carbo., 2 g fiber, 24 g pro.

Christmas Morning Strata

Sausage, Broccoli, and Eggs Brunch Casserole

Sweet Italian sausage links and a rich cheese sauce spiked with honey mustard pack this satisfying casserole with plenty of robust flavors.

Prep: 40 minutes **Bake:** 35 minutes
Oven: 350°F **Makes:** 6 servings

 12 ounces sweet Italian sausage links,
       cut into ½-inch slices
    2 cups mushrooms, quartered (such as
       cremini, brown, and/or button)
    1 medium onion, cut into thin wedges
    8 eggs
  ¼ cup milk
  ¼ teaspoon salt
 1½ cups frozen cut broccoli, thawed
    2 tablespoons butter
    2 tablespoons all-purpose flour
  ¼ teaspoon ground black pepper
 1⅓ cups milk
    6 ounces process Gruyère or Swiss cheese,
       shredded (1½ cups)
    2 teaspoons honey mustard
  ¾ cup soft bread crumbs

1. Preheat oven to 350°F. Grease bottom of a 2-quart rectangular baking dish; set aside.

2. In a 12-inch skillet cook sausage, mushrooms, and onion until meat is brown and onion is tender. Drain off fat. In a large bowl whisk together eggs, the ¼ cup milk, and the salt; add to skillet along with broccoli. Cook, without stirring, until egg mixture begins to set on the bottom and around the edges. Using a large spatula, lift and fold the partially cooked egg mixture so the uncooked portion flows underneath. Continue cooking just until egg mixture is cooked through but still glossy and moist. Transfer to a bowl; set aside.

3. For sauce, in a large saucepan melt butter over medium heat. Stir in flour and pepper. Add the 1⅓ cups milk. Cook and stir until mixture is thickened and bubbly. Add 1 cup of the cheese and the honey mustard; cook and stir just until cheese melts. Remove from heat. Gently fold in egg mixture. Turn into prepared dish.

4. Cover and bake for 25 minutes. In a small bowl combine the remaining ½ cup cheese and the bread crumbs. Uncover casserole and sprinkle with crumb mixture. Bake, uncovered, for 10 to 15 minutes more or until heated through and crumb topping is light brown.

Per serving: 412 cal., 31 g total fat (12 g sat. fat), 343 mg chol., 721 mg sodium, 12 g carbo., 1 g fiber, 21 g pro.

Baked Italian Omelet

When you're entertaining guests for breakfast or brunch, bypass the fussy omelets. This fix-and-forget egg dish bakes while you mingle.

Prep: 20 minutes **Bake:** 30 minutes
Stand: 10 minutes **Oven:** 325°F
Makes: 6 to 8 servings

- 1 **10-ounce package frozen chopped spinach, thawed**
- 8 **eggs, beaten**
- 1 **cup ricotta cheese**
- ½ **cup milk**
- ½ **teaspoon dried basil, crushed**
- ¼ **teaspoon salt**

Baked Italian Omelet

- ¼ **teaspoon fennel seeds, crushed**
- ¼ **teaspoon ground black pepper**
- 1 **cup chopped tomato**
- 1 **cup shredded mozzarella cheese (4 ounces)**
- ½ **cup thinly sliced green onion**
- ½ **cup diced salami or ham**
- ¼ **cup finely shredded Parmesan cheese**

1. Preheat oven to 325°F. Drain thawed spinach well, pressing out excess liquid; set aside. In a large bowl combine eggs and ricotta cheese; beat just until combined. Stir in milk, basil, salt, fennel seeds, and pepper. Stir in spinach, tomato, mozzarella cheese, green onion, and salami.

2. Pour mixture into a greased 3-quart rectangular baking dish. Sprinkle with Parmesan cheese. Bake for 30 to 35 minutes or until a knife inserted near the center comes out clean. Let stand for 10 minutes before serving.

Per serving: 281 cal., 18 g total fat (8 g sat. fat), 318 mg chol., 620 mg sodium, 8 g carbo., 1 g fiber, 22 g pro.

 ## All-Time Favorite Quiche Lorraine

Quiche was all over the place in the '70s—and it didn't take long before the Test Kitchen was all over the recipe. And while some wonderful versions of the French egg pie have been published over the years, this recipe may well be the gold standard.

Prep: 20 minutes **Bake:** 1 hour **Cook:** 10 minutes
Stand: 10 minutes **Oven:** 450°F/325°F
Makes: 6 servings

- 1 recipe Pastry Shell
- 8 slices bacon
- 1 medium onion, thinly sliced
- 4 eggs, beaten
- 1 cup half-and-half or light cream
- 1 cup milk
- ¼ teaspoon salt
  Dash ground nutmeg
- 1½ cups shredded Swiss cheese (6 ounces)
- 1 tablespoon all-purpose flour

1. Preheat oven to 450°F. Prepare Pastry Shell. Line the unpricked pastry shell with a double thickness of heavy-duty foil. Bake for 8 minutes. Remove foil. Bake for 4 to 5 minutes more or until pastry is set and dry. Remove from oven. Reduce oven temperature to 325°F. (Pastry shell should still be hot when filling is added; do not partially bake pastry shell ahead of time.)

2. Meanwhile, in a large skillet cook bacon until crisp. Drain, reserving 2 tablespoons of the drippings in skillet. Finely crumble bacon; set aside. Cook sliced onion in reserved drippings over medium heat until tender; drain.

3. In a medium bowl stir together eggs, half-and-half, milk, salt, and nutmeg. Stir in the crumbled bacon and onion. In a small bowl toss together cheese and flour. Add to egg mixture; mix well.

4. Pour egg mixture into the hot, baked pastry shell. Bake in the 325°F oven for 50 to 60 minutes or until a knife inserted near the center comes out clean. Let stand for 10 minutes before serving.

Pastry Shell: In a medium bowl stir together 1¼ cups all-purpose flour and ¼ teaspoon salt. Using a pastry blender, cut in ⅓ cup shortening until

pieces are pea size. Sprinkle 1 tablespoon cold water over part of the flour mixture; gently toss with a fork. Push moistened dough to the side of the bowl. Repeat moistening flour mixture, using 1 tablespoon cold water at a time, until all is moistened (4 or 5 tablespoons cold water total). Form dough into a ball. On a lightly floured surface, use your hands to slightly flatten dough. Roll dough from center to edges into a circle about 12 inches in diameter. To transfer pastry, wrap it around the rolling pin. Unroll pastry into a 9-inch quiche dish. Ease pastry into dish, being careful not to stretch pastry. Trim pastry even with top of dish. Crimp edge as desired. Do not prick pastry. Bake as directed.

Per serving: 524 cal., 37 g total fat (16 g sat. fat), 198 mg chol., 501 mg sodium, 26 g carbo., 1 g fiber, 20 g pro.

 ## Mushroom, Spinach, And Havarti Quiche

The quiche recipes developed over the years often reflect popular ingredients of their time. This brand-new version takes advantage of the wonderful array of fresh mushrooms that are widely available now.

Prep: 50 minutes **Bake:** 30 minutes
Stand: 10 minutes **Oven:** 450°F/350°F
Makes: 8 servings

- 1 recipe Cornmeal Pastry (see page 65)
- 2 cloves garlic, minced
- 1 tablespoon butter
- 2½ cups sliced fresh assorted mushrooms (such as cremini, oyster, and/or button)
- ½ cup chopped shallot
- 3 cups lightly packed fresh baby spinach
- 4 ounces Havarti or brick cheese, shredded (1 cup)
- 2 eggs, beaten
- 1 cup half-and-half or light cream
- 1 tablespoon snipped fresh dill or 1 teaspoon dried dill
- ¼ teaspoon salt
- ⅛ teaspoon freshly ground black pepper

1. Preheat oven to 450°F. Prepare Cornmeal Pastry. On a lightly floured surface, use your hands to slightly flatten dough. Roll dough from center to edges into a circle about 13 inches in diameter. To transfer pastry, wrap it around the rolling pin. Unroll pastry into a 10-inch tart pan with a removable bottom. Press pastry onto bottom and up side of the pan. Trim pastry even with top of pan. Line pastry with a double thickness of foil. Bake for 8 minutes. Remove foil. Bake 4 to 5 minutes more or until pastry is set and dry. Remove and set aside. Reduce oven temperature to 350°F.

2. Meanwhile, in a large skillet cook garlic in hot butter for 30 seconds. Add mushrooms and shallot. Cook and stir until mushrooms are tender. Remove from heat. Add spinach, tossing just until wilted. Arrange mushrooms and spinach in bottom of hot crust. Sprinkle with cheese.

3. In a large bowl stir together eggs, half-and-half, dill, salt, and pepper. Place tart pan on oven rack. Carefully pour egg mixture over spinach, mushrooms, and cheese in crust. Bake for 30 to 35 minutes or until a knife inserted near the center

comes out clean. Transfer to a wire rack and let stand for 10 minutes. Remove sides of tart pan. To serve, cut into wedges.

Cornmeal Pastry: In a medium bowl stir together 1¼ cups all-purpose flour, ¼ cup yellow cornmeal, and ¼ teaspoon salt. Using a pastry blender, cut in ½ cup butter until pieces are pea size. In a small bowl lightly beat together 1 egg yolk and 3 tablespoons cold water. Add to flour mixture and gently toss with a fork; if necessary, add more water, 1 teaspoon at a time, to completely moisten dough. Using your hands, gently knead the dough just until a ball forms. If necessary, cover dough with plastic wrap and chill for 30 to 60 minutes or until dough is easy to handle.

Per serving: 339 cal., 25 g total fat (11 g sat. fat), 141 mg chol., 350 mg sodium, 22 g carbo., 1 g fiber, 10 g pro.

Mushroom, Spinach, and Havarti Quiche

Enduring and Endearing
Holiday Breads

Feather Rolls, a favorite from years past, lead this parade of heartwarming breads for gift giving and serving at your holiday table. Start Christmas Day with a batch of Creamy Cinnamon Rolls—they'll bring as much delight as Santa's special deliveries! Add appeal to the meals of the season with Cheddar Batter Bread, Cottage Cheese-Chive Biscuits, or other hearty loaves. Stop by a friend's house with Brandied Apricot Loaves or Cocoa Ripple Ring and linger over treats and tea. The holidays are all about enjoying the company of loved one and there's no better way to do that than over these luscious goodies.

Onion and Olive Focaccia, page 70

Cheddar Batter Bread

Cheddar Batter Bread

This yummy loaf has all the home-baked goodness of a tricky yeast bread but with none of the fuss.

Prep: 15 minutes **Rise:** 20 minutes
Bake: 40 minutes **Oven:** 350°F
Makes: 1 loaf (16 slices)

- 1 **tablespoon cornmeal**
- 2 **cups all-purpose flour**
- 1 **package fast-rising active dry yeast**
- ¼ **teaspoon onion powder**
- ¼ **teaspoon ground black pepper**
- 1 **cup milk**
- 2 **tablespoons sugar**
- 2 **tablespoons butter**
- ½ **teaspoon salt**
- 1 **egg**
- ¾ **cup shredded cheddar cheese (3 ounces)**
- ½ **cup cornmeal**

1. Grease the bottom and ½ inch up the sides of an 8×4×2-inch loaf pan. Sprinkle with the 1 tablespoon cornmeal; set aside. In a large mixing bowl stir together 1½ cups of the flour, the yeast, onion powder, and pepper; set aside.

2. In a small saucepan combine milk, sugar, butter, and salt; heat and stir over medium heat just until mixture is warm (120°F to 130°F) and butter almost melts. Add milk mixture and egg to flour mixture. Beat with an electric mixer on low to medium speed for 30 seconds, scraping bowl. Beat on high speed for 3 minutes. Stir in cheese and the ½ cup cornmeal. Stir in remaining flour. (The batter will be soft and sticky.) Spread batter evenly in prepared pan. Cover and let rise in a warm place until nearly double in size (about 20 minutes).

3. Meanwhile, preheat oven to 350°F. Bake about 40 minutes or until bread sounds hollow when lightly tapped. If necessary to prevent overbrowning, cover with foil for the last 15 minutes of baking. Remove bread from the pan. Cool on a wire rack. Serve warm.

Per slice: 124 cal., 4 g total fat (2 g sat. fat), 24 mg chol., 127 mg sodium, 17 g carbo., 1 g fiber, 4 g pro.

Dill Batter Bread

Here's another standout in the batter bread hall of fame. This one has a hearty onion-dill flavor. Try it with winter soups and stews.

Prep: 15 minutes **Rise:** 50 minutes
Bake: 25 minutes **Oven:** 375°F
Makes: 1 loaf (8 slices)

- 2 cups all-purpose flour
- 1 package active dry yeast
- ½ cup water
- ½ cup cream-style cottage cheese
- 1 tablespoon sugar
- 1 tablespoon dillseeds or caraway seeds
- 1 tablespoon butter
- 1 teaspoon dried minced onion
- 1 teaspoon salt
- 1 egg, beaten
- ½ cup toasted wheat germ

1. Grease a 9×1½-inch round baking pan or a 1-quart soufflé dish; set aside. In a large mixing bowl stir together 1 cup of the flour and the yeast; set aside.

2. In a medium saucepan combine the water, cottage cheese, sugar, dillseeds, butter, dried minced onion, and salt; heat and stir just until warm (120°F to 130°F) and butter almost melts. Add cottage cheese mixture to flour mixture along with the egg. Beat with an electric mixer on low to medium speed for 30 seconds, scraping sides of bowl frequently. Beat on high speed for 3 minutes. Using a wooden spoon, stir in the wheat germ and the remaining flour (batter will be stiff).

3. Spoon batter into the prepared pan or casserole, spreading to the edges. Cover and let rise in a warm place until double in size (50 to 60 minutes).

4. Preheat oven to 375°F. Bake for 25 to 30 minutes or until golden brown. Immediately remove from pan. Serve warm, or cool on a wire rack.

Per slice: 185 cal., 4 g total fat (2 g sat. fat), 33 mg chol., 369 mg sodium, 30 g carbo., 8 g pro.

Cottage Cheese-Chive Biscuits

What's cottage cheese doing in a biscuit? Making it creamy and dreamy, that's what! You'll also love the way these drop from a spoon—no rolling and cutting needed. No wonder it's a favorite!

Prep: 20 minutes **Bake:** 15 minutes
Oven: 425°F **Makes:** 12 biscuits

- 2 cups all-purpose flour
- 2½ teaspoons baking powder
- ¼ teaspoon salt
- 6 tablespoons butter
- ¾ cup small-curd cream-style cottage cheese
- ⅔ cup milk
- 2 tablespoons snipped fresh chive or thinly sliced green onion tops

1. Preheat oven to 425°F. Line a baking sheet with parchment paper; set aside.

2. In a medium bowl stir together flour, baking powder, and salt. Using a pastry blender, cut in butter until mixture resembles coarse crumbs. Make a well in the center of the flour mixture; set aside.

3. In a small bowl combine cottage cheese, milk, and chives. Add mixture all at once to flour mixture. Using a fork, stir just until moistened.

4. Drop dough by generous tablespoonfuls onto prepared baking sheet. Bake for 15 to 18 minutes or until golden brown. Remove from parchment to wire rack; serve warm.

Per biscuit: 144 cal., 7 g total fat (4 g sat. fat), 19 mg chol., 254 mg sodium, 16 g carbo., 1 g fiber, 4 g pro.

Onion and Olive Focaccia

Onion and Olive Focaccia

This is a favorite of food editor Wini Moranville. She recommends serving slices of the olive-topped version alongside wedges of blue cheese, crackers, and an array of imported olives. Open a bottle of wine and let the fun begin!

Prep: 30 minutes **Rise:** 1⅓ hours
Bake: 25 minutes **Oven:** 375°F
Makes: 2 rounds (24 wedges)

3¼ to 3¾ cups bread flour or all-purpose flour
  1 package active dry yeast
1¼ cups warm water (120°F to 130°F)
  1 tablespoon olive oil or cooking oil
  1 teaspoon salt
  2 tablespoons olive oil or cooking oil
1½ cups chopped onion
  2 cloves garlic, minced
  1 cup sliced pitted ripe olives and/or snipped
     oil-packed dried tomato, drained
  2 tablespoons snipped fresh rosemary or
     2 teaspoons dried rosemary, crushed

1. In a large mixing bowl combine 1¼ cups of the flour and the yeast. Add the warm water, the 1 tablespoon oil, and the salt to the flour mixture. Beat with an electric mixer on low to medium speed for 30 seconds, scraping sides of bowl frequently. Beat on high speed for 3 minutes. Stir in as much of the remaining flour as you can.

2. Turn out dough onto a lightly floured surface. Knead in enough of the remaining flour to make a stiff dough that is smooth and elastic (about 8 to 10 minutes total). Shape dough into a ball. Place in a lightly greased bowl; turn once to grease surface. Cover and let rise in a warm place until double in size (about 1 hour).

3. Punch dough down. Turn out onto a floured surface. Divide in half. Shape each portion of the dough into a ball. Place on two lightly greased baking sheets. Cover; let rest for 10 minutes.

4. Meanwhile, in a medium skillet heat the 2 tablespoons oil over low heat. Add onion and garlic; cover and cook for 3 to 5 minutes or until onion is tender, stirring occasionally. Uncover; cook and stir just until onion begins to brown. Remove from heat. If using olives, stir into onion mixture; set aside.

5. Using your hands, flatten each ball to about 10 inches in diameter. With your fingertips, make ½-inch-deep indentations every 2 inches. Spoon onion mixture over dough. Sprinkle with rosemary. Cover and let rise in a warm place for 20 minutes.

6. Meanwhile, preheat oven to 375°F. Bake about 25 minutes or until golden. If using dried tomato, sprinkle over bread for the last 5 minutes of baking. Remove from baking sheet; cool on wire racks.

Per wedge: 94 cal., 3 g total fat (0 g sat. fat), 0 mg chol., 147 mg sodium, 15 g carbo., 1 g fiber, 3 g pro.

Blue Cheese and Walnut Focaccia: Prepare as directed, except omit the onion, garlic, olives and/or tomato, and rosemary. Brush the shaped dough with the 2 tablespoons olive oil or cooking oil. Sprinkle with 1½ cups chopped walnuts and 1 cup crumbled blue cheese or shredded Swiss cheese. Cover and let rise in a warm place for 20 minutes. Continue as directed in step 6.

Per wedge: 148 cal., 8 g total fat (2 g sat. fat), 4 mg chol., 164 mg sodium, 15 g carbo., 1 g fiber, 4 g pro.

Feather Rolls

You'll see at once how these rolls from 1934 received their name. They're so tender and light, they just might float right off the dinner table. Mashed potatoes are the secret ingredient.

Prep: 30 minutes **Chill:** 2 hours
Rise: 40 minutes **Bake:** 25 minutes
Oven: 400°F **Makes:** 15 rolls

4¼	to 4¾ cups all-purpose flour
1	package active dry yeast
1½	cups warm water (120°F to 130°F)
½	cup mashed cooked potato
⅓	cup butter, melted
¼	cup sugar
1¼	teaspoons salt
2	tablespoons butter, melted

1. In a large mixing bowl combine 2 cups of the flour and the yeast. In a medium bowl combine the warm water, mashed potato, the ⅓ cup melted butter, the sugar, and salt. Add potato mixture to flour mixture. Beat with an electric mixer on low speed for 30 seconds, scraping sides of bowl frequently. Beat on high speed for 3 minutes, scraping sides of bowl occasionally. Using a wooden spoon, stir in as much of the remaining flour as you can.

2. Turn out dough onto a lightly floured surface. Knead in enough of the remaining flour to make a moderately soft dough that is smooth and elastic (3 to 5 minutes total). Place dough in a greased bowl, turning once to grease the surface. Cover; chill for 2 to 24 hours.

3. Punch dough down. Turn out onto a lightly floured surface. Cover; let rest for 10 minutes. Meanwhile, grease a 13×9×2-inch baking pan. With lightly floured hands, shape dough into 15 rolls. Arrange rolls in prepared pan. Cover; let rise in a warm place until nearly double in size (about 40 minutes).

4. Preheat oven to 400°F. Bake about 25 minutes or until rolls are golden brown and sound hollow when lightly tapped. Brush tops with the 2 tablespoons melted butter. Immediately remove from pan. Invert so tops face up. Serve warm.

Per roll: 188 cal., 6 g total fat (4 g sat. fat), 15 mg chol., 256 mg sodium, 29 g carbo., 1 g fiber, 4 g pro.

Feather Rolls

Spoon Bread Soufflé

This dish hails from the 1940s. It makes a rich and intriguing side dish to serve in place of mashed potatoes. Also try the maple syrup option with eggs, sausages, and toast in place of breakfast potatoes.

Prep: 25 minutes **Bake:** 1 hour **Stand:** 30 minutes
Oven: 325°F **Makes:** 8 servings

- 3 **egg yolks**
- 3 **egg whites**
- 4 **cups milk**
- 1 **cup yellow cornmeal**
- ¼ **cup chopped onion**
- ¼ **cup chopped celery**
- 1 **tablespoon sugar**
- 1¼ **teaspoons salt**
  Dash ground black pepper
- 1 **tablespoon butter**
  Butter (optional)
  Maple syrup (optional)

1. Allow the egg yolks and egg whites to stand at room temperature for 30 minutes. Beat egg yolks; set aside.

2. Preheat oven to 325°F. Grease a 2-quart casserole; set aside. In a large saucepan combine milk, cornmeal, onion, celery, sugar, salt, and pepper. Cook and stir over medium-high heat about

10 minutes or until thickened and bubbly. Reduce heat to low; cook for 2 minutes more, stirring frequently (watch carefully as cornmeal mixture may bubble). Remove from heat. Gradually add 1 cup of the cornmeal mixture to beaten egg yolks; return to cornmeal mixture in the saucepan.

3. In a large mixing bowl beat the egg whites with an electric mixer on medium to high speed until stiff peaks form (tips stand straight). Fold egg whites into the hot mixture. Turn into prepared casserole. Dot with the 1 tablespoon butter.

4. Bake about 1 hour or until a knife inserted near the center comes out clean. Serve warm. If desired, serve with additional butter and maple syrup. (The soufflé will settle as it stands.)

Per serving: 172 cal., 6 g total fat (3 g sat. fat), 90 mg chol., 451 mg sodium, 22 g carbo., 1 g fiber, 8 g pro.

Now **Apples and Cheese Spoon Bread**

Calling for a packaged corn muffin mix, this satisfying spoon bread recipe proves that beautiful holiday food need not be stressful. Imagine how lovely it will look on a holiday buffet table. It's perfect alongside roast pork.

Prep: 25 minutes **Bake:** 50 minutes
Cool: 15 minutes **Oven:** 375°F **Makes:** 8 servings

- ¼ **cup butter**
- 1 **large red onion, chopped**
- 1 **8½-ounce package corn muffin mix**
- 1 **egg**
- 2 **4-ounce containers applesauce**
- 1 **8-ounce carton dairy sour cream**
- 1 **cup shredded sharp cheddar cheese
  (4 ounces)**
- ⅓ **cup water**
- 1 **teaspoon snipped fresh sage
  Few dashes ground black pepper**
- 1 **medium red apple, very thinly sliced
  (optional)**
  Melted butter (optional)
  Fresh sage leaves (optional)

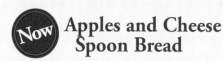
Apples and Cheese Spoon Bread

1. Preheat oven to 375°F. In a medium skillet melt the ¼ cup butter over medium heat. Add red onion; cook about 5 minutes or just until tender. In a large bowl stir together corn muffin mix, egg, applesauce, sour cream, cheddar cheese, the water, sage, and pepper. Stir in onion mixture. Pour mixture into a 2-quart square baking dish.

2. Bake for 50 to 55 minutes or until golden across the top. If desired, brush apple slices with melted butter and arrange apples on spoon bread for the last 25 minutes of baking. Let cool in pan on a wire rack for 15 minutes (the spoon bread may sink slightly in center while cooling). If desired, garnish with a few sage leaves.

Per serving: 328 cal., 20 g total fat (10 g sat. fat), 70 mg chol., 367 mg sodium, 29 g carbo., 1 g fiber, 8 g pro.

Brandied Apricot Loaves

Brandied Apricot Loaves

Hailing from Austria and Germany, this bread bursts with fruity flavor. If your recipient's tastes lean more toward the mellow side, try a mix of half apricot nectar and half brandy in the batter.

Prep: 20 minutes **Bake:** 40 minutes
Stand: 15 minutes **Oven:** 350°F
Makes: two 7½×3½×2-inch loaves (12 slices each) or six 4½×2½×1½-inch loaves (6 slices each)

- ½ cup snipped dried apricot
- ¼ cup golden raisins or snipped dried apricot
- ¼ cup apricot brandy or apricot nectar
- 2 cups all-purpose flour
- 1 cup sugar
- 2 teaspoons baking powder
- ½ teaspoon salt
- ¼ teaspoon ground cinnamon
- ¼ teaspoon ground mace
- 1 cup apricot nectar
- 2 eggs, beaten
- ⅓ cup butter, melted
- ½ cup sliced almonds, toasted
- 1 recipe Apricot Icing
- 2 tablespoons finely snipped dried apricots
- 2 tablespoons sliced almonds, toasted

1. Grease bottom and ½ inch up the sides of two 7½×3½×2-inch loaf pans or six 4½×2½×1½-inch loaf pans. Set aside. In a small bowl combine the ½ cup dried apricot, the raisins, and apricot brandy; let stand for 15 minutes.

2. Preheat oven to 350°F. In a large bowl stir together flour, sugar, baking powder, salt, cinnamon, and mace. Make a well in the center of the flour mixture. Set aside.

3. In a medium bowl combine apricot nectar, eggs, and melted butter. Add egg mixture all at once to flour mixture. Stir just until moistened (batter should be lumpy). Fold in soaked fruit mixture and the ½ cup almonds. Spoon batter evenly into prepared pans.

4. Bake until a toothpick inserted near the centers comes out clean. Allow 40 to 45 minutes for the 7½×3½×2-inch loaf pans or 35 to 40 minutes for the 4½×2½×1½-inch loaf pans. Cool in pans on wire racks for 10 minutes. Remove from pans. Cool on wire racks. Wrap each loaf in foil or plastic wrap and store overnight.

5. Drizzle Apricot Icing over bread; sprinkle with the 2 tablespoons dried apricots and 2 tablespoons sliced almonds.

Apricot Icing: In a small bowl combine 1 cup powdered sugar, 1 tablespoon apricot nectar, and ¼ teaspoon vanilla. Stir in additional apricot nectar, 1 teaspoon at a time, to reach drizzling consistency.

Per slice: 160 cal., 5 g total fat (2 g sat. fat), 24 mg chol., 93 mg sodium, 26 g carbo., 1 g fiber, 3 g pro.

Cocoa Ripple Ring

Cocoa Ripple Ring

This nutty coffee cake caught the fancy of readers when it first appeared in the 1950s because it used presweetened instant cocoa powder—a new ingredient at the time. Take it to the office sometime this holiday season. Your coworkers will be glad you did!

Prep: 30 minutes **Bake:** 45 minutes
Stand: 5 minutes **Cool:** 30 minutes
Oven: 350°F **Makes:** 12 servings

- 1½ **cups all-purpose flour**
- 1 **teaspoon baking powder**
- ½ **teaspoon salt**
- ½ **cup butter, softened**
- ¾ **cup sugar**
- 2 **eggs**
- ¾ **cup milk**
- ⅓ **cup presweetened instant cocoa powder**
- ⅓ **cup broken walnuts**
- 1 **recipe Chocolate Glaze**

1. Preheat oven to 350°F. Grease a 6-cup fluted tube pan or a 9×9×2-inch baking pan. Set aside. In a small bowl stir together flour, baking powder, and salt. Set aside.

2. In a large mixing bowl beat butter with an electric mixer on medium to high speed for 30 seconds. Add sugar; beat on medium speed until well mixed. Add

eggs; beat until light and fluffy. Add flour mixture and milk alternately to the egg mixture, beating well after each addition.

3. If using a fluted tube pan, spoon one-third of the batter into it. In a small bowl combine cocoa powder and walnuts; sprinkle half of the nut mixture over batter in pan. Repeat layers, ending with batter. (If using a 9×9×2-inch baking pan, spoon half of the batter into it. Sprinkle with all of the walnut mixture; top with remaining batter.)

4. Bake until a wooden toothpick inserted into the center of the coffee cake comes out clean. Allow about 45 minutes for the fluted tube pan or about 35 minutes for the 9×9×2-inch baking pan. Let stand for 5 minutes; turn out of tube pan (leave in 9×9×2-inch pan). Cool for 30 minutes. Spoon Chocolate Glaze over coffee cake.

Chocolate Glaze: In a small saucepan combine ¼ cup semisweet chocolate pieces, 1 tablespoon half-and-half or light cream, 1½ teaspoons sugar, and ¼ teaspoon vanilla. Heat and stir over low heat until melted and smooth.

Per serving: 255 cal., 13 g total fat (6 g sat. fat), 59 mg chol., 239 mg sodium, 32 g carbo., 1 g fiber, 4 g pro.

Cowboy Coffee Cake

This rich, buttery coffee cake was a star in the 1930s; what it has to do with cowboys was, unfortunately, lost to history. What is known without question, however, is that it's absolutely delicious and so easy to make.

Prep: 15 minutes **Bake:** 25 minutes
Oven: 375°F **Makes:** 9 servings

- 1½ **cups all-purpose flour**
- 1 **cup packed brown sugar**
- ⅓ **cup butter**
- 1 **teaspoon baking powder**
- ¼ **teaspoon baking soda**
- ¼ **teaspoon ground cinnamon**
- ¼ **teaspoon ground nutmeg**
- ½ **cup buttermilk or sour milk***
- 1 **egg, beaten**

1. Preheat oven to 375°F. Grease an 8×8×2-inch baking pan; set aside. In a medium bowl stir together flour and brown sugar. Using a pastry blender, cut in butter until mixture resembles fine crumbs; set aside ½ cup of the crumb mixture to sprinkle over batter. To remaining crumb mixture, add baking powder, baking soda, cinnamon, and nutmeg; stir to combine. Stir in buttermilk and egg.

2. Pour into prepared baking pan; spread evenly. Sprinkle with reserved crumb mixture. Bake about 25 minutes or until a wooden toothpick inserted near the center comes out clean. Serve warm.

*Note: To make ½ cup sour milk, place 1½ teaspoons lemon juice or vinegar into a glass measuring cup. Add enough milk to make ½ cup total liquid; stir. Let mixture stand for 5 minutes before using.

Per serving: 246 cal., 8 g total fat (5 g sat. fat), 43 mg chol., 184 mg sodium, 41 g carbo., 1 g fiber, 3 g pro.

Raspberry-Almond Rolls

Instead of the cinnamon-brown sugar filling of cinnamon rolls, these sinfully luscious buns are packed with a sensational filling of raspberry jam and almond paste. A bite of these breakfast beauties will get any morning off to a great start!

Prep: 50 minutes **Rise:** 1½ hours **Bake:** 18 minutes
Cool: 5 minutes **Oven:** 350°F **Makes:** 12 rolls

3½	to 4 cups all-purpose flour
1	package active dry yeast
1	cup warm water (120°F to 130°F)
¼	cup sugar
2	tablespoons cooking oil
1	egg
½	teaspoon salt
½	teaspoon almond extract
3	tablespoons raspberry jam or blackberry jam
1	8-ounce can almond paste*
1	recipe Powdered Sugar Icing

1. In a large mixing bowl combine 1 cup of the flour and the yeast. Add the water, sugar, oil, egg, salt, and almond extract. Beat with an electric mixer on low speed for 30 seconds, scraping the sides of the bowl. Beat on high speed for 3 minutes. Using a wooden spoon, stir in as much of the remaining flour as you can.

2. Turn out dough onto a lightly floured surface. Knead in enough of the remaining flour to make a moderately soft dough that is smooth and elastic (3 to 5 minutes total). Shape dough into a ball. Place in a greased bowl; turn once. Cover and let rise in a warm place until double in size (about 1 hour).

3. Punch dough down (dough may be sticky). Cover; let rest for 10 minutes. Grease two large baking sheets or one 13×9×2-inch baking pan; set aside.

4. On a lightly floured surface, roll dough to a 12×10-inch rectangle. Spread jam evenly over dough. Crumble almond paste into very small pieces; sprinkle over dough. Starting from a long side, roll up dough; seal seam. Cut into twelve 1-inch-thick slices. Place rolls, cut sides down, 2 inches apart on prepared baking sheets for single rolls or arrange in prepared baking pan. Cover; let rise in a warm place until nearly double in size (about 30 minutes).

5. Meanwhile, preheat oven to 350°F. Bake until golden brown. For individual rolls, place the two baking sheets on separate racks in the oven and bake for 10 minutes; switch sheets to opposite racks and bake for 8 to 10 minutes more. For the 13×9×2-inch pan, bake about 25 minutes. Cool on wire rack(s) for 5 minutes; transfer to a platter. Drizzle with Powdered Sugar Icing. Serve warm.

Powdered Sugar Icing: In a medium bowl stir together 1½ cups powdered sugar, 1 tablespoon milk, and ½ teaspoon vanilla until well mixed. Stir in enough additional milk, ½ teaspoon at a time, to make icing of drizzling consistency.

*Note: For best results, use an almond paste made without syrup or liquid glucose.

Per roll: 328 cal., 8 g total fat (1 g sat. fat), 18 mg chol., 108 mg sodium, 58 g carbo., 2 g fiber, 6 g pro.

Classic Cinnamon Rolls

Nut-and-raisin-studded cinnamon rolls are an all-time favorite Christmas morning treat, and this is one of the best recipes. Make them the day before so your holiday crew can munch away while checking their Christmas stockings.

Prep: 45 minutes **Rise:** 1½ hours **Bake:** 20 minutes
Stand: 10 minutes **Oven:** 375°F **Makes:** 24 rolls

- 4 **to 4½ cups all-purpose flour**
- 1 **package active dry yeast**
- 1 **cup milk**
- ⅓ **cup granulated sugar**
- ⅓ **cup butter**
- ½ **teaspoon salt**
- 2 **eggs**
- ¾ **cup packed brown sugar**
- ¼ **cup all-purpose flour**
- 1 **tablespoon ground cinnamon**
- ⅓ **cup butter**
- ½ **cup golden raisins (optional)**
- ½ **cup chopped pecans, toasted (optional)**
- 1 **recipe Cream Cheese Icing**

1. In a large mixing bowl combine 2 cups of the flour and the yeast; set aside. In a saucepan heat and stir milk, granulated sugar, the ⅓ cup butter, and the salt just until warm (120°F to 130°F) and butter almost melts. Add to flour mixture along with eggs. Beat with an electric mixer on low speed for 30 seconds, scraping sides of bowl. Beat on high speed for 3 minutes. Stir in as much of the remaining 2 to 2½ cups flour as you can.

2. Turn out dough onto a floured surface. Knead in enough of the remaining flour to make a moderately soft dough that is smooth and elastic (3 to 5 minutes total). Shape dough into a ball. Place dough in a lightly greased bowl, turning once to grease dough surface. Cover; let rise in a warm place until double in size (1 to 1½ hours).

3. Punch dough down. Turn out onto a lightly floured surface. Divide in half. Cover and let rest for 10 minutes. Lightly grease two 8×8×2- or 9×9×2-inch baking pans or two 9×1½-inch round baking pans; set aside. For filling, in a bowl stir together brown sugar, the ¼ cup flour, and the cinnamon; cut in ⅓ cup butter until the mixture resembles coarse crumbs. If desired, stir in raisins and pecans.

4. Roll each portion of the dough into a 12×8-inch rectangle. Sprinkle filling over dough, leaving a 1-inch space on one of the long sides. Starting from the long side opposite the space, roll up each rectangle. Pinch dough to seal seam. Slice each roll into 12 pieces. Arrange in prepared pans. Cover and let rise in a warm place until nearly double in size (about 30 minutes).

5. Preheat oven to 375°F. Bake for 20 to 25 minutes or until golden brown. Cool for 5 minutes; remove from pans. Spread with Cream Cheese Icing. If desired, serve warm.

Cream Cheese Icing: In a small bowl beat together one 3-ounce package softened cream cheese, 2 tablespoons softened butter, and 1 teaspoon vanilla. Gradually beat in 2½ cups powdered sugar until smooth. Beat in enough milk, 1 teaspoon at a time, to make spreading consistency.

Per roll: 233 cal., 8 g total fat (4 g sat. fat), 39 mg chol., 118 mg sodium, 36 g carbo., 1 g fiber, 3 g pro.

Creamy Cinnamon Rolls

Here's another favorite cinnamon roll recipe. Readers love the way it starts with frozen sweet bread dough and how the whipping cream creates a luscious caramel mixture while the rolls bake.

Prep: 20 minutes **Rise:** 1 hour **Bake:** 20 minutes
Oven: 350°F **Makes:** 20 rolls

- 1 **16-ounce loaf frozen sweet bread dough, thawed**
- 2 **tablespoons butter, melted**
- ⅔ **cup packed brown sugar**
- ½ **cup chopped walnuts**
- 1 **teaspoon ground cinnamon**
- ½ **cup whipping cream**
- ⅔ **cup powdered sugar**
-   **Milk**

1. Lightly grease two 8×1½-inch round baking pans; set aside. On a lightly floured surface, roll dough to a 20×8-inch rectangle. Brush with melted butter. In a small bowl combine brown sugar, nuts, and cinnamon; sprinkle evenly over dough. Starting from a long side, roll up dough. Moisten edges and seal. Cut into 20 slices. Place rolls, cut sides down, in prepared pans. Cover and let rise in a warm place until nearly double (1 to 1½ hours).

2. Preheat oven to 350°F. Slowly pour whipping cream over rolls. Bake about 20 minutes or until golden. Let stand for 1 minute. Loosen edges; invert onto serving plates. Scrape any caramel mixture left in pans onto rolls.

3. For glaze, in a small bowl combine powdered sugar and enough milk (3 to 4 teaspoons) to make drizzling consistency. Drizzle glaze over warm rolls.

Per roll: 160 cal., 7 g total fat (3 g sat. fat), 16 mg chol., 131 mg sodium, 23 g carbo., 1 g fiber, 3 g pro.

Up-and-Down Biscuits

Up-and-Down Biscuits

This recipe from 1950 imparts cinnamon-sugar goodness in a cleverly shaped quick bread.

Prep: 20 minutes Bake: 10 minutes
Oven: 425°F Makes: 12 biscuits

2	cups all-purpose flour
3	tablespoons sugar
1	tablespoon baking powder
½	teaspoon cream of tartar
½	teaspoon salt
½	cup shortening
⅔	cup milk
3	tablespoons butter, melted
¼	cup sugar
2	teaspoons ground cinnamon
1	recipe Vanilla Icing

1. Preheat oven to 425°F. Grease twelve 2½-inch muffin cups. Set aside.

2. In a medium bowl stir together flour, the 3 tablespoons sugar, the baking powder, cream of tartar, and salt. Using a pastry blender, cut in shortening until mixture resembles coarse crumbs. Make a well in the center of the flour mixture. Add milk all at once. Using a fork, stir just until moistened.

3. Turn out dough onto a lightly floured surface. Quickly knead dough by gently folding and pressing for 10 to 12 strokes or until nearly smooth.

Divide dough in half. Roll half of the dough to a 12×10-inch rectangle.* Brush dough with half of the melted butter. In a small bowl stir together the ¼ cup sugar and the cinnamon; sprinkle half over the dough. Cut rectangle lengthwise into five 2-inch-wide strips. Stack the five strips on top of each other. Cut stack into six 2-inch squares. Place squares, cut sides down, in prepared muffin cups. Repeat with remaining dough, remaining butter, and remaining cinnamon mixture.

4. Bake for 10 to 12 minutes or until golden. Drizzle with Vanilla Icing. Serve warm.

Vanilla Icing: In a small bowl combine 1 cup powdered sugar, ¼ teaspoon vanilla, and 1 tablespoon milk. Stir in additional milk, 1 teaspoon at a time, until icing reaches drizzling consistency.

***Note:** For a rectangular shape, trim uneven edges from around the outside of the dough. These can be placed in the center and rolled back into the dough.

Per biscuit: 246 cal., 12 g total fat (4 g sat. fat), 9 mg chol., 184 mg sodium, 33 g carbo., 1 g fiber, 3 g pro.

Unforgettable Desserts

From the first prizewinning cake in 1928 to the recently perfected biggest, richest, moistest chocolate cake, this selection of dessert perfection sweetly spans the decades. Of course, the choices go well beyond cakes because there are so many kinds of dessert lovers out there. Some like their sweets ooey, gooey, and oh-so-sweet; for them, nothing hits the spot like the Ultimate Nut and Chocolate Chip Tart. For old-fashioned appeal, sample the Baked Apples or Apple-Cranberry Deep-Dish Pie. Around the holidays, you can always find a winner with pumpkin—serve it in Maple-Pumpkin Cheesecake, one of the finest pumpkin desserts ever. Choices, choices!

Peppermint Swirl Chiffon Cake, page 86

Apple-Cranberry Deep-Dish Pie

1. In a large bowl combine the ¼ cup sugar, the flour, apple pie spice, and orange peel. Stir in cranberry sauce. Add apple; gently toss to coat. Transfer to a 9-inch deep-dish pie plate or a 1½-quart casserole.

2. Preheat oven to 375°F. Prepare Pastry for Single-Crust Pie. On a lightly floured surface, flatten pastry dough. Roll dough from center to edge into a 14-inch circle. Using cookie cutters, cut shapes from pastry, rerolling and cutting trimmings as necessary. Arrange cutouts on apple mixture so the edges overlap.

3. In a small bowl stir together egg yolk and the water; brush onto pastry cutouts. Sprinkle with the 1 tablespoon sugar. Place pie on a baking sheet. Bake for 50 to 55 minutes or until top is golden and apples are tender. Cool slightly on a wire rack; serve warm. If desired, serve with vanilla ice cream.

Pastry for Single-Crust Pie: In a large bowl stir together 1¼ cups all-purpose flour and ¼ teaspoon salt. Using a pastry blender, cut in ⅓ cup shortening until pieces are pea size. Sprinkle 1 tablespoon cold water over part of the mixture; gently toss with a fork. Push moistened dough to side of bowl. Repeat moistening dough, using 1 tablespoon cold water at a time, until all the dough is moistened (4 to 5 tablespoons cold water total). Form dough into a ball.

Per slice: 323 cal., 9 g total fat (2 g sat. fat), 26 mg chol., 92 mg sodium, 59 g carbo., 4 g fiber, 3 g pro.

Apple-Cranberry Deep-Dish Pie

This pretty pie combines two favorite fall/winter flavors in one unforgettable dessert. Spoon it into your prettiest dessert dishes and top it with scoops of vanilla ice cream.

Prep: 50 minutes **Bake:** 50 minutes
Oven: 375°F **Makes:** 8 slices

¼ cup sugar
3 tablespoons all-purpose flour
1 teaspoon apple pie spice or
   ¼ teaspoon ground nutmeg
1 teaspoon finely shredded orange peel
1 16-ounce can whole cranberry sauce
7 cups thinly sliced, peeled cooking apple
   (such as Granny Smith) (about 2¼ pounds)
1 recipe Pastry for Single-Crust Pie
1 egg yolk
1 tablespoon water
1 tablespoon sugar
   Vanilla ice cream (optional)

Apricot-Almond Crunch Pie

Originally, this pie was developed to showcase summer's ripe, juicy apricots. When apricots aren't in season, try the canned-apricot option.

Prep: 35 minutes **Bake:** 45 minutes
Oven: 375°F **Makes:** 8 slices

1 recipe Pastry for Single-Crust Pie
   (see recipe, above)
¾ cup sugar
⅓ cup all-purpose flour
4 cups sliced, pitted apricot (about
   1¾ pounds) or three 11½-ounce cans
   apricots, drained and sliced
½ teaspoon almond extract
1 recipe Crumb Topping (see page 81)

1. Preheat oven to 375°F. Prepare Pastry for Single-Crust Pie. On a lightly floured surface, flatten pastry dough. Roll dough from center to edges into a circle about 12 inches in diameter. Line a 9-inch pie plate with the pastry. Trim and crimp edge as desired.

2. In a large bowl combine sugar and flour. Add apricot and almond extract. Gently toss until coated.

3. Transfer apricot mixture to pastry-lined pie plate. Sprinkle Crumb Topping over filling.

4. To prevent overbrowning, cover edges of the pie with foil.* Bake for 25 minutes. Remove foil. Bake for 20 to 25 minutes more or until top is golden. Cool on a wire rack.

Crumb Topping: In a medium bowl stir together ½ cup all-purpose flour and ½ cup packed brown sugar. Using a pastry blender, cut in 3 tablespoons cold butter until mixture resembles coarse crumbs. Stir in ¼ cup slivered almonds.

***Note:** To make foil cover for pie, fold a 12-inch square of foil into quarters. Cut a 7-inch hole out of the center. Unfold and loosely mold the foil over the edge of the pie.

Per slice: 408 cal., 16 g total fat (5 g sat. fat), 11 mg chol., 110 mg sodium, 64 g carbo., 3 g fiber, 5 g pro.

Chocolaty Bourbon And Nut Pie

A favorite since 1996, this dessert indulgence is comparable to a pecan pie with a bonus layer of chocolate and a hint of bourbon. If that all sounds like a keeper, it is! Many readers continue to request this recipe when they misplace their copies.

Prep: 30 minutes **Bake:** 45 minutes
Oven: 350°F **Makes:** 10 slices

- 1 **recipe Pastry for Single-Crust Pie**
  (see recipe, page 80)
- 3 **eggs, slightly beaten**
- ¾ **cup light-colored corn syrup**
- 3 **tablespoons granulated sugar**
- 3 **tablespoons packed brown sugar**
- 3 **tablespoons butter, softened**

- 1 **teaspoon vanilla**
- ⅛ **teaspoon salt**
- ½ **cup finely chopped pecans**
- ⅓ **cup bourbon**
- 1 **cup semisweet chocolate pieces (6 ounces)**
- 1⅓ **cups pecan halves**

1. Prepare Pastry for Single-Crust Pie. On a lightly floured surface, roll dough from center to edges into a circle about 12 inches in diameter. Line a 9-inch pie plate with the pastry. Trim to ½ inch beyond edges. Fold under extra pastry and flute edge. Do not prick pastry.

2. Preheat oven to 350°F. For filling, in a large bowl combine eggs, corn syrup, granulated sugar, brown sugar, butter, vanilla, and salt; mix well. Stir in the chopped pecans and bourbon.

3. Lightly pat chocolate pieces onto bottom of pastry shell. Pour filling over chocolate pieces. Arrange pecan halves on filling.

4. Bake for 45 to 60 minutes or until a knife inserted near the center comes out clean. To prevent overbrowning, cover edges of pie loosely with foil (see note, left) for the last 30 minutes of baking.

Per slice: 494 cal., 30 g total fat (8 g sat. fat), 73 mg chol., 156 mg sodium, 51 g carbo., 3 g fiber, 6 g pro.

Picking the Perfect Plate

For a golden brown and flaky bottom crust, choose the right pie plate for the job. Here's what to look for when selecting:

- **Surface:** Always use a standard glass or dull metal pie plate. Shiny metal pie pans—which work fine for crumb-crust pies—can result in a soggy bottom crust.

- **Size:** Although they may be pretty, ceramic or pottery pie plates aren't always standard size (a standard-size plate holds about 3¾ cups liquid). If you use a larger ceramic plate, adjust the amount of filling and the baking time.

- **Foil:** Disposable foil pans are usually smaller than standard pie plates; deep-dish foil pie pans are closer to standard size.

Macaroon Brownie Pie

If you can't decide between cookies, brownies, or pie, just combine all three with this decadent dessert! Packed with chewy chocolate goodness, no wonder it's a holiday favorite!

Prep: 30 minutes **Bake:** 40 minutes
Stand: 30 minutes **Chill:** 3 hours
Oven: 350°F **Makes:** 10 slices

1¼	cups all-purpose flour
1	tablespoon sugar
⅛	teaspoon salt
6	tablespoons butter
4	eggs, slightly beaten
½	cup sugar
½	cup light-colored corn syrup
4	ounces semisweet chocolate, chopped
¾	cup shredded coconut
¼	cup butter, melted
1	tablespoon maraschino cherry juice
¼	teaspoon almond extract

1. In a large bowl stir together flour, the 1 tablespoon sugar, and the salt. Using a pastry blender, cut in the 6 tablespoons butter until pieces are pea size. Stir in 1 of the eggs. Gently knead to form a ball. If necessary, cover and chill for 30 to 60 minutes or until easy to handle.

2. Preheat oven to 350°F. On a lightly floured surface, roll dough into a circle about 12 inches in diameter. Line a 9-inch pie plate with pastry. Trim pastry to ½ inch beyond edges. Fold under extra pastry and flute edges. Do not prick pastry.

3. In a medium saucepan combine the ½ cup sugar and the corn syrup. Cook and stir until mixture begins to boil. Remove from heat. Stir in the 4 ounces chocolate and the coconut. Stir in the remaining 3 eggs, the ¼ cup melted butter, the cherry juice, and almond extract. Pour into pastry shell. To prevent overbrowning, cover edges of pie with foil (see note, page 81).

4. Bake for 40 to 50 minutes or until a knife inserted near the center comes out clean. Cool on a wire rack. Cover and chill for 3 to 24 hours. Let stand at room temperature for 30 minutes before serving. If desired, garnish with *whipped cream* and *maraschino cherries*.

Per slice: 357 cal., 19 g total fat (12 g sat. fat), 115 mg chol., 162 mg sodium, 44 g carbo., 2 g fiber, 5 g pro.

Chocolate-Peanut Mousse Pie

This recipe crosses chocolate mousse—an airy treat—with a down-home swirl of peanuts and peanut butter candy. Although this pie is not difficult to make, it does require some extra time for each step.

Prep: 1 hour **Bake:** 5 minutes **Cook:** 20 minutes
Freeze: 35 minutes **Chill:** 4½ hours **Oven:** 375°F
Makes: 16 slices

1¼	cups crushed chocolate graham crackers
3	tablespoons sugar
⅓	cup butter, melted
3¾	cups whipping cream
4	ounces bittersweet chocolate, finely chopped (about ¾ cup)
1	cup chopped peanuts
1⅓	cups peanut butter-flavor pieces

1. Preheat oven to 375°F. For crust, in a small bowl combine graham crackers and sugar; stir in melted butter. Press onto bottom and up sides of a 9-inch pie plate. Bake for 5 minutes; cool on a wire rack for 15 minutes.

Chocolate-Peanut Mousse Pie

2. Meanwhile, in a small saucepan combine ¾ cup of the whipping cream and the chocolate; cook and stir over low heat until mixture is smooth. Stir in ¾ cup of the peanuts. Pour half of the chocolate mixture over crust. Place in freezer and chill about 20 minutes or until set, then place in refrigerator. (Cover and refrigerate remaining chocolate mixture.)

3. Meanwhile, in a medium saucepan combine 1 cup of the remaining whipping cream and the peanut butter pieces; cook and stir over low heat until mixture is smooth. Cover and chill about 30 minutes or until cool but not stiff, stirring occasionally.

4. In a chilled medium mixing bowl beat the remaining 2 cups whipping cream with chilled beaters of an electric mixer on medium speed until soft peaks form (tips curl). Fold about one-third of the whipped cream into the peanut butter mixture; gently fold in remaining whipped cream. Spoon 3 cups of the mixture over the chocolate in crust. Place in freezer about 15 minutes or until set. (Cover and refrigerate remaining peanut butter mixture.)

5. Spread remaining chocolate mixture over peanut butter mixture in crust. Pipe or spoon remaining peanut butter mixture around edge of pie. Sprinkle with remaining ¼ cup peanuts. If desired, garnish with *chocolate curls*. Chill for 4 to 24 hours.

Per slice: 448 cal., 37 g total fat (20 g sat. fat), 87 mg chol., 184 mg sodium, 25 g carbo., 2 g fiber, 8 g pro.

Fudge Ribbon Pie

Looking for a holiday dessert that's both refreshing and indulgent? Consider this 1968 classic—a decadent swirl of homemade fudge sauce ribbons through a brisk peppermint ice cream filling. Top it all off with a fluffy meringue or mounds of sweetened whipped cream.

Prep: 50 minutes **Bake:** 3 minutes **Freeze:** 7 hours
Oven: 475°F **Makes:** 8 slices

- 1 cup sugar
- 1 5-ounce can evaporated milk (⅔ cup)
- 2 tablespoons butter
- 2 ounces unsweetened chocolate, cut up
- 1 teaspoon vanilla
- 2 pints (4 cups) peppermint ice cream
- 1 9-inch baked pastry shell,* cooled
- ¾ cup sugar
- ½ cup boiling water
- ¼ cup meringue powder**
- ¼ cup crushed peppermint-stick candy

1. For fudge sauce, in a small saucepan combine the 1 cup sugar, the evaporated milk, butter, and chocolate. Cook and stir over medium heat until bubbly; reduce heat. Boil gently for 4 to 5 minutes or until mixture is thickened and reduced to 1½ cups; stir occasionally. Remove from heat; stir in vanilla. If necessary, beat until smooth with wire whisk or rotary beater. Set aside to cool completely.

2. In a chilled bowl stir 1 pint of the ice cream until softened. Spread into cooled pastry shell. Cover with half of the cooled fudge sauce. Freeze until nearly firm. Repeat with remaining ice cream and fudge sauce. Return to freezer while preparing meringue.

3. For meringue, in a medium mixing bowl dissolve the ¾ cup sugar in the boiling water. Cool to room temperature. Add meringue powder. Beat on low speed until combined; beat on high speed until stiff peaks form (tips stand straight). Using a wooden spoon, fold in 3 tablespoons of the crushed candy. Spread meringue over chocolate sauce layer, sealing to edge. Sprinkle top with remaining crushed candy. Freeze until firm (4 hours or overnight).

4. Preheat oven to 475°F. Bake for 3 to 4 minutes or just until meringue is light brown. Cover loosely; freeze for 3 hours or overnight before serving.

*Note: For a 9-inch baked pastry shell, use your favorite pastry recipe, bake a 9-inch frozen deep-dish piecrust according to package directions, or prepare and bake half of a 15-ounce package (1 crust) rolled refrigerated unbaked piecrust according to package directions.

**Note: Look for meringue powder in the cake decorating department of hobby and specialty cooking stores.

Per slice: 564 cal., 24 g total fat (12 g sat. fat), 43 mg chol., 198 mg sodium, 83 g carbo., 2 g fiber, 6 g pro.

Snowdrift Coconut Cream Pie

Dreaming of a white Christmas? Even if it doesn't snow outside, your day can be dreamy if you end the meal with this spectacular white chocolate cream pie. Heap the pie with piles of elegant fresh coconut curls to create the effect of winsome snowdrifts.

Prep: 45 minutes **Bake:** 10 minutes **Chill:** 2½ hours
Oven: 350°F **Makes:** 8 slices

  2 **cups flaked coconut**
  ½ **cup finely crushed graham crackers**
  ¼ **cup butter, melted**
  2 **cups milk**
  1 **cup flaked coconut**
  6 **egg yolks**
  ¾ **cup granulated sugar**
  ½ **cup all-purpose flour**
  2 **tablespoons crème de cacao**
  1 **tablespoon butter**
  4 **1-ounce squares white chocolate baking squares (with cocoa butter)**
1½ **cups whipping cream**
  2 **tablespoons powdered sugar**
  1 **tablespoon crème de cacao (optional)**

1. Preheat oven to 350°F. For the coconut-cracker crust, in a medium bowl stir together the 2 cups coconut, the crushed graham crackers, and the ¼ cup melted butter. Press onto bottom and side of a 9-inch pie plate. Bake for 10 minutes. Cool on a wire rack.

2. For filling, in a large heavy saucepan combine milk and the 1 cup coconut; heat just until simmering, stirring occasionally.

3. Meanwhile, in a large mixing bowl combine egg yolks, granulated sugar, and flour. Beat with an electric mixer on medium-high speed until combined. Gradually stir 1 cup of the hot milk mixture into the egg mixture. Stir egg mixture into the remaining mixture in saucepan. Cook and stir until mixture comes to a boil. Cook and stir for 2 minutes more. Remove from heat. Stir in the 2 tablespoons crème de cacao and the 1 tablespoon butter until melted. Transfer to a bowl. Cover the surface with plastic wrap; cool.

4. Meanwhile, in a small saucepan combine white chocolate and 2 tablespoons of the whipping cream; heat over low heat until white chocolate is melted, stirring constantly. Using a spoon, drizzle onto the bottom and sides of piecrust. Chill until chocolate is firm. Pour filling into crust. Cover and chill for 2 to 4 hours.

5. In a chilled large mixing bowl combine the remaining whipping cream, the powdered sugar, and, if desired, the 1 tablespoon crème de cacao; beat with an electric mixer on medium to high speed until stiff peaks form (tips stand straight). Swirl whipped cream over chilled filling. (If pie isn't served all at once, top only the pieces to be served with whipped cream. Refrigerate remaining whipped cream and pie separately.) Cover and chill for 30 minutes. If desired, garnish with *toasted coconut shreds*.

Per slice: 717 cal., 49 g total fat (33 g sat. fat), 242 mg chol., 259 mg sodium, 63 g carbo., 3 g fiber, 11 g pro.

Ultimate Nut and Chocolate Chip Tart

Start with a purchased piecrust, then fill it with caramel-custard filling that's amazingly easy to stir together. That's about all there is to this sweet, gooey, all-time-favorite tart.

Prep: 30 minutes **Bake:** 40 minutes
Oven: 350°F **Makes:** 8 to 10 slices

  ½ **of a 15-ounce package (1 crust) rolled refrigerated unbaked piecrust**
  3 **eggs**
  1 **cup light-colored corn syrup**
  ½ **cup packed brown sugar**
  ⅓ **cup butter, melted and cooled**
  1 **teaspoon vanilla**
  1 **cup coarsely chopped salted dry roasted mixed nuts**
  ½ **cup miniature semisweet chocolate pieces**
  ⅓ **cup miniature semisweet chocolate pieces**
  1 **tablespoon shortening**
     Sweetened whipped cream (optional)

1. Let refrigerated piecrust stand at room temperature according to package directions. On a lightly floured surface, roll out dough to a 12-inch diameter. Ease piecrust into an 11-inch tart pan with a removable bottom. Trim piecrust even with the rim of the pan. Do not prick piecrust; set aside.

2. Preheat oven to 350°F. In a large bowl beat eggs slightly with a rotary beater or fork. Stir in corn syrup. Add brown sugar, melted butter, and vanilla, stirring until sugar is dissolved. Stir in the nuts and the ½ cup chocolate pieces.

3. Place pastry-lined tart pan on a baking sheet on an oven rack. Carefully pour filling into pan. Bake about 40 minutes or until a knife inserted near the center comes out clean. Cool on a wire rack.

4. To serve, cut tart into slices and transfer to dessert plates. In a small heavy saucepan combine the ⅓ cup chocolate pieces and the shortening; cook and stir over very low heat until chocolate begins to melt. Immediately remove from heat and stir until smooth. Cool slightly. Transfer chocolate mixture to a clean, small resealable plastic bag. Snip a very small hole in one corner of the bag. Drizzle the melted chocolate across each tart slice.

5. If desired, serve tart with sweetened whipped cream. Cover and refrigerate any leftover tart for up to 2 days.

Per slice: 581 cal., 31 g total fat (12 g sat. fat), 104 mg chol., 231 mg sodium, 74 g carbo., 3 g fiber, 7 g pro.

Ultimate Nut and Chocolate Chip Tart

1. Preheat oven to 325°F. For crust, in a medium bowl combine crushed graham crackers, the ⅓ cup sugar, and the melted butter. Press crumb mixture onto the bottom and about 2 inches up the sides of an ungreased 9-inch springform pan. Bake for 8 minutes. Cool in pan on a wire rack.

2. For filling, in a large mixing bowl combine cream cheese, 1 cup sugar, pumpkin, whipping cream, vanilla, and allspice; beat on medium speed with an electric mixer until combined. Add eggs; beat on low speed just until combined.

Maple-Pumpkin Cheesecake

A pumpkin cheesecake won Better Homes and Gardens® *magazine's Prize Tested Recipe contest in 1971 and became a year-after-year favorite after that. This recent version updates the tradition with maple flavor and a caramel drizzle.*

3. Spoon filling into crust-lined pan. Place springform pan into a shallow baking pan. Bake about 1 hour or until center appears nearly set when gently shaken.

4. Cool in springform pan on a wire rack for 15 minutes. Loosen crust from side of pan with a thin-bladed knife; cool for 30 minutes more. Remove side of pan; cool for 1 hour. Cover and chill for 4 to 48 hours. Just before serving, spoon caramel ice cream topping over top of cheesecake.

Prep: 35 minutes **Bake:** 1 hour **Cool:** 1¾ hours
Chill: 4 hours **Oven:** 325°F **Makes:** 12 slices

1½ **cups finely crushed graham crackers (about 20 squares)**
⅓ **cup maple sugar or granulated sugar**
½ **cup butter, melted**
3 **8-ounce packages cream cheese, softened**
1 **cup maple sugar or granulated sugar**
1 **cup canned pumpkin**
1 **tablespoon whipping cream**
1½ **teaspoons vanilla**
¾ **teaspoon ground allspice**
3 **eggs, slightly beaten**
½ **cup caramel ice cream topping**

Per slice: 475 cal., 31 g total fat (18 g sat. fat), 139 mg chol., 362 mg sodium, 44 g carbo., 1 g fiber,

# Grapefruit Chiffon Cake

Chiffon cakes are richer than angel food cakes but just as airy and light. This grapefruit-sparked version will nicely complement richer choices on a holiday dessert table.

Prep: 45 minutes **Bake:** 65 minutes
Stand: 30 minutes **Cool:** 2 hours
Oven: 325°F **Makes:** 12 servings

> 7 **eggs**
> 2¼ **cups sifted cake flour or 2 cups sifted**
>   **all-purpose flour**
> 1½ **cups sugar**
> 1 **tablespoon baking powder**
> ¼ **teaspoon salt**
> ¾ **cup cold water**
> ½ **cup cooking oil**
> 1 **teaspoon vanilla**
> 1 **tablespoon finely shredded grapefruit peel**
> ½ **teaspoon cream of tartar**
> 1 **recipe Grapefruit-Cream Cheese Frosting**

1. Separate eggs. Allow egg whites and yolks to stand at room temperature for 30 minutes. Meanwhile, in a large mixing bowl combine flour, sugar, baking powder, and salt. Make a well in the center of the flour mixture. Add the cold water, oil, egg yolks, and vanilla. Beat with an electric mixer on low speed until combined. Beat on high speed about 5 minutes or until smooth. Stir in grapefruit peel.

2. Preheat oven to 325°F. Thoroughly wash and dry the beaters. In a very large bowl combine egg whites and cream of tartar; beat on medium speed until stiff peaks form (tips stand straight). Pour egg yolk mixture in a thin stream over beaten egg whites; fold in gently. Pour into an ungreased 10-inch tube pan.

3. Bake for 65 to 70 minutes or until top springs back when lightly touched. Immediately invert cake (leave in pan); cool completely. Loosen sides of cake from pan; remove cake. Frost with Grapefruit-Cream Cheese Frosting. Cover and store the frosted cake in the refrigerator.

Grapefruit-Cream Cheese Frosting: In a medium mixing bowl combine half of an 8-ounce package cream cheese, softened; 2 tablespoons butter, softened; and ½ teaspoon vanilla. Beat with an electric mixer on medium speed until light and fluffy. Gradually beat in 2 cups powdered sugar. Beat in enough grapefruit juice (1 to 2 teaspoons) to make spreading consistency; stir in 1½ teaspoons finely shredded grapefruit peel.

Per serving: 420 cal., 17 g total fat (6 g sat. fat), 139 mg chol., 192 mg sodium, 61 g carbo., 0 g fiber, 6 g pro.

# Peppermint Swirl Chiffon Cake

In this update of the popular mid-20th-century chiffon cake, peppermint adds a holiday angle, while the Chocolate Ganache Glaze adds extra richness. To serve, dip a knife into warm water before cutting each slice.

Prep: 35 minutes **Bake:** 65 minutes
Stand: 40 minutes **Oven:** 325°F
Makes: 16 servings

> 7 **eggs**
> 2¼ **cups sifted cake flour or 2 cups**
>   **sifted all-purpose flour**
> 1½ **cups sugar**
> 1 **tablespoon baking powder**
> ¼ **teaspoon salt**
> ¾ **cup cold water**
> ½ **cup cooking oil**
> 1 **teaspoon vanilla**
> ½ **teaspoon cream of tartar**
> ½ **teaspoon peppermint extract**
> ¼ **teaspoon red food coloring**
> 1 **recipe Chocolate Ganache Glaze**
>   **(see page 87)**
> ½ **cup coarsely chopped peppermint**
>   **sticks, candy canes, and/or other**
>   **hard peppermint candies (3 ounces)**

1. Separate eggs. Allow egg whites and egg yolks to stand at room temperature for 30 minutes.

2. Preheat oven to 325°F. Meanwhile, in a large mixing bowl stir together flour, sugar, baking powder, and salt. Make a well in the center of flour mixture. Add egg yolks, the cold water, the oil, and vanilla. Beat with an electric mixer on low speed until combined. Beat on high speed about 5 minutes more or until very smooth.

3. Thoroughly wash and dry the beaters. In a very large mixing bowl combine egg whites and cream of tartar; beat on medium speed until stiff peaks form (tips stand straight). Pour egg yolk batter in a thin stream over beaten egg whites. Fold in gently.

4. Transfer one-third of the batter (about 3 cups) to a medium bowl. Gently fold in peppermint extract and the food coloring.

5. Turn half of the white batter into an ungreased 10-inch tube pan. Top with half of the red batter. Repeat layers of white and red batters. With a narrow spatula, gently swirl through batters to marble, leaving distinctive white and red areas throughout.

6. Bake for 65 to 70 minutes or until top springs back when lightly touched. Immediately invert cake in pan; cool completely. Loosen sides of cake from pan; remove cake from pan and place on a pedestal cake stand or plate.

7. Prepare Chocolate Ganache Glaze. Spread evenly with a thin spatula over top and sides of cake. Let stand for 5 minutes. Sprinkle with chopped peppermint candies.*

Chocolate Ganache Glaze: In a medium saucepan bring 1 cup whipping cream just to boiling over medium-high heat. Remove from heat. Add 12 ounces bittersweet or semisweet chocolate, chopped (do not stir). Let stand for 5 minutes. Stir until smooth. Cool for 10 minutes. Spread evenly over top and sides of cooled cake.

*Note: To serve clean slices from this cake, cut it with a warm wet knife.

Per serving: 395 cal., 22 g total fat (10 g sat. fat), 113 mg chol., 122 mg sodium, 48 g carbo., 2 g fiber, 6 g pro.

Peppermint Swirl Chiffon Cake

Mocha and Cherry Cake

With ricotta cheese, chocolate, cherries, and a terrific mocha frosting, this chocolate cake is fit for royalty! Even the most determined dessert dodgers find it hard to resist. (See photos, front cover and below.)

Prep: 50 minutes **Bake:** 25 minutes **Chill:** 1 hour
Oven: 350°F **Makes:** 14 to 16 servings

     Unsweetened cocoa powder
 2   cups sugar
 1¾ cups all-purpose flour
 ¾   cup unsweetened cocoa powder
 2   teaspoons baking soda
 1   teaspoon baking powder
 ½   teaspoon salt
 2   eggs
 1   cup buttermilk
 1   cup strong coffee, cooled
 ½   cup cooking oil
 2   teaspoons vanilla
 1   recipe Ricotta Filling
 1   recipe Mocha Frosting

1. Preheat oven to 350°F. Grease two 9×1½-inch round cake pans; sprinkle with cocoa powder, tilting each pan to evenly distribute the powder. Set aside.

2. In a large mixing bowl combine sugar, flour, the ¾ cup cocoa powder, the baking soda, baking powder, and salt. Add eggs, buttermilk, coffee, oil, and vanilla. Beat with an electric mixer on low speed for 30 seconds or until combined; beat on medium speed for 2 minutes. Spread evenly into prepared pans.

3. Bake for 25 to 30 minutes or until a toothpick inserted near the centers comes out clean. Cool in pans on wire racks for 10 minutes. Remove from pans. Cool completely on wire racks. Split each cake layer horizontally to make a total of four layers.

4. Place one cake layer, cut side up, on a serving plate; carefully spread with one-third of the Ricotta Filling. Top with another layer. Continue layering filling and cake layers, ending with a cake layer, top side up.

5. Frost top and sides of cake with Mocha Frosting. If desired, garnish with *chocolate curls* and *maraschino cherries*. Cover; chill for 1 to 24 hours.

Ricotta Filling: In a medium bowl stir together 2½ cups ricotta cheese, ½ cup sugar, and ½ cup miniature semisweet chocolate pieces. Gently stir in ½ cup maraschino cherries, drained and chopped.

Mocha Frosting: In a small bowl stir 1 teaspoon instant coffee crystals into ½ cup milk until dissolved; set aside. In a large mixing bowl beat ⅔ cup softened butter with an electric mixer on medium speed until fluffy. Gradually add 3¾ cups powdered sugar and ½ cup unsweetened cocoa powder. Slowly beat in half of the milk mixture and 2 teaspoons vanilla. Beat in another 3¾ cups powdered sugar. Beat in remaining milk mixture. If necessary, beat in additional milk, 1 teaspoon at a time, to make frosting of spreading consistency.

Per serving: 755 cal., 26 g total fat (12 g sat. fat), 77 mg chol., 414 mg sodium, 121 g carbo., 1 g fiber, 11 g pro.

Mocha and Cherry Cake

Chocolate-Mousse Torte

This prizewinning recipe from the 1990s starts with a cake mix but ends up nothing less than spectacular. The creamy mousse makes all the difference. Don't heat the fudge sauce before spreading onto the cake—it's easier to spread straight from the jar.

Prep: 25 minutes **Bake:** per cake mix directions
Chill: 2 hours 35 minutes **Makes:** 10 servings

 1   package 1-layer-size devil's food cake mix*
 ⅓   cup chocolate fudge sauce
 4   ounces semisweet chocolate

Chocolate-Mousse Torte

2   tablespoons powdered sugar
2   tablespoons coffee liqueur or strong
      brewed coffee, cooled
2   tablespoons whipping cream
2   egg yolks
⅔ cup whipping cream
      Fresh raspberries (optional)
      Fresh mint leaves (optional)

1. Prepare and bake cake mix according to package directions, using an 8×1½- or 9×1½-inch round cake pan. Cool in pan on a wire rack for 15 minutes. Remove cake from pan; cool completely. Place cake on a serving platter. Spread top with the chocolate fudge sauce. Chill until needed.

2. For chocolate mousse, in a small saucepan melt semisweet chocolate over low heat, stirring often. Stir in powdered sugar, coffee liqueur, the 2 tablespoons whipping cream, and the egg yolks. Cook and stir over low heat about 8 minutes or until an instant-read thermometer registers 160°F. Remove from heat. Chill chocolate mousse for 30 minutes, stirring occasionally.

3. In a small mixing bowl beat the ⅔ cup whipping cream with an electric mixer on medium speed just until soft peaks form (tips curl). Fold half of the whipped cream into the chocolate mixture until combined. Fold in remaining whipped cream. Cover and chill for 5 to 10 minutes or until mixture mounds. Spread onto cake top to within 1 inch of edges. Cover and chill for 2 to 4 hours.

4. If desired, garnish cake with fresh raspberries and mint leaves.

*Note: Or use a 2-layer-size devil's food cake mix and save the second baked layer for another use.

Per serving: 264 cal., 14 g total fat (7 g sat. fat), 82 mg chol., 195 mg sodium, 31 g carbo., 1 g fiber, 3 g pro.

Best-Ever Chocolate Cake

The name of this cake says it all!

Prep: 30 minutes **Stand:** 30 minutes
Bake: 35 minutes **Oven:** 350°F
Makes: 12 to 16 servings

¾ cup butter, softened
3 eggs
2 cups all-purpose flour
¾ cup unsweetened cocoa powder
1 teaspoon baking soda
¾ teaspoon baking powder
½ teaspoon salt
2 cups sugar
2 teaspoons vanilla
1½ cups milk
1 recipe Chocolate-Sour Cream Frosting

1. Preheat oven to 350°F. Allow butter and eggs to stand at room temperature for 30 minutes. Meanwhile, lightly grease bottoms of two 8×8×2-inch square or 9×1½-inch round cake pans. Line bottom of pans with waxed paper. Grease and lightly flour waxed paper and sides of pans. (Or grease one 13×9×2-inch baking pan.) Set pan(s) aside.

2. In a medium bowl stir together flour, cocoa powder, baking soda, baking powder, and salt; set aside.

3. In a large bowl beat butter with an electric mixer on medium to high speed for 30 seconds. Gradually add sugar, about ¼ cup at a time, beating on medium speed until well mixed (3 to 4 minutes). Scrape sides of bowl; continue beating on medium speed for 2 minutes. Add eggs 1 at a time, beating after each addition (about 1 minute total). Beat in vanilla.

4. Alternately add flour mixture and milk to beaten mixture, beating on low speed just until combined after each addition. Beat on medium to high speed for 20 seconds more. Spread batter evenly into the prepared pan(s).

5. Bake for 35 to 40 minutes for 8-inch pans and the 13×9×2-inch pan or 30 to 35 minutes for 9-inch pans or until a wooden toothpick inserted in the center comes out clean. Cool cake layers in pans on wire racks for 10 minutes; remove from pans and peel off waxed paper. Cool completely on wire racks. (Or

place 13×9×2-inch cake in pan on a wire rack; cool completely.) Fill and frost with Chocolate-Sour Cream Frosting. If desired, arrange *walnut halves* around the top edges of the cake. Cover and store frosted cake in the refrigerator.

Chocolate-Sour Cream Frosting: In a large saucepan combine one 12-ounce package semisweet chocolate pieces and ½ cup butter; cook and stir over low heat until melted and smooth. Cool for 5 minutes. Stir in one 8-ounce carton dairy sour cream. Gradually add 4½ cups powdered sugar (about 1 pound), beating with an electric mixer on medium speed until smooth.

Per serving: 360 cal., 15 g total fat (8 g sat. fat), 88 mg chol., 382 mg sodium, 51 g carbo., 1 g fiber, 6 g pro.

Chocolate-Cherry Bread Pudding

This is the kind of wintertime dessert that makes you feel all warm and happy inside.

Prep: 25 minutes **Bake:** 1 hour **Stand:** 2 hours
Oven: 350°F **Makes:** 12 servings

⅔ cup Kirsch or orange juice
1½ cups dried tart cherries or dried plums
     (prunes), snipped (about 8 ounces)
1 16-ounce loaf country Italian bread or
     baguette, cut into 1- to 1½-inch pieces
     (about 11 cups)
¼ cup butter, melted
8 ounces bittersweet chocolate,
     coarsely chopped
6 eggs, slightly beaten
3 cups milk
2 cups half-and-half or light cream
1 cup sugar
1 teaspoon vanilla

1. In a small saucepan heat Kirsch over medium-low heat until simmering; remove from heat. Add cherries; let stand, covered, for 1 hour. Do not drain.

2. Preheat oven to 350°F. In a very large bowl toss bread with melted butter until coated. Divide bread cubes evenly between two 1½-quart casseroles or place in one 3-quart rectangular baking dish.

Sprinkle half of the coarsely chopped chocolate evenly over bread in casseroles; set aside remaining chocolate. Spoon half of the fruit and liquid evenly over the chocolate layer; set aside remaining half of the fruit and liquid. Top with remaining bread.

3. In a large bowl whisk together eggs, milk, half-and-half, sugar, and vanilla until combined. Slowly pour egg mixture evenly over the layers in the casseroles or baking dish. Press layers down lightly.

4. Bake, covered, for 45 minutes. Uncover and bake for 15 to 20 minutes more for the 1½-quart casseroles or 30 minutes more for the baking dish or until the egg portion in the center appears set. Evenly sprinkle remaining chocolate and fruit-liquid mixture over top. Let stand for 1 hour. Serve warm.

Per serving: 506 cal., 20 g total fat (11 g sat. fat), 137 mg chol., 342 mg sodium, 67 g carbo., 3 g fiber, 11 g pro.

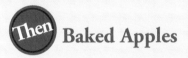 **Baked Apples**

When only a delightfully old-fashioned, comforting dessert will do, reach for this classic.

Prep: 15 minutes **Bake:** 40 minutes
Oven: 350°F **Makes:** 4 servings

 4 **medium cooking apples (such as Jonathan)**
 ½ **cup raisins, snipped pitted whole dates, or mixed dried fruit bits**

Chocolate-Cherry Bread Pudding

 2 **tablespoons packed brown sugar**
 ½ **teaspoon ground cinnamon**
 ¼ **teaspoon ground nutmeg**
 ⅓ **cup apple juice, apple cider, or water**
   Vanilla ice cream or half-and-half (optional)

1. Preheat oven to 350°F. Core apples; peel a strip from the top of each apple. Place apples in a 2-quart casserole. In a small bowl combine raisins, brown sugar, cinnamon, and nutmeg; spoon into centers of apples. Pour apple juice into casserole.

2. Bake for 40 to 45 minutes or until the apples are tender, basting occasionally with liquid in casserole. If desired, serve warm with ice cream or half-and-half.

Per serving: 164 cal., 1 g total fat (0 g sat. fat), 0 mg chol., 5 mg sodium, 42 g carbo., 5 g fiber, 1 g pro.

 **Molasses-Fig Baked Apples**

Though savored since ancient times, figs are enjoying a renaissance in up-to-date bistro cooking. In this dish, they are sensational when combined with apples!

Prep: 20 minutes **Bake:** 25 minutes
Oven: 350°F **Makes:** 6 to 8 servings

 ½ **cup mild-flavored molasses**
 ½ **cup snipped dried figs**
 ¼ **cup packed brown sugar**
 ¼ **cup chopped walnuts**
 1 **tablespoon butter, melted**
 2 **pounds cooking apples (such as McIntosh, or Jonathan), peeled if desired, cored, and each cut into 8 wedges**

1. Preheat oven to 350°F. In a large bowl stir together molasses, figs, brown sugar, walnuts, and butter. Add apple wedges; toss to coat. Spoon mixture into a 2-quart rectangular baking dish.

2. Bake for 25 to 30 minutes or until apples are tender, stirring once. Cool slightly before serving. Serve with a slotted spoon.

Per serving: 242 cal., 6 g total fat (1 g sat. fat), 5 mg chol., 31 mg sodium, 50 g carbo., 4 g fiber, 2 g pro.

80 Years of Amazing Cookies

No one knows cookies like the food editors and Test Kitchen pros from the Better Homes and Gardens® family of publications. Here are the cream-of-the-crop choices from 80 years of great baking. Some, such as Peanut Butter Blossoms, Cherry Winks, and Pecan Crispies, are delightfully old-fashioned—sure to warm the heart. Others, such as Coffeehouse Crisps and Chocolate Truffle Winks, are thoroughly modern—new classics you'll enjoy for years to come. In between, you will find plenty of elegant gems and sweet kid pleasers to make this year's selections your best cookie collection ever.

Cherry-Nut Rum Balls, page 102,
Coffeehouse Crisps, page 109, and
Hickory Nut Macaroons, page 105

Toy Cookie Bouquet

This delicious bouquet is the perfect gift for anyone— big or small, old or young—during the holiday season. The cookies are cut into the shapes of old-fashioned Christmas toys, but try any other theme you like, including beautifully decorated flower cookies for May Day or heart cookies for St. Valentine's Day.

Prep: 3 hours **Chill:** 2 hours
Bake: 10 minutes per batch
Cool: 5 minutes per batch **Stand:** 2 hours
Oven: 375°F **Makes:** 24 cookie lollipops

  1 recipe Sugar Cookie Dough
     Assorted 2½- to 3-inch toy-shape
       cookie cutters*
     Lollipop sticks*
  1 recipe Royal Icing
     Assorted gel or paste food coloring*
     Small clean artist's paintbrushes
     Pastry bag fitted with a small
       round tip**
     Fine sanding sugar or edible glitter
       (optional)*
     Modeling clay
     Several small decorated boxes
     Paper confetti or tissue paper

1. Prepare and chill Sugar Cookie Dough.

2. Preheat oven to 375°F. On a lightly floured surface, roll out half of the dough to ⅛-inch thickness. Using desired cookie cutters, cut out pairs of toy shapes. For each cookie lollipop, place one cutout on cookie sheet. Place the end of a lollipop stick on the middle of the cookie. Top with matching cookie cutout. Repeat with remaining cookie cutouts and lollipop sticks. Bake about 10 minutes or just until edges begin to brown. Cool on cookie sheet for 5 to 10 minutes or until firm. Transfer to a wire rack; let cool.

3. Prepare Royal Icing. Set aside about ⅔ cup of the icing for piping. Divide remaining icing among several small bowls for tinting. (Keep icing covered when not using.) Tint bowls of icing as desired with food coloring. Stir in a small amount of water a few drops at a time until tinted icings are thinned to a paint consistency. Using paintbrushes, paint different colors of tinted icings onto cooled cookies. Let stand about 1 hour or until dry.

4. Place the reserved ⅔ cup white icing in a decorating bag fitted with a small round tip. Pipe outlines and details onto painted cookies. If desired, while white icing is still wet, sprinkle with sanding sugar. Let stand about 1 hour or until dry.

5. To assemble each cookie bouquet, arrange modeling clay in the bottom of a decorated box. Poke the sticks of the cookie lollipops into the clay, arranging cookies as desired. Fill the box with paper confetti to cover up the modeling clay.

Sugar Cookie Dough: In a medium mixing bowl combine 4 cups flour and 1 teaspoon baking powder; set aside. In a medium saucepan combine 1 cup butter, 1 cup sugar, and ⅔ cup light-colored corn syrup; cook and stir over medium heat until sugar dissolves. Pour butter mixture into a large bowl. Stir in 1 teaspoon vanilla. Cool for 5 minutes. Add 1 beaten egg to butter mixture; mix well. Stir in flour mixture until well mixed. Divide dough in half. Cover and chill for at least 2 hours or overnight. (If chilled overnight, let dough stand at room temperature for 15 to 30 minutes before rolling.)

Royal Icing: In a medium mixing bowl combine ½ cup warm water and 3 tablespoons meringue powder.* Add one 16-ounce package powdered sugar, 1 teaspoon vanilla, and ½ teaspoon cream of tartar. Beat with an electric mixer on low speed until combined; beat on high speed for 7 to 10 minutes or until mixture is very stiff. (Icing may thin while standing. If necessary, beat icing until very stiff.)

***Note:** Find cookie cutters, lollipop sticks, meringue powder, gel or paste food coloring, and fine sanding sugar or edible glitter in the hobby department of local department stores or in the cake decorating department of hobby stores.

****Note:** If you don't own a pastry bag, use a heavy-duty resealable plastic bag. Fill the bag with icing, then cut a small hole in one corner of the bag. Pipe icing onto cookies as desired.

Per cookie lollipop: 273 cal., 8 g total fat (5 g sat. fat), 29 mg chol., 79 mg sodium, 49 g carbo., 1 g fiber, 2 g pro.

Toy Cookie Bouquet

Sugar Cookie Star Cutouts

Sugar Cookie Star Cutouts

Dozens of sugar cookie cutout recipes have been published and made better over the years. Here's a sure-fire standout. (See photo, front cover and above.)

Prep: 30 minutes **Chill:** 1 hour
Bake: 8 minutes per batch **Oven:** 375°F
Makes: about 48 (2½-inch) cookies or about 16 (5-inch) cookies

- ⅓ **cup butter, softened**
- ⅓ **cup shortening**
- ¾ **cup sugar**
- 1 **teaspoon baking powder**
- 1 **egg**
- 1 **teaspoon vanilla**
- 2 **cups all-purpose flour**
- 1 **recipe Royal Icing Glaze**
- 1 **recipe Luster Dust Topper (optional)**

1. In a medium mixing bowl combine butter and shortening; beat with an electric mixer on medium to high speed for 30 seconds. Add sugar, baking powder, and a dash of *salt*. Beat until combined, scraping sides of bowl occasionally. Beat in egg and vanilla until combined. Beat in as much of the flour as you can with the mixer. Using a wooden spoon, stir in any remaining flour. Cover; chill about 1 hour or until dough is easy to handle.

2. Preheat oven to 375°F. Divide dough into thirds. On a lightly floured surface, roll dough, one portion at a time, to ¼-inch thickness. Cut dough using 2½- to 5-inch star-shape cutters. Place star cutouts on an ungreased cookie sheet.

3. Bake for 8 to 10 minutes or until edges are firm and bottoms are very light brown. Cool on cookie sheet for 1 minute. Transfer cookies to wire racks; let cool.

4. Frost and pipe cookies with Royal Icing Glaze as desired. If desired, sprinkle with *sanding sugar* or use a small clean artist's paintbrush to paint the piped designs with Luster Dust Topper.

Royal Icing Glaze: In a small mixing bowl combine 2 cups powdered sugar, 4 teaspoons meringue powder, and ¼ teaspoon cream of tartar. Stir in ¼ cup warm water. Beat with an electric mixer on low speed until combined, then on high speed for 7 to 10 minutes or until very stiff. Add 1 to 2 tablespoons additional warm water, 1 teaspoon at a time, until icing is of glazing consistency.

Per cookie: 74 cal., 3 g total fat (1 g sat. fat), 8 mg chol., 19 mg sodium, 12 g carbo., 0 g fiber, 1 g pro.

Luster Dust Topper: Place ½ teaspoon gold, silver, red, or green luster dust in a custard cup.* Stir in 2 teaspoons vodka. (The vodka will evaporate, leaving a dry mixture that you can paint onto icing.)

*Note: Look for luster dust in the cake decorating department of hobby or department stores.

Mix Now, Bake Later

If you think you're too busy to bake this holiday season, why not separate your cookie making into two steps: Mix one day, bake another. Most cookie doughs (except bar batters and meringue mixtures) can be mixed, then refrigerated or frozen to bake later. Simply pack your favorite dough into freezer containers or shape slice-and-bake dough into rolls and wrap. Store in a tightly covered container in the refrigerator for up to 1 week or freeze up to 6 months. Before baking, thaw the frozen dough in the container in the refrigerator. If the dough is still too stiff, let the thawed dough stand at room temperature to soften.

Chocolate Rum and Butter Cookies

Recipe developer Jennifer Peterson modeled this recipe after a treat she discovered on childhood trips to Canada. "My sister and I were in love with the rum and butter candy bars we could find only on our family vacations there," she says.

Prep: 45 minutes **Bake:** 7 minutes per batch
Chill: 3 hours **Oven:** 375°F
Makes: about 48 cookies

- 1 **cup butter, softened**
- 1½ **cups sugar**
- ⅓ **cup unsweetened cocoa powder**
- 2 **teaspoons cream of tartar**
- 1 **teaspoon baking soda**
- ½ **teaspoon salt**
- 3 **eggs**
- 1 **teaspoon vanilla**
- ½ **teaspoon rum flavoring**
- 3¼ **cups all-purpose flour**
- ½ **cup crushed hard butterscotch candies**
- 3 **ounces semisweet or bittersweet chocolate**
- 1 **tablespoon shortening**

1. In a large mixing bowl beat butter with an electric mixer on medium to high speed for 30 seconds. Add sugar, cocoa powder, cream of tartar, baking soda, and salt. Beat until combined, scraping sides of bowl occasionally. Beat in eggs, vanilla, and rum flavoring until combined. Beat in flour until well mixed.

2. Divide dough into thirds. Wrap each dough portion in plastic wrap and chill about 3 hours or until easy to handle.

3. Preheat oven to 375°F. Line cookie sheets with foil; set aside. On a lightly floured surface, roll each dough portion to ¼-inch thickness. Using 3-inch round or square cookie cutters, cut out dough and place on prepared cookie sheets. Using 1-inch round or square cutters, cut out center of each cookie. Fill the cutouts with crushed butterscotch candy. Reroll scraps and centers; cut out and fill as directed.

4. Bake for 7 to 9 minutes or until edges are firm and candy is melted. Transfer foil sheet with cookies to a wire rack. Cool completely. Carefully peel foil from cookies.

5. In a small microwave-safe bowl combine chocolate and shortening. Microwave on 100% power (high) for 1 to 1½ minutes or until melted, stirring every 30 seconds. Drizzle melted chocolate mixture over cookies.

Per cookie: 112 cal., 5 g total fat (3 g sat. fat), 23 mg chol., 83 mg sodium, 15 g carbo., 0 g fiber, 2 g pro.

Chocolate Rum and Butter Cookies

Orange-Chocolate Rounds

Checkerboard cookies stand out on a holiday cookie tray. Even after these rounds have vanished, the memory of their chocolaty, buttery, citrusy goodness will linger.

Prep: 30 minutes **Chill:** 2½ hours
Bake: 7 minutes per batch **Oven:** 375°F
Makes: about 72 cookies

- 1 **cup butter, softened**
- 1½ **cups sugar**
- 1½ **teaspoons baking powder**
- ¼ **teaspoon salt**
- 1 **egg**
- 1 **teaspoon vanilla**
- 2½ **cups all-purpose flour**
- 2 **teaspoons finely shredded orange peel**
- 2 **ounces unsweetened chocolate, melted and cooled**

1. In a large mixing bowl beat butter with an electric mixer on medium speed for 30 seconds. Add sugar, baking powder, and salt. Beat until combined, scraping sides of bowl occasionally. Beat in egg and vanilla until combined. Beat in as much of the flour as you can with the mixer. Using a wooden spoon, stir in any remaining flour.

2. Divide dough in half. Stir orange peel into half of the dough. Stir melted chocolate into the other half of the dough. If necessary, cover and chill dough about 1 hour or until easy to handle.

3. Shape each dough half into a 10-inch-long roll. Wrap in plastic wrap or waxed paper. Chill for 2 to 24 hours or until firm enough to slice.

4. Cut rolls lengthwise into quarters. Reassemble rolls, alternating chocolate and orange quarters. Wrap and chill about 30 minutes more or until firm enough to slice.

5. Preheat oven to 375°F. Cut rolls into ¼-inch-thick slices. Place slices 1 inch apart on ungreased cookie sheet. Bake for 7 to 9 minutes or until edges are firm and bottoms are light brown. Transfer cookies to a wire rack; let cool.

Per cookie: 58 cal., 3 g total fat (2 g sat. fat), 10 mg chol., 32 mg sodium, 7 g carbo., 0 g fiber, 1 g pro.

Almond-Cinnamon Cookies

Browned butter frosting is one of the all-time best ways to top a cookie, and when the cookie in question is a buttery, almondy delight, it's bound to be a hit.

Prep: 30 minutes **Bake:** 13 minutes per batch
Oven: 375°F **Makes:** about 42 cookies

- ¾ **cup butter, softened**
- 1½ **cups sugar**
- ½ **teaspoon baking soda**
- ½ **teaspoon cream of tartar**
- ½ **teaspoon ground cinnamon**
- 1 **egg**
- 1 **teaspoon vanilla**
- ½ **cup blanched almonds, ground**
- 2 **cups all-purpose flour**
- 1 **recipe Browned Butter Drizzle (see page 99)**

1. In a large mixing bowl beat butter with an electric mixer on medium to high speed for 30 seconds. Add the sugar, baking soda, cream of tartar, and cinnamon. Beat until combined, scraping side of bowl occasionally. Beat in egg and vanilla until combined. Beat in ground almonds. Beat in as much of the flour as you can with the mixer. Using a wooden spoon, stir in any remaining flour.

2. Preheat oven to 375°F. With hands, shape dough into 1-inch balls, or scoop dough with a 1-inch cookie scoop. Place balls 2 inches apart on ungreased cookie sheets. Bake about 13 minutes or until cookies are light brown. Transfer to a wire rack; let cool.

3. Drizzle cookies with Browned Butter Drizzle.

Orange-Chocolate Rounds

Peanut Butter Munchies

Browned Butter Drizzle: In a saucepan heat 2 tablespoons butter over medium heat until butter turns the color of light brown sugar, stirring frequently. Remove from heat. Slowly stir in 1½ cups powdered sugar, 1 teaspoon vanilla, and enough milk (about 2 tablespoons) to make drizzling consistency.

Per cookie: 109 cal., 5 g total fat (3 g sat. fat), 15 mg chol., 44 mg sodium, 16 g carbo., 0 g fiber, 1 g pro.

Peanut Butter Munchies

When making cookies for a Christmas gift-giving list, be sure to include this peanut butter-filled gem!

Prep: 35 minutes **Bake:** 8 minutes per batch
Cool: 1 minute per batch **Oven:** 350°F
Makes: 32 cookies

- 1½ cups all-purpose flour
- ½ cup unsweetened cocoa powder
- ½ teaspoon baking soda
- ½ cup butter, softened
- ½ cup granulated sugar
- ½ cup packed brown sugar
- ¼ cup peanut butter
- 1 egg
- 1 tablespoon milk
- 1 teaspoon vanilla
- ¾ cup powdered sugar
- ½ cup peanut butter
- 2 tablespoons granulated sugar

1. In a medium bowl stir together flour, cocoa powder, and baking soda; set aside.

2. In a large mixing bowl combine butter, the ½ cup granulated sugar, the brown sugar, and the ¼ cup peanut butter; beat with an electric mixer until combined. Add egg, milk, and vanilla; beat well. Beat in as much of the flour mixture as you can with mixer. Using a wooden spoon, stir in any remaining flour mixture. Shape dough into 32 balls, each about 1¼ inches in diameter. Set aside.

3. For peanut butter filling, in a medium bowl combine powdered sugar and the ½ cup peanut butter; beat until smooth, kneading by hand if necessary. Shape mixture into 32 balls.

4. Preheat oven to 350°F. On a work surface, slightly flatten a chocolate dough ball and top with a peanut butter filling ball. Shape the chocolate dough over the peanut butter filling, completely covering the filling. Roll dough into a ball. Repeat with the remaining chocolate dough and peanut butter filling balls.

5. Place balls 2 inches apart on ungreased cookie sheet. Lightly flatten with bottom of a glass dipped in the 2 tablespoons granulated sugar.

6. Bake about 8 minutes or just until set and surface is slightly cracked. Cool on cookie sheet 1 minute. Transfer cookies to wire racks; cool completely.

Per cookie: 127 cal., 5 g total fat (3 g sat. fat), 14 mg chol., 72 mg sodium, 15 g carbo., 1 g fiber, 3 g pro.

White Chocolate Kisses and Peanut Butter Blossoms

 Peanut Butter Blossoms

These days, they're known as Peanut Butter Blossoms, but your grandmother probably called them Black-Eyed Susans, thanks to their resemblance to daisies.

Prep: 30 minutes **Bake:** 10 minutes per batch
Oven: 350°F **Makes:** about 54 cookies

  ½ cup shortening
  ½ cup peanut butter
  ½ cup granulated sugar
  ½ cup packed brown sugar
  1 teaspoon baking powder
  ⅛ teaspoon baking soda
  1 egg
  2 tablespoons milk
  1 teaspoon vanilla
  1¾ cups all-purpose flour
  ¼ cup granulated sugar
     Milk chocolate kisses or stars

1. In a large mixing bowl combine shortening and peanut butter; beat with an electric mixer on medium to high speed for 30 seconds. Add the ½ cup granulated sugar, the brown sugar, baking powder, and baking soda. Beat until combined, scraping sides of bowl occasionally. Beat in egg, milk, and

vanilla until combined. Beat in as much of the flour as you can with the mixer. Using a wooden spoon, stir in any remaining flour.

2. Preheat oven to 350°F. Shape dough into 1-inch balls. Roll balls in the ¼ cup granulated sugar. Place balls 2 inches apart on an ungreased cookie sheet.

3. Bake for 10 to 12 minutes or until edges are firm and bottoms are lightly browned. Immediately press a chocolate kiss into the center of each cookie. Transfer cookies to a wire rack; let cool.

Per cookie: 83 cal., 4 g total fat (2 g sat. fat), 4 mg chol., 27 mg sodium, 10 g carbo., 0 g fiber, 1 g pro.

 White Chocolate Kisses

Modeled after the enduring Peanut Butter Blossom, this attractive version specifies some of the newfangled versions of kisses now available at the supermarket.

Prep: 45 minutes **Chill:** 2 hours
Bake: 7 minutes per batch
Cool: 1 minute per batch
Oven: 375°F **Makes:** about 50 cookies

  1½ ounces white chocolate baking
      squares (with cocoa butter), melted
      and cooled slightly
  ¼ cup butter, softened
  ¼ cup shortening
  ½ cup sugar
  ⅛ teaspoon baking soda
  ⅛ teaspoon salt
  1 egg yolk
  1 tablespoon milk
  ½ teaspoon vanilla
  1½ cups all-purpose flour
  50 assorted candy kisses, unwrapped
      (such as white chocolate striped, milk
      chocolate, and/or dark chocolate)

1. In a heavy small saucepan melt white chocolate over low heat, stirring frequently. Let cool slightly.

2. In a large mixing bowl combine butter and shortening; beat with an electric mixer on medium to high speed for 30 seconds. Add sugar, baking soda, and salt. Beat until well mixed, scraping sides of bowl occasionally. Beat in the white chocolate, egg yolk, milk, and vanilla. Beat in as much of the flour as you can with the mixer. Using a wooden spoon, stir in any remaining flour. Cover and chill dough about 2 hours or until easy to handle.

3. Preheat oven to 375°F. Shape dough into 1-inch balls. Place balls 1 inch apart on ungreased cookie sheet. Bake for 7 to 9 minutes or just until tops are set. Cool cookies on cookie sheet on a wire rack for 1 minute. Gently press a candy kiss into the center of each cookie. Transfer cookies to a wire rack; let cool (candies will soften after placing on cookies but will firm while cooling).

Per cookie: 72 cal., 4 g total fat (2 g sat. fat), 8 mg chol., 22 mg sodium, 8 g carbo., 0 g fiber, 1 g pro.

Chocolate-Mint Creams

Chocolate and mint are a favorite candy duo—a perfect combo in this 1985 cookie. Look for the mints in the cake decorating department of hobby stores.

Prep: 25 minutes **Stand:** 10 minutes
Chill: 1 hour **Bake:** 10 minutes
Oven: 350°F **Makes:** about 48 cookies

1¼ cups all-purpose flour
½ teaspoon baking soda
⅔ cup packed brown sugar
6 tablespoons butter
1 tablespoon water
1 6-ounce package semisweet chocolate pieces (1 cup)
1 egg
8 to 12 ounces pastel-color cream mint kisses

1. In a medium bowl stir together flour and baking soda; set aside. In a medium saucepan combine brown sugar, butter, and the water; cook and stir over low heat until butter melts. Add chocolate pieces; cook and stir until melted. Pour chocolate mixture into a large bowl; let stand at room temperature for 10 to 15 minutes or until cool.

2. Using a wooden spoon, beat egg into the chocolate mixture. Stir in the flour mixture until well mixed. (Dough will be soft.) Cover and chill for 1 to 2 hours or until dough is easy to handle.

3. Preheat oven to 350°F. Shape dough into 1-inch balls. Place balls 2 inches apart on an ungreased cookie sheet. Bake for 8 minutes. Remove from oven and immediately top each cookie with a mint kiss. Bake about 2 minutes more or until edges are set. Swirl the melted mints with a knife to "frost" cookies. Transfer cookies to wire racks and let cool until mints are firm.

Per cookie: 76 cal., 4 g total fat (2 g sat. fat), 8 mg chol., 34 mg sodium, 10 g carbo., 0 g fiber, 1 g pro.

Chocolate-Mint Creams

Cherry-Nut Rum Balls

Covered with a luscious white coating and drizzled with chocolate, these little bites look just like truffles. (See photo, front cover and page 108.)

Prep: 1 hour **Stand:** 2 hours **Chill:** 15 minutes
Makes: about 45 rum balls

- ¾ cup chopped dried tart cherries
- ¼ cup dark rum
- 2 cups finely crushed vanilla wafers (about 54)
- ¾ cup ground pecans, almonds, or walnuts
- ¼ cup powdered sugar
- ¼ cup butter, melted
- 2 tablespoons frozen orange juice concentrate, thawed
- 1⅔ cups white baking pieces
- 2 tablespoons shortening
- 1 cup semisweet chocolate pieces
- 2 teaspoons shortening

1. In a small bowl combine cherries and rum; cover and let stand for 1 hour. Line two cookie sheets with waxed paper; set aside.

2. In a large bowl combine crushed wafers, ground pecans, and powdered sugar. Add undrained cherry mixture, melted butter, and orange juice concentrate; stir until combined. Shape mixture into 1-inch balls. Place balls on prepared cookie sheets; let stand about 1 hour or until dry.

3. In a small heavy saucepan combine baking pieces and the 2 tablespoons shortening; cook and stir over medium-low heat until melted. Remove from heat. Dip rum balls in the mixture, turning each ball to coat completely. Remove each ball with a fork and return to baking sheets. Drizzle with any remaining melted mixture. Chill about 15 minutes or until coating is set.

4. Meanwhile, in another small heavy saucepan combine semisweet chocolate pieces and the 2 teaspoons shortening; cook and stir over low heat until melted, stirring constantly until smooth. Place chocolate mixture in a small resealable plastic bag. Seal bag. Snip off a small corner of the bag. Drizzle chocolate over rum balls. Let stand until set.

Holiday-Color Drizzle: For red- and green-colored drizzle, melt red- and green-colored candy coating. Continue as directed in step 4. (Find colored candy coating at cake decorating and hobby stores.)

Per rum ball: 140 cal., 8 g total fat (4 g sat. fat), 3 mg chol., 42 mg sodium, 18 g carbo., 1 g fiber, 1 g pro.

Key Lime Snowballs

Sometimes you want something with a little citrus flavor on the Christmas cookie tray to help balance all the sweetness from the other treats. This recent recipe will do the trick!

Prep: 45 minutes **Bake:** 20 minutes per batch
Cool: 1 minute per batch **Oven:** 325°F
Makes: about 36 cookies

- ⅓ cup granulated sugar
- 1 teaspoon finely shredded Key lime or regular lime peel
-    Green and yellow gel or paste food colorings (optional)
- ¾ cup butter, softened
- 1 3-ounce package cream cheese, softened
- ¾ cup powdered sugar
- 1 tablespoon Key lime or regular lime juice
- 2½ cups all-purpose flour
- ¾ cup finely chopped macadamia nuts
- 1 tablespoon finely shredded Key lime or regular lime peel

1. In a food processor or blender combine the granulated sugar, the 1 teaspoon lime peel, and if desired, a small dot of green and a small dot of yellow food coloring. Cover and process or blend until well mixed. Place in a small bowl; set aside.

2. Preheat oven to 325°F. In a large mixing bowl combine butter and cream cheese; beat with an electric mixer on medium to high speed for 30 seconds. Add powdered sugar. Beat until combined, scraping sides of bowl occasionally. Beat in lime juice until combined. Beat in as much of the flour as you can with mixer. Using a wooden spoon, stir in any remaining flour, the macadamia nuts, and the 1 tablespoon lime peel.

3. Shape dough into 1¼-inch balls. Place balls 1 inch apart on an ungreased cookie sheet. Bake for 20 to 25 minutes or until bottoms are golden (do not underbake). Cool cookies on cookie sheet on a wire rack for 1 minute.

4. Roll warm cookies in the granulated sugar mixture until coated. Place on a wire rack to cool.

Per cookie: 108 cal., 7 g total fat (3 g sat. fat), 13 mg chol., 42 mg sodium, 11 g carbo., 1 g fiber, 0 g pro.

French Pistachio Buttercreams

This recent addition to the list of all-time favorites is buttery and elegant. Bon appétit!

Prep: 35 minutes **Bake:** 8 minutes per batch
Chill: 1 hour 40 minutes **Oven:** 350°F
Makes: 30 sandwich cookies

French Pistachio Buttercreams

- 1½ **cups all-purpose flour**
- ½ **teaspoon salt**
- ¾ **cup unsalted butter, softened**
- ½ **cup powdered sugar**
- 1 **egg**
  Granulated sugar
- ¼ **cup unsalted butter, softened**
- ½ **cup powdered sugar**
- 1 **teaspoon rum, cognac, or milk**
- 6 **ounces semisweet chocolate pieces or white baking pieces, melted**
- ½ **cup shelled pistachio nuts, chopped**

1. In a small bowl combine flour and salt; set aside. In a medium mixing bowl combine the ¾ cup butter and ½ cup powdered sugar; beat with an electric mixer on medium to high speed until combined. Add the egg and beat until combined. Add flour mixture; beat on low speed just until combined. Cover and chill about 1 hour or until easy to handle.

2. Preheat oven to 350°F. Shape dough into sixty balls (each about ¾ inch in diameter). Place balls about 2 inches apart on an ungreased cookie sheet. Dip the bottom of a glass in granulated sugar and use to flatten each ball to a 1½-inch circle (about ⅛ inch thick). Bake about 8 minutes or until cookie bottoms are light brown. Transfer cookies to wire racks; let cool.

3. Meanwhile, for the filling, in a small mixing bowl combine the ¼ cup butter, ½ cup powdered sugar, and rum; beat with an electric mixer on medium to high speed until combined.

4. To assemble cookies, spread rum filling on the flat sides of half of the cookies. Top each cookie with filling with another cookie, flat side down, to make a sandwich cookie. Chill about 30 minutes or until filling is set. Spread sandwich cookies with melted chocolate and sprinkle with nuts. Chill about 10 minutes or until chocolate is set.

Per cookie: 134 cal., 9 g total fat (5 g sat. fat), 24 mg chol., 42 mg sodium, 13 g carbo., 1 g fiber, 2 g pro.

Pink Peppermint Twists

For some people it isn't Christmas without peppermint candy. If you are in that camp, call on this pretty cookie to indulge your peppermint craving!

Prep: 45 minutes **Bake:** 8 minutes per batch
Oven: 350°F **Makes:** 56 cookies

- 1½   **cups butter, softened**
- 2½   **cups powdered sugar**
- ¼   **teaspoon salt**
- 1   **egg**
- 1   **teaspoon vanilla**
- ¾   **teaspoon peppermint extract**
  Few drops red food coloring
- 3   **cups all-purpose flour**
- 3   **ounces white chocolate, melted and slightly cooled**
  Crushed peppermint candy canes*

1. In a large mixing bowl beat butter with an electric mixer on medium to high speed for 30 seconds. Add powdered sugar and salt; beat until combined, scraping sides of bowl occasionally. Beat in egg, vanilla, and peppermint extract. Beat in enough red food coloring to tint dough pink. Beat in as much of the flour as you can with the mixer. Using a wooden spoon, stir in any remaining flour.

2. Preheat oven to 350°F. Shape dough into 1-inch balls. On a lightly floured surface, roll each ball into a 6-inch-long rope. Gently fold rope in half and twist once or twice. Place twists 1 inch apart on ungreased cookie sheets.

The Right White Chocolate

Cooks can sometimes find baking with white chocolate a little tricky because different products react differently when baked. The trick is in choosing the right "white" product. Some products contain cocoa butter, while others do not. Only products having cocoa butter can truly be labeled "white chocolate." Read the recipe to know what product to buy. If the recipe specifies white chocolate, check the label ingredient listing for the words "cocoa butter."

3. Bake for 8 to 10 minutes or until light brown on bottom. Transfer to wire rack; let cool. When cool, spread or drizzle with melted white chocolate. Sprinkle with crushed candy canes.

***Note:** To crush candy canes, place in a heavy plastic bag and tap with the flat side of a meat mallet until crushed into ⅛- to ¼-inch pieces. Shake crushed candy in a fine wire sifter to remove candy dust.

Per cookie: 96 cal., 6 g total fat (4 g sat. fat), 17 mg chol., 49 mg sodium, 11 g carbo., 0 g fiber, 1 g pro.

Brownie Meringues

Crisp and delicate on the outside with melt-in-your mouth centers, these chocolate meringue cookies are a delightful melding of textures.

Prep: 20 minutes **Stand:** 30 minutes
Bake: 10 minutes per batch **Oven:** 350°F
Makes: about 24 cookies

- 2   **egg whites**
- ½   **teaspoon vinegar**
- ½   **teaspoon vanilla**
  Dash salt
- ½   **cup sugar**
- 1   **cup semisweet chocolate pieces, melted and cooled**
- ¾   **cup chopped walnuts**
- ½   **cup semisweet chocolate pieces**
- 1   **teaspoon shortening**

1. In a large mixing bowl let egg whites stand at room temperature for 30 minutes. Meanwhile, lightly grease a cookie sheet; set aside.

2. Preheat oven to 350°F. Add vinegar, vanilla, and salt to egg whites. Beat with an electric mixer on medium speed until soft peaks form (tips curl). Gradually add the sugar, 1 tablespoon at a time, beating on high speed about 4 minutes or until stiff peaks form (tips stand straight) and the sugar is almost dissolved. Fold in the melted chocolate and the walnuts.

3. Drop mixture by teaspoons 2 inches apart onto prepared cookie sheets. Bake for 10 to 12 minutes or until edges are firm. (Cookies puff and sides split during baking.) Transfer cookies to a wire rack; let cool.

4. In a small heavy saucepan combine the ½ cup chocolate pieces and the shortening; heat and stir until melted. Drizzle chocolate mixture over cookies; let stand until set.

Per cookie: 95 cal., 5 g total fat (2 g sat. fat), 0 mg chol., 11 mg sodium, 8 g carbo., 2 g fiber, 1 g pro.

Hickory Nut Macaroons

Forgotten for decades, this recipe made a recent comeback when a Better Homes and Gardens® *magazine food editor was leafing through a 1925 issue of the magazine. He asked the Test Kitchen to retest the recipe and was struck by the cookie's elegance. (See photo, page 108.)*

Prep: 25 minutes Bake: 15 minutes per batch
Oven: 325°F Makes: about 36 cookies

- 4 egg whites
- 4 cups powdered sugar
- 2 cups chopped hickory nuts, black walnuts, or toasted pecans

1. Preheat oven to 325°F. Line cookie sheet with foil; grease foil. Set aside.

2. In a large mixing bowl beat egg whites with an electric mixer on high speed until soft peaks form (tips curl). Gradually add powdered sugar, about ¼ cup at a time, beating on medium speed just until well mixed. Beat on high speed until stiff peaks form (tips stand straight). Using a wooden spoon, fold in nuts. Drop mixture by rounded teaspoons 2 inches apart on prepared sheet.

3. Bake about 15 minutes or until very light brown (cookies will puff and sides will split during baking). Transfer to wire racks; let cool.

Per cookie: 86 cal., 4 g total fat (0 g sat. fat), 0 mg chol., 6 mg sodium, 12 g carbo., 1 g fiber, 1 g pro.

Golden Macaroons

This is the best macaroon recipe ever! These heavenly bites have everything you want in the classic cookie—a crispy outside, a moist chewy center, and plenty of coconut flavor!

Prep: 20 minutes Chill: 30 minutes
Bake: 17 minutes per batch
Oven: 300°F Makes: about 40 cookies

- 2½ cups sweetened flaked coconut (about 7 ounces)
- 2 cups unsweetened finely shredded coconut*
- 1 cup sugar
- 3 tablespoons all-purpose flour
- ¼ teaspoon salt
- 4 egg whites
- 1 tablespoon honey
- 1 teaspoon vanilla

1. In a large bowl combine flaked and shredded coconut until evenly mixed. (Flaked coconut should be broken into separate flakes with only a few very small clumps.)

2. In a medium bowl combine sugar, flour, and salt. Add egg whites, honey, and vanilla. Whisk until smooth. Pour sugar mixture over coconut mixture. Stir with a wooden spoon, then use your hands to blend until evenly mixed. Cover with plastic wrap; chill for 30 minutes.

3. Preheat oven to 300°F. Line a large cookie sheet with foil. Drop batter by rounded tablespoons 2 inches apart onto prepared cookie sheet. Bake for 17 to 19 minutes or until golden. Immediately transfer cookies to a wire rack and let cool.

*****Note:** Look for unsweetened finely shredded coconut in health food stores or in the bulk-food section of your supermarket.

Per cookie: 73 cal., 4 g total fat (3 g sat. fat), 0 mg chol., 41 mg sodium, 9 g carbo., 1 g fiber, 1 g pro.

Chocolate-Peanut Blowouts

Stir honey-roasted peanuts, chocolate pieces, and chopped peanut butter cups into the dough for a sensational snack that tastes great with cold milk.

Prep: 25 minutes **Bake:** 10 minutes per batch
Oven: 350°F **Makes:** about 30 cookies

- ½ cup butter, softened
- ½ cup peanut butter
- ½ cup packed brown sugar
- ¼ cup granulated sugar
- 1 teaspoon baking soda
- ¼ teaspoon salt
- 1 egg
- ¼ cup milk
- 1 teaspoon vanilla
- 2 cups all-purpose flour
- ¾ cup semisweet chocolate pieces
- ¾ cup honey-roasted peanuts
- ¾ cup coarsely chopped bite-size chocolate-covered peanut butter cups (about 15)*

1. Preheat oven to 350°F. In a large mixing bowl combine butter and peanut butter; beat with an electric mixer on medium speed for 30 seconds. Add brown sugar, granulated sugar, baking soda, and salt. Beat until combined, scraping sides of bowl occasionally.

2. Beat in egg, milk, and vanilla until combined. Beat in as much of the flour as you can with the mixer. Using a wooden spoon, stir in any remaining flour. Stir in chocolate pieces, peanuts, and chopped peanut butter cups.

3. Drop dough by generously rounded teaspoons 2 inches apart onto an ungreased cookie sheet. Bake about 10 minutes or until light brown. Transfer cookies to a wire rack; let cool.

***Note:** For easier chopping, freeze the bite-size chocolate-covered peanut butter cups in their wrappers for 1 hour. Remove wrappers before chopping the candies.

Per cookie: 159 cal., 9 g total fat (4 g sat. fat), 15 mg chol., 131 mg sodium, 18 g carbo., 1 g fiber, 3 g pro.

Then Cherry Winks

Cookies that have tiny dents filled with jellies and jams are called by many names—Thumbprints, Thimble Cookies, and Wee Tom Thumbs. In this playfully named 1945 recipe from the prizewinning archives, candied cherries stand in for the jelly.

Prep: 30 minutes **Bake:** 7 minutes per batch
Oven: 400°F **Makes:** 36 cookies

- ½ cup sugar
- ⅓ cup shortening
- ½ teaspoon baking powder
- ¼ teaspoon salt
- 1 egg
- 1 tablespoon milk
- 1 teaspoon vanilla
- 1 cup all-purpose flour
- ½ cup chopped raisins
- ½ cup chopped walnuts
- 1 teaspoon finely shredded lemon peel
- 2 cups wheat flakes cereal, crushed
- 18 candied cherries, halved

1. Preheat oven to 400°F. In a large mixing bowl combine sugar, shortening, baking powder, and salt; beat with an electric mixer on medium to high speed for 30 seconds. Beat in the egg, milk, and vanilla until combined. Beat in as much of the flour as you can with the mixer. Stir in any remaining flour. Stir in raisins, walnuts, and lemon peel.

2. Drop a teaspoonful of dough into crushed cereal; toss lightly to coat dough with flakes. Repeat with remaining dough. Place cookies 2 inches apart on an ungreased cookie sheet. Top each cookie with a candied cherry half. Bake for 7 to 8 minutes or until bottoms are light brown. Transfer cookies to wire racks; let cool.

Per cookie: 77 cal., 3 g total fat (1 g sat. fat), 6 mg chol., 34 mg sodium, 12 g carbo., 0 g fiber, 1 g pro.

Now Chocolate Truffle Winks

These sinfully rich cookies are similar in style to the Cherry Winks—but all grown-up with sophisticated chocolate-truffle centers.

Prep: 45 minutes **Bake:** 9 minutes per batch
Oven: 350°F **Makes:** about 48 cookies

- ½ cup chopped dried tart cherries
- 2 tablespoons Kirsch
- ½ cup butter, softened
- ½ cup granulated sugar
- ¼ cup packed brown sugar
- 1 teaspoon baking soda
- 2 ounces unsweetened chocolate, melted and cooled slightly
- 1 egg
- 1 teaspoon vanilla
- 1¼ cups all-purpose flour
- 4 ounces semisweet chocolate
- 1 tablespoon butter
- 1 tablespoon light-colored corn syrup
- 1 tablespoon milk

1. Preheat oven to 350°F. Lightly grease cookie sheets; set aside. In a small microwave-safe bowl combine cherries and Kirsch. Microwave on 100% power (high) for 20 to 30 seconds or until warm. Stir; let stand while preparing dough.

2. In a large mixing bowl beat the ½ cup butter with an electric mixer on medium to high speed for 30 seconds. Add granulated sugar, brown sugar, and baking soda. Beat until combined, scraping sides of bowl occasionally. Beat in the melted unsweetened chocolate, the egg, and vanilla until combined. Beat in as much of the flour as you can with the mixer. Using a wooden spoon, stir in any remaining flour and the undrained cherry mixture.

3. Drop dough by rounded teaspoons about 2 inches apart onto prepared cookie sheets. Bake for 9 to 11 minutes or until edges are firm and centers are just set. Remove from oven. With the back of a small metal measuring teaspoon, make an indentation in the center of each warm cookie. Transfer cookies to a wire rack; let cool.

4. For truffle filling, in a small heavy saucepan combine the semisweet chocolate and the 1 tablespoon butter. Heat over low heat until melted, stirring frequently. Remove pan from heat; stir in corn syrup and milk until smooth. Spoon about ½ teaspoon of the truffle filling into the center of each baked cookie.

Per cookie: 69 cal., 4 g total fat (2 g sat. fat), 10 mg chol., 45 mg sodium, 9 g carbo., 1 g fiber, 1 g pro.

Chocolate Truffle Winks and Cherry Winks

The Drop Method

Drop cookies are favored for their ease and homespun appeal. Here are some tips for the best drop cookies ever:

- If a recipe calls for greased baking sheets, use only a very light coating or your cookies may spread too much during baking.
- If your electric mixer begins to strain while mixing dough, stir in the last bit of flour with a wooden spoon.
- Drop the dough using spoons from your flatware, not measuring spoons, to get the right number of cookies from each batch.
- Let baking sheets cool between batches to prevent the dough from spreading too much.
- Bake on only one oven rack at a time for even browning.
- Generally, drop cookies are done when the dough looks set and the edges and bottoms are light brown.

Cherry-Nut Rum Balls, page 102, Coffeehouse Crisps, page 109, and Hickory Nut Macaroons, page 105

Then Pecan Crispies

Sometimes simplicity wins! Just a handful of ingredients—many of which you probably have on hand if you enjoy baking—transforms into a buttery, nutty cookie that's been a favorite since the 1950s.

Prep: 20 minutes **Bake:** 12 minutes per batch
Oven: 350°F **Makes:** about 60 cookies

- ½ cup shortening
- ½ cup butter
- 2½ cups packed brown sugar
- ½ teaspoon baking soda
- ¼ teaspoon salt
- 2 eggs
- 2½ cups all-purpose flour
- 1 cup chopped pecans

1. Preheat oven to 350°F. Grease a large cookie sheet; set aside.

2. In a large mixing bowl combine shortening and butter; beat with an electric mixer on medium to high speed for 30 seconds. Add brown sugar, baking soda, and salt; beat until combined, scraping sides of bowl occasionally. Beat in eggs until combined. Beat in as much of the flour as you can with the mixer. Stir in any remaining flour. Stir in pecans.

3. Drop dough by rounded teaspoons about 2 inches apart onto prepared cookie sheet. Bake about 12 minutes or until light brown and edges are set.*

***Note:** For cookies with chewier centers and crisp edges, bake for 10 minutes.

Per cookie: 96 cal., 5 g total fat (2 g sat. fat), 11 mg chol., 37 mg sodium, 13 g carbo., 0 g fiber, 1 g pro.

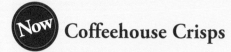

Coffeehouse Crisps

To update the famous Pecan Crispies recipe, cookie expert Jennifer Peterson sprinkled in hazelnuts, peanut brittle candy, and a few extra spices. "They're terrific with coffee or tea," she says.

Prep: 30 minutes **Cook:** 12 minutes per batch
Oven: 350°F **Makes:** about 48 cookies

- ½ cup butter, softened
- ½ cup shortening
- 2½ cups packed dark brown sugar
- ½ teaspoon baking soda
- ½ teaspoon ground cardamom
- ¼ teaspoon salt
- ¼ teaspoon ground nutmeg
- 2 eggs
- 2½ cups all-purpose flour
- 1 cup chopped hazelnuts, toasted
- ½ cup crushed peanut brittle or toffee bits

1. Preheat oven to 350°F. Grease a large cookie sheet; set aside. In a large mixing bowl combine butter and shortening; beat with an electric mixer on medium to high speed for 30 seconds. Add brown sugar, baking soda, cardamom, salt, and nutmeg; beat until mixture is combined, scraping sides of bowl occasionally. Beat in eggs until combined. Beat in as much of the flour as you can with the mixer. Using a wooden spoon, stir in any remaining flour. Stir in hazelnuts and peanut brittle.

2. Drop dough by rounded teaspoons about 2 inches apart onto prepared cookie sheets. Bake about 12 minutes or until light brown and edges are set. Immediately transfer to a wire rack; let cool.

Per cookie: 130 cal., 6 g total fat (2 g sat. fat), 14 mg chol., 54 mg sodium, 17 g carbo., 0 g fiber, 1 g pro.

Spiced Apple Drops

Apples and spice and everything nice—that's what makes these cookies special. The apple frosting gives them an extra dose of irresistible flavor.

Prep: 30 minutes **Bake:** 10 minutes per batch
Oven: 375°F **Makes:** about 40 cookies

- ½ cup butter, softened
- ⅔ cup granulated sugar
- ⅔ cup packed brown sugar
- 1 teaspoon ground cinnamon
- ½ teaspoon baking soda
- ½ teaspoon ground nutmeg
- ⅛ teaspoon ground cloves
- 1 egg
- ¼ cup apple juice or apple cider
- 2 cups all-purpose flour
- 1 cup finely chopped, peeled apple
- 1 cup chopped walnuts
- 1 recipe Apple Frosting

1. Preheat oven to 375°F. Grease a large cookie sheet; set aside.

2. In a large mixing bowl beat butter with an electric mixer on medium speed for 30 seconds. Add granulated sugar, brown sugar, cinnamon, baking soda, nutmeg, and cloves. Beat until combined, scraping sides of bowl occasionally. Beat in egg and apple juice until combined. Beat in as much of the flour as you can with the mixer. Using a wooden spoon, stir in any remaining flour, the chopped apple, and walnuts.

3. Drop dough by rounded teaspoons 2 inches apart onto prepared cookie sheet. Bake for 10 to 12 minutes or until edges are lightly browned. Cool on cookie sheet for 1 minute. Transfer cookies to a wire rack; let cool. Frost with Apple Frosting; let frosting dry.

Apple Frosting: In a large mixing bowl beat 4 cups sifted powdered sugar, ¼ cup softened butter, 1 teaspoon vanilla, and enough apple juice (3 to 4 tablespoons) with an electric mixer to make a smooth, spreadable frosting.

Per cookie: 138 cal., 5 g total fat (2 g sat. fat), 15 mg chol., 54 mg sodium, 22 g carbo., 0 g fiber, 1 g pro.

Raspberry-Almond Tassies

The almond filling in these tarts may remind you of the classic Dutch Letter pastry. The filling covers a touch of raspberry jam, creating a gem of a cookie.

Prep: 35 minutes **Chill:** 1 hour **Bake:** 23 minutes
Oven: 400°F **Makes:** 18 tassies

- 1 cup all-purpose flour
- ¼ teaspoon salt
- 6 tablespoons butter
- 3 to 4 tablespoons cold water
- 4½ teaspoons seedless raspberry jam
- ½ cup sugar
- 3 tablespoons butter, softened
- ⅔ cup ground almonds
- ¼ teaspoon almond extract
- 1 egg, slightly beaten
  Powdered sugar (optional)

1. In a medium bowl stir together flour and salt. Using a pastry blender, cut in the 6 tablespoons butter until mixture resembles coarse crumbs. Add the water, 1 tablespoon at a time, gently tossing mixture with a fork until all of the flour mixture is moistened. Form dough into a ball. Wrap in waxed paper. Chill for 1 hour.

2. On a floured surface, roll dough to ⅛-inch thickness. Using a 2¾-inch round cookie cutter, cut 18 circles. Fit the circles into 1¾-inch muffin cups. Place ¼ teaspoon of the jam in each pastry shell. (Do not add more or the jam will burn.)

3. Preheat oven to 450°F. In a small mixing bowl combine sugar and the 3 tablespoons butter; beat with an electric mixer on low speed until creamy. Stir in almonds, almond extract, and egg. Spoon 1 tablespoon of the almond mixture over jam in each pastry shell.

4. Bake for 23 to 25 minutes or until golden brown. Carefully remove from muffin cups. Cool on a wire rack. If desired, sift powdered sugar over tops.

Per tassie: 133 cal., 9 g total fat (4 g sat. fat), 27 mg chol., 78 mg sodium, 12 g carbo., 1 g fiber, 2 g pro.

Trilevel Brownies

This brownie recipe from 1963 boasts three sweet layers for one solid-gold treat.

Prep: 15 minutes **Bake:** 35 minutes
Oven: 350°F **Makes:** 24 brownies

- 1 cup quick-cooking rolled oats
- ½ cup all-purpose flour
- ½ cup packed brown sugar
- ¼ teaspoon baking soda
- ½ cup butter, melted
- 1 egg
- ¾ cup granulated sugar
- ⅔ cup all-purpose flour
- ¼ cup milk
- ¼ cup butter, melted
- 1 ounce unsweetened chocolate, melted
  and cooled
- 1 teaspoon vanilla
- ¼ teaspoon baking powder
- ½ cup chopped walnuts
- 1 ounce unsweetened chocolate
- 2 tablespoons butter
- 1½ cups powdered sugar
- ½ teaspoon vanilla

1. Preheat oven to 350°F. For the bottom layer, in a medium bowl stir together oats, the ½ cup flour, the brown sugar, and baking soda. Stir in the ½ cup melted butter. Pat mixture into the bottom of an ungreased 11×7×1½-inch baking pan. Bake for 10 minutes.

2. Meanwhile, for the middle layer, stir together the egg, granulated sugar, the ⅔ cup flour, the milk, the ¼ cup melted butter, the 1 ounce melted chocolate, the 1 teaspoon vanilla, and the baking powder until smooth. Fold in nuts. Spread batter evenly over baked layer in pan. Bake for 25 minutes more. Place on a wire rack while preparing top layer.

3. For the top layer, in a saucepan combine the 1 ounce chocolate and the 2 tablespoons butter; heat and stir over low heat until melted. Stir in the powdered sugar and the ½ teaspoon vanilla. Stir in enough *hot water* (1 to 2 tablespoons) to make a mixture that is almost pourable. Spread over brownies. Cool in pan on wire rack.

Per brownie: 195 cal., 10 g total fat (5 g sat. fat), 27 mg chol., 70 mg sodium, 26 g carbo., 1 g fiber, 2 g pro.

Triple-Chocolate Coffee Brownies

This brownie recipe is a favorite because it starts with a mix and combines three kinds of luscious chocolate.

Prep: 15 minutes **Bake:** 30 minutes
Oven: 350°F **Makes:** 36 brownies

- ¼ cup water
- 2 teaspoons instant espresso coffee powder or 1 tablespoon instant coffee crystals
- 1 egg, beaten
- 1 19- to 21½-ounce package fudge brownie mix
- ¼ cup cooking oil
- ¼ cup coffee liqueur or water
- ¾ cup milk chocolate pieces
- ¾ cup white baking pieces
- ½ cup semisweet chocolate pieces
- ½ cup chopped walnuts or pecans

1. Preheat oven to 350°F. Grease a 13×9×2-inch baking pan; set aside.

2. In a large bowl combine the water and the espresso powder; stir until dissolved. Stir in the egg, brownie mix, oil, liqueur, milk chocolate pieces, white baking pieces, semisweet chocolate pieces, and nuts. Stir just until combined. Spread batter into prepared baking pan. Bake for 30 minutes. Cool in pan on a wire rack.

Per brownie: 125 cal., 6 g total fat (2 g sat. fat), 6 mg chol., 48 mg sodium, 17 g carbo., 1 g fiber, 1 g pro.

Marmalade-Nut Brownies

Around the holidays, orange and chocolate are a star flavor combination. Combined with walnuts and chocolate bits, the combo is even more spectacular.

Prep: 20 minutes **Bake:** 30 minutes
Oven: 350°F **Makes:** 32 or 36 brownies

- 1½ cups sugar
- 1 cup butter, melted
- 3 eggs
- ½ cup orange marmalade
- 1 teaspoon vanilla

Marmalade-Nut Brownies

- 1 cup all-purpose flour
- ¾ cup unsweetened cocoa powder
- 1 teaspoon baking powder
- ¼ teaspoon salt
- ¼ teaspoon cayenne pepper
- 1 cup semisweet or milk chocolate pieces
- ½ cup chopped walnuts, toasted
- ½ teaspoon shortening

1. Preheat oven to 350°F. Line a 13×9×2-inch baking pan with foil, extending it over ends of pan. Grease foil; set aside.

2. In a large bowl stir together sugar and melted butter. Stir in eggs, 1 at a time, beating well after each addition. Stir in marmalade and vanilla. Stir in flour, cocoa powder, baking powder, salt, and cayenne pepper until well mixed. Stir in ½ cup of the chocolate pieces and the nuts.

3. Spread batter evenly into prepared pan. Bake about 30 minutes or until center is set. Transfer to a wire rack; let cool.

4. Use foil edges to remove brownies from pan. Remove foil. Transfer brownies to a large cutting board. Cut baked brownies into 32 or 36 pieces.

5. In a small saucepan combine the remaining ½ cup chocolate pieces and the shortening. Cook and stir over low heat until melted. Cool slightly. Transfer melted chocolate mixture to a resealable plastic bag. Snip off a small corner of bag; drizzle chocolate mixture over the top of the brownies. Chill until chocolate sets.

Per brownie: 162 cal., 9 g total fat (5 g sat. fat), 35 mg chol., 76 mg sodium, 20 g carbo., 1 g fiber, 2 g pro.

Gifts
for the
Season

When it's time to give a gift straight from the heart, go directly to the kitchen. You'll find recipes to help you share holiday joy with friends, neighbors, and coworkers for decades. Who wouldn't love to receive a batch of Buttery Cashew Brittle, Snowy White Truffles, Hazelnut Toffee, or other time-honored gifts? If there are kids on your list, opt for Rainbow Cookies in a Jar or Chocolaty Candy Cane Drops. For the adults, a beautiful bottle of Almond Cream Liqueur or Very Berry Martinis definitely will help spread seasonal cheer.

Very Berry Martinis, page 121

Chocolaty Candy Cane Drops

Two favorite flavors—chocolate and peppermint—star in this easy, no-bake treat. Chocolate sandwich cookies make them extra indulgent!

Prep: 45 minutes **Chill:** 30 minutes
Makes: 40 treats

- 40 small foil or paper candy cups
- 6 ounces chocolate-flavored candy coating, chopped
- 1 cup semisweet chocolate pieces
- 1 tablespoon shortening
- ¾ cup finely crushed candy canes
- 40 tiny chocolate sandwich cookies with white filling

1. Line a baking sheet with candy cups; set aside. In a medium saucepan combine candy coating, chocolate pieces, and shortening; heat and stir over low heat until melted and smooth. Remove from heat. Add ½ cup of the crushed candy canes; stir gently to coat.

2. Drop chocolate mixture from a teaspoon into candy cups. Press a sandwich cookie, one edge down, into each cup. Sprinkle with remaining crushed candy canes. Chill about 30 minutes or until firm.

Chocolaty Candy Cane Drops

To Store: Place candy in paper cups in layers separated by waxed paper in an airtight container; cover. Store in the refrigerator for up to 1 week.

Per treat: 71 cal., 3 g total fat (2 g sat. fat), 0 mg chol., 19 mg sodium, 11 g carbo., 0 g fiber, 1 g pro.

Mocha Fudge

This recipe from 1961 results in a smooth, coffee-flavored, nut-studded candy that's slightly softer than classic chocolate fudge.

Prep: 35 minutes **Cool:** 1 hour **Chill:** overnight
Makes: 2 pounds (36 pieces)

-   Butter
- 3 cups sugar
- 1¼ cups half-and-half, light cream, or milk
- 2 tablespoons instant coffee crystals
- 1 tablespoon light-colored corn syrup
- ¼ teaspoon salt
- 3 tablespoons butter
- 1 teaspoon vanilla
- ½ cup miniature semisweet chocolate pieces
- ½ cup chopped pecans, toasted
-   Pecan halves, toasted (optional)

1. Line an 8×8×2-inch pan with foil, extending foil over edges of pan. Butter the foil; set aside. Butter the sides of a 3-quart heavy saucepan. In the saucepan combine sugar, half-and-half, coffee crystals, corn syrup, and salt. Heat and stir over medium-high heat until sugar dissolves and mixture comes to boiling. Clip a candy thermometer to the pan. Reduce heat to medium; continue boiling at a moderate, steady rate, stirring frequently, until thermometer registers 234°F, soft-ball stage (10 to 15 minutes).

2. Immediately remove saucepan from heat; add the 3 tablespoons butter but do not stir. Cool to lukewarm (110°F) without stirring (60 to 65 minutes). Add vanilla. Beat vigorously until fudge becomes very thick and starts to lose its gloss (about 10 minutes). Immediately stir in chocolate pieces and the chopped pecans. Quickly spread into prepared pan. Score into squares while warm and, if desired, top each square with a pecan half. Cover and chill overnight.

3. Use foil to lift fudge from pan. Peel off foil and cut fudge into squares.

To Store: Store in an airtight container in the refrigerator for up to 1 week.

Per piece: 104 cal., 4 g total fat (2 g sat. fat), 6 mg chol., 27 mg sodium, 19 g carbo., 0 g fiber, 1 g pro.

White Coconut Fudge

Colorful green and red candied cherries create a creamy coconut candy perfectly colored for the holidays. For the nut lovers in your crowd, make another batch with toasted macadamia nuts.

Prep: 20 minutes **Chill:** 4 hours
Makes: 2½ pounds fudge (64 pieces)

   Butter
3 **cups white baking pieces**
1 **14-ounce can sweetened condensed milk**
⅛ **teaspoon salt**
½ **cup chopped green candied cherries**
½ **cup chopped red candied cherries**
¼ **cup flaked coconut**
1½ **teaspoons coconut extract**

1. Line an 8×8×2-inch or 9×9×2-inch baking pan with foil, extending foil over edges of pan. Butter foil; set pan aside.

2. In a medium saucepan combine baking pieces, sweetened condensed milk, and salt. Cook and stir over low heat until baking pieces are melted and smooth. Remove pan from heat; stir in candied cherries, coconut, and coconut extract. Spread fudge evenly in prepared pan. Cover and chill about 4 hours or until firm.

3. When fudge is firm, use foil to lift it from pan. Peel off foil and cut fudge into squares.

Toasted Nutty White Fudge: Prepare as directed, except substitute 1 cup chopped toasted macadamia or other nuts for the cherries. Spread fudge evenly in prepared pan. If desired, top with ¼ cup chopped toasted nuts.

**Toasted Nutty White Fudge
and White Coconut Fudge**

To Store: Store in an airtight container in the refrigerator for up to 1 week.

Per piece: 93 cal., 4 g total fat (3 g sat. fat), 2 mg chol., 32 mg sodium, 13 g carbo., 0 g fiber, 1 g pro.

3. Butter the sides of a 2-quart heavy saucepan. In the saucepan combine powdered sugar, milk, and the ¼ cup butter. Cook and stir over medium-high heat until mixture boils and sugar dissolves. Reduce heat to medium-low. Boil gently, without stirring, for 5 minutes.

4. Reduce heat to low. Add the white chocolate. Stir until white chocolate is melted and mixture is smooth and creamy. Remove from heat; stir in dried fruit, almonds, and, if desired, almond extract. Immediately spread fudge in prepared pan. Cover and chill about 6 hours or until firm.

5. When fudge is firm, use foil to lift it out of pan. Peel off foil; cut fudge into 1-inch squares or triangles.

To Store: Store in an airtight container in the refrigerator for up to 1 week.

Per piece: 67 cal., 3 g total fat (2 g sat. fat), 3 mg chol., 12 mg sodium, 9 g carbo., 0 g fiber, 1 g pro.

White Christmas Cherry-Almond Fudge

Looking for an easier way to make homemade fudge? This recipe doesn't even require a candy thermometer! Packed full of luscious dried cherries and crunchy almonds, this fudge is a festive and simple gift.

Prep: 30 minutes **Chill:** 6 hours **Oven:** 350°F
Makes: about 2 pounds (64 pieces)

- ¾ **cup sliced almonds**
  Butter
- 2½ **cups powdered sugar**
- ⅔ **cup milk**
- ¼ **cup butter**
- 12 **ounces white chocolate baking squares (with cocoa butter), coarsely chopped**
- ¾ **cup snipped dried tart red cherries or dried cranberries**
- ½ **teaspoon almond extract (optional)**

1. Preheat oven to 350°F. Spread almonds in a shallow baking pan. Bake for 5 to 10 minutes or until toasted, stirring occasionally. Remove from oven; let cool.

2. Line an 8×8×2-inch baking pan with foil, extending foil over edges of pan. Butter the foil; set pan aside.

Snowy White Truffles

When you're aiming for elegance, offer a gift of these dreamy gems!

Prep: 1 hour **Chill:** 3 hours 10 minutes
Freeze: 15 minutes **Makes:** about 60 truffles

- 4 **6-ounce packages white chocolate baking squares (with cocoa butter) or white baking bars, chopped**
- ¼ **cup whipping cream**
- ¼ **cup cream of coconut**
- 1 **tablespoon butter**
- 2 **tablespoons white crème de cacao**
- 2 **tablespoons shortening**
- 3½ **cups flaked coconut**

1. For filling, place half of the chopped white chocolate in a food processor. Cover and process until finely chopped. In a small saucepan combine whipping cream, cream of coconut, and butter; heat and stir until hot but not boiling. Remove from heat. With the food processor running, carefully pour hot mixture through the feed tube into finely chopped white chocolate. Process until smooth, scraping sides of bowl if necessary. Stir in crème de cacao. Transfer white chocolate mixture to a medium bowl. Cover and chill filling about 3 hours or until firm. Shape filling into ¾-inch balls. Freeze for 15 minutes.

2. Meanwhile, in a 4-cup glass measure combine the remaining chopped white chocolate and the shortening. In a large glass bowl pour very warm tap water (100°F to 110°F) to a depth of 2 inches. Place glass measure containing the white chocolate inside the large bowl. (Water should cover bottom half of the glass measure.) Using a rubber spatula, stir white chocolate constantly until completely melted and smooth. (This takes about 20 minutes; don't rush. If the water cools, remove glass measure. Discard cool water; add warm water. Return glass measure to bowl of water.)

3. Line a baking sheet with waxed paper. Use a fork to dip frozen balls into melted white chocolate, allowing excess white chocolate to drip back into the glass measure. Roll in coconut. Place truffles on the prepared baking sheet. Chill about 10 minutes or until set.

To Store: Place truffles in layers separated by waxed paper in an airtight container; cover. Store in the refrigerator for up to 2 weeks or freeze for up to 3 months. Let stand at room temperature for 30 minutes before serving.

Per truffle: 111 cal., 7 g total fat (5 g sat. fat), 4 mg chol., 33 mg sodium, 10 g carbo., 0 g fiber, 2 g pro.

Snowy White Truffles

Hazelnut Toffee

This hazelnut-topped treasure captured the attention (and taste buds) of Better Homes and Gardens® *magazine editors in 1995, when it won the magazine's Prize Tested Recipe® Contest.*

Prep: 30 minutes **Cook:** 40 minutes
Makes: about 2 pounds (about 40 pieces)

        Nonstick cooking spray
    1 **cup finely chopped, toasted* hazelnuts**
        Butter
    1 **cup butter**
    1¼ **cups packed brown sugar**
    3 **tablespoons water**
    1 **tablespoon light-colored corn syrup**
    1 **tablespoon hazelnut liqueur**
    2 **cups semisweet chocolate pieces**
        (12 ounces)

1. Line a 13×9×2-inch baking pan with foil, extending foil over the edges. Lightly coat foil with nonstick cooking spray. Sprinkle ½ cup of the nuts evenly in the pan; set aside.

2. Butter the sides of a heavy 2-quart saucepan. In the saucepan melt the 1 cup butter. Stir in brown sugar, the water, and corn syrup. Bring to boiling over medium-high heat, stirring constantly. Clip a candy thermometer to the side of the pan. Reduce heat to medium-low. Cook to 290°F, soft-crack stage, stirring occasionally. Mixture should boil at a moderate, steady rate across the surface. (This should take 40 to 45 minutes.) Remove pan from heat; remove thermometer.

3. Immediately stir in liqueur; pour over nuts in pan, spreading to edges of pan. Sprinkle with chocolate pieces. Let stand about 2 minutes or until chocolate is soft; spread to cover. Sprinkle evenly with remaining ½ cup nuts. Cool. (Or chill several minutes to harden chocolate.) Lift foil lining and candy from pan. Remove candy from foil. Break into pieces.

*Note: To toast hazelnuts, bake in a 350°F oven for 8 to 10 minutes or until toasted. Rub warm nuts in a clean kitchen towel to remove skins.

Per piece: 126 cal., 9 g total fat (4 g sat. fat), 12 mg chol., 36 mg sodium, 13 g carbo., 1 g fiber, 1 g pro.

Buttery Cashew Brittle

This 1974 recipe one-ups the usual peanut brittle by substituting rich, buttery cashews. Readers loved it—the recipe generated a substantial amount of fan mail in its day!

Prep: 10 minutes **Cook:** 45 minutes
Makes: about 2½ pounds (72 servings)

   Butter
2 **cups sugar**
1 **cup light-colored corn syrup**
½ **cup water**
1 **cup butter**
3 **cups raw cashews (about 12 ounces)**
1 **teaspoon baking soda, sifted**

1. Butter two large baking sheets or two 15×10×1-inch pans. Set aside. Butter the sides of a 3-quart saucepan. In saucepan combine sugar, corn syrup, and the water. Cook and stir until sugar dissolves. Bring mixture to boiling. Add the 1 cup butter; stir until butter is melted. Clip a candy thermometer to the side of the pan. Reduce heat to medium-low; continue boiling at a moderate, steady rate, stirring occasionally, until thermometer registers 280°F, soft-crack stage (about 35 minutes).

2. Stir in cashews; continue cooking over medium-low heat, stirring until the thermometer registers 300°F, hard-crack stage (10 to 15 minutes more).

3. Remove saucepan from heat; remove thermometer. Quickly sprinkle baking soda over mixture, stirring constantly. Pour mixture onto prepared baking sheets or pans.

4. Use two forks to lift and pull candy as it cools. Loosen from pans as soon as possible; pick up sections and break them into bite-size pieces.

To Store: Store in an airtight container for up to 1 week.

Per serving: 90 cal., 5 g total fat (2 g sat. fat), 7 mg chol., 47 mg sodium, 11 g carbo., 0 g fiber, 1 g pro.

Buttery Cashew Brittle

Christmas Pound Cake

This cake makes an indulgent treat for teatime—so rich, in fact, it can be served without the Raspberry Sauce. When serving it as dessert, you may wish to add the colorful sauce as a finishing touch.

Prep: 30 minutes **Bake:** 1 hour 5 minutes
Oven: 325°F **Makes:** 16 servings

2¼ **cups granulated sugar**
 ¾ **cup butter, softened**
  4 **eggs**
  1 **egg yolk**
  3 **cups all-purpose flour**
 ¼ **teaspoon baking soda**
 ¼ **teaspoon baking powder**
    Dash salt
 ⅔ **cup dairy sour cream**
 ⅓ **cup apricot brandy or apricot nectar**
  1 **teaspoon vanilla**
 ¾ **teaspoon orange extract or orange flavoring**
    Powdered sugar
  1 **recipe Raspberry Sauce
     (see page 119) (optional)**

1. Preheat oven to 325°F. Grease and flour a 10-inch fluted tube pan; set aside. In a large mixing bowl combine granulated sugar and butter; beat with an electric mixer on medium to high speed until well mixed. Add eggs and egg yolk, one at a time, beating well after each addition. In a medium bowl stir together flour, baking soda, baking powder, and salt. In a small bowl combine sour cream, brandy, vanilla, and orange extract. Alternately add flour mixture and sour cream mixture to butter mixture, beating on low speed after each addition just until combined. Turn into prepared pan.

2. Bake about 65 minutes or until a toothpick inserted in the center of the cake comes out clean. Cool in pan on a wire rack 15 minutes. Loosen sides. Turn out of pan. Place, right side up, on wire rack; cool completely. To serve, sprinkle with powdered sugar. If desired, serve with Raspberry Sauce.

Per serving: 315 cal., 12 g total fat (7 g sat. fat), 92 mg chol., 116 mg sodium, 45 g carbo., 1 g fiber, 4 g pro.

Raspberry Sauce: Thaw two 12-ounce packages frozen raspberries. Place berries in a blender. Cover and blend until smooth. Press pureed berries through a fine-mesh sieve. Discard seeds. In a medium saucepan combine ⅔ cup sugar and 2 teaspoons cornstarch. Add sieved berries. Cook and stir over medium heat until thickened and bubbly. Cook and stir for 2 minutes more. Transfer to a bowl. Cover and chill for 1 to 24 hours. Makes 2½ cups.

Peanut Butter Banana Bread

This recipe from the 1990s adds chocolate pieces and peanut butter for a whole new take on banana bread! For a simpler, unadorned bread, you can skip the Peanut Butter Glaze.

Prep: 35 minutes **Bake:** 40 minutes
Stand: overnight **Oven:** 350°F
Makes: 2 loaves (32 slices)

2½ **cups all-purpose flour**
 ½ **cup granulated sugar**
 ½ **cup packed brown sugar**
 1 **tablespoon baking powder**
 ¾ **teaspoon salt**
 ¼ **teaspoon ground cinnamon**
 2 **large bananas, mashed (1 cup)**
 1 **cup milk**

 ¾ **cup chunky peanut butter**
 3 **tablespoons cooking oil**
 1 **teaspoon vanilla**
 1 **egg, slightly beaten**
 1 **cup milk chocolate pieces**
 1 **recipe Peanut Butter Glaze**
    Finely chopped peanuts (optional)

1. Preheat oven to 350°F. Grease the bottoms and ½ inch up the sides of two 8×4×2-inch or 9×5×3-inch loaf pans; set aside. In a large bowl stir together flour, granulated sugar, brown sugar, baking powder, salt, and cinnamon. Make a well in the center of flour mixture; set aside.

2. In a medium bowl combine mashed bananas, milk, peanut butter, oil, vanilla, and egg. Add banana mixture to flour mixture; stir just until moistened. Stir in chocolate pieces. Spoon batter evenly into prepared pans.

3. Bake for 40 to 45 minutes or until a toothpick inserted near the center of each loaf comes out clean. Cool in pans on wire racks for 10 minutes. Remove from pans; cool on wire racks. Wrap in plastic wrap and store overnight before slicing. Before serving, spread with Peanut Butter Glaze. If desired, top with peanuts.

Peanut Butter Glaze: In a small saucepan combine 3 tablespoons chunky peanut butter and 2 tablespoons butter; heat and stir until melted. Remove from heat; stir in 1 cup powdered sugar and 1 teaspoon vanilla. Stir in 1 tablespoon milk. (Glaze will thicken as it cools.) Makes about ⅔ cup.

Per slice: 170 cal., 8 g total fat (2 g sat. fat), 10 mg chol., 128 mg sodium, 23 g carbo., 1 g fiber, 4 g pro.

Rainbow Cookies in a Jar

3. Attach baking directions and give as a gift. (Or store at room temperature for up to 1 month.)

Baking Directions: Preheat oven to 375°F. Empty contents of jar into a large bowl. Stir in 1 beaten egg, 1 tablespoon milk, and 1 teaspoon vanilla. Drop by rounded teaspoons 2 inches apart onto an ungreased cookie sheet. Bake for 8 to 10 minutes or until edges are golden. Let stand on cookie sheet for 1 minute. Transfer to a wire rack and let cool.

Per cookie: 77 cal., 4 g total fat (1 g sat. fat), 9 mg chol., 36 mg sodium, 10 g carbo., 0 g fiber, 1 g pro.

Rainbow Cookies in a Jar

When gift-giving time rolls around, readers often request "cookies in a jar" recipes. And why not? At a time when everyone seems inundated with sweets, a mix is most welcome. With a shelf life of up to one month, this kid-pleasing version lets recipients bake the cookies fresh whenever they're craving sweets.

Start to Finish: 10 minutes **Makes:** 24 cookies

  1   **cups all-purpose flour**
  ¼   **teaspoon baking powder**
  ¼   **teaspoon baking soda**
  ⅓   **cup shortening**
 1½   **cups fruit-flavored crisp rice cereal**
  ½   **cup packed brown sugar**
  ¼   **cup coconut**

1. In a bowl stir together flour, baking powder, and baking soda. Using a pastry blender, cut in shortening until the mixture resembles coarse crumbs.

2. Layer ingredients in a 1-quart glass jar or canister in the following order: one-third of the cereal, the flour mixture, another one-third of the cereal, brown sugar, coconut, and remaining cereal. Tap jar gently on the counter to settle each layer before adding the next. Cover jar.

Pear-Cherry Chutney

Present this sweet-tart gift in a beribboned jar alongside a small wheel of Brie or Camembert cheese and a package of fancy crackers. Voila—a beautiful appetizer gift your friends will love!

Prep: 20 minutes **Cook:** 10 minutes
Chill: 2 hours **Makes:** 4½ cups chutney

  ½   **cup sugar**
  1   **cup dried tart red cherries**
  2   **teaspoons finely shredded lemon peel**
  ⅓   **cup lemon juice**
  ½   **teaspoon ground cinnamon**
  ½   **teaspoon ground allspice**
  5   **cups chopped, peeled firm pears**

1. In a large saucepan combine sugar, dried cherries, lemon peel, lemon juice, cinnamon, and allspice. Bring to boiling; reduce heat to medium. Simmer, uncovered, for 5 minutes, stirring occasionally. Stir in pear; return to boiling. Simmer, uncovered, about 5 minutes or just until pear is tender. Let cool.

2. Transfer to a storage container. Cover and chill for 2 hours. Serve with a slotted spoon as a topper for cheese or as a condiment with beef or pork.

To Store: Store in an airtight container in the refrigerator for up to 2 weeks or in a freezer container in the freezer for up to 6 months.

Per ¼-cup serving: 71 cal., 0 g total fat (0 g sat. fat), 0 mg chol., 0 mg sodium, 18 g carbo., 1 g fiber, 0 g pro.

Almond Cream Liqueur

This smooth, rich drink makes a lovely hostess gift. When buying the whipping cream, be sure to check the date on the carton. Purchase cream that will still be fresh for up to one week after you give the gift.

Start to Finish: 10 minutes **Makes:** about 4 cups

- 2 **cups whipping cream**
- 1 **14-ounce can sweetened condensed milk (1¼ cups)**
- 1 **cup crème d'amande**

1. In a large pitcher stir together whipping cream, sweetened condensed milk, and liqueur. Pour into clean, decorative bottles. Cover and store in the refrigerator for up to 1 week.

Per ¼-cup serving: 246 cal., 13 g total fat (8 g sat. fat), 50 mg chol., 44 mg sodium, 21 g carbo., 0 g fiber, 3 g pro.

Orange-Mocha Cream Liqueur: Prepare as directed, except omit crème d'amande and add ½ cup coffee liqueur, ¼ cup orange liqueur, and ¼ cup chocolate-flavored syrup. Combine all ingredients in a blender or food processor. Cover and blend or process just until smooth. Makes about 4 cups.

Per ¼-cup serving: 235 cal., 13 g total fat (8 g sat. fat), 50 mg chol., 47 mg sodium, 23 g carbo., 0 g fiber, 3 g pro.

 Very Berry Martinis

A pretty jar of these fun little martinis will make a winsome and sophisticated present for just about any adult on your gift list.

Start to Finish: 10 minutes
Makes: three 1-pint gift jars (15 servings)

- 3 **cups cranberry-raspberry drink**
- 1½ **cups lemon-flavored vodka**
- ¾ **cups raspberry liqueur**
  Fresh raspberries (optional)

1. In a large pitcher stir together cranberry-raspberry drink, vodka, and raspberry liqueur. Divide mix-

ture among three clean 1-pint glass jars with lids. If desired, add a skewer threaded with 3 raspberries to each jar. Cover and store in the refrigerator for up to 1 week.

Preparation Directions: Add ice cubes to a martini shaker. Add ⅓ cup of the Very Berry Martinis mix to the shaker. Cover and shake well. If desired, dip the rim of a chilled martini glass in water, then in granulated or coarse sugar. Strain the martini mixture into the glass. If desired, garnish with fresh raspberries. Serve immediately.

Per serving: 111 cal., 0 g total fat (0 g sat. fat), 0 mg chol., 7 mg sodium, 11 g carbo., 0 g fiber, 0 g pro.

Very Berry Martinis

 **Bridge Party Mix**

The game of bridge may not be as popular as it once was, but the distinction of this irresistible party mix hasn't waned a bit!

Prep: 20 minutes **Bake:** 45 minutes **Oven:** 300°F
Makes: 16 to 18 cups

- 5 cups pretzel sticks
- 4 cups round toasted oat cereal
- 4 cups bite-size wheat or bran square cereal
- 4 cups bite-size rice or corn square cereal or bite-size shredded wheat biscuits
- 3 cups mixed nuts
- 1 cup butter or margarine
- ¼ cup Worcestershire sauce
- 1 teaspoon garlic powder
  Several drops bottled hot pepper sauce

1. Preheat oven to 300°F. In a large roasting pan combine pretzels, oat cereal, wheat cereal, rice cereal, and nuts. Set aside.

2. In a small saucepan combine butter, Worcestershire sauce, garlic powder, and hot pepper sauce; heat and stir until butter melts. Drizzle butter mixture over cereal mixture; stir gently to coat.

3. Bake for 45 minutes, stirring every 15 minutes. Spread on a large piece of foil to cool.

To Store: Store in an airtight container at room temperature for up to 2 weeks or in the freezer for up to 3 months.

Per ½-cup serving: 171 cal., 11 g total fat (4 g sat. fat), 12 mg chol., 264 mg sodium, 16 g carbo., 2 g fiber, 3 g pro.

 **Tropical Fruit and Nut Party Mix**

With a clever combination of sweet and nutty ingredients, this addictive recipe takes the bridge mix concept to a whole new level!

Prep: 5 minutes **Bake:** 20 minutes
Oven: 300°F **Makes:** about 15 cups

- 5 cups bite-size rice square cereal
- 5 cups bite-size honey-nut shredded wheat biscuits
- 1 cup whole cashews, whole blanched almonds, and/or macadamia nuts
- 1 cup raw chip coconut
- 1 cup dried banana chips
- ½ cup dried pineapple
- 1 cup packed brown sugar
- ½ cup butter
- ¼ cup light-colored corn syrup
- 1½ cups white baking pieces

1. Preheat oven to 300°F. In a large roasting pan combine rice cereal, wheat biscuits, cashews, coconut, banana chips, and pineapple; set aside.

2. In a medium saucepan combine brown sugar, butter, and corn syrup. Cook and stir over medium heat until mixture boils. Boil at a moderate, steady rate, without stirring, for 5 minutes. Pour over cereal mixture; stir gently to coat.

3. Bake for 15 minutes; stir cereal mixture and bake for 5 minutes more. Remove from oven. Spread on a large piece of buttered foil to cool. Break into pieces. Stir in white baking pieces.

To Store: Store in an airtight container for up to 1 week.

Per 1-cup serving: 475 cal., 22 g total fat (14 g sat. fat), 16 mg chol., 220 mg sodium, 66 g carbo., 3 g fiber, 4 g pro.

Bridge Party Mix and Tropical Fruit and Nut Party Mix

Favorite Fireside Suppers

In between the grand and glamorous feasts of the holidays come smaller occasions—chances to share quiet, meaningful evenings with family and close friends. These recipes are perfect for those times. Everyone wants to come home after a busy day of shopping to a slow cooker full of Hot and Spicy Sloppy Joes or Super-Simple Beef Stew. After trimming the tree, enjoy a hearty bowl of Cheesy Chicken Corn Chowder and reward everyone for a job well done with the Busy-Day Cake. If you're lucky enough to have a white Christmas season, many of these dishes are perfect after-sledding suppers too.

Deep-Dish Chicken Pie, page 129

Super-Simple Beef Stew

Super simple is right! It's hard to believe that so few ingredients result in such a satisfying one-dish winner. A can of soup is the legendary shortcut.

Prep: 15 minutes **Cook:** Low 8 hours, High 4 hours; plus 10 minutes on High
Makes: 4 servings

- 1 pound beef stew meat
- 12 ounces small red potatoes, quartered (about 2 cups)
- 4 medium carrots, cut into ½-inch pieces
- 1 small red onion, cut into wedges
- 1 10¾-ounce can condensed cream of mushroom or cream of celery soup
- 1 cup beef broth
- ½ teaspoon dried thyme, crushed
- 1 9-ounce package frozen cut green beans, thawed

1. In a 3½- or 4-quart slow cooker combine stew meat, potato, carrot, onion, cream of mushroom soup, beef broth, and marjoram.

2. Cover and cook on low-heat setting for 8 to 9 hours or on high-heat setting for 4 to 4½ hours.

3. If using low-heat setting, turn to high-heat setting. Stir in thawed green beans. Cover and cook for 10 minutes or just until green beans are tender.

Per serving: 316 cal., 11 g total fat (3 g sat. fat), 38 mg chol., 766 mg sodium, 31 g carbo., 6 g fiber, 24 g pro.

 ### Spicy Beef Stew with Pesto Mashed Potatoes

Here a home-style classic is combined with a little spice and pesto mashed potatoes for a tasty update.

Prep: 45 minutes **Cook:** Low 10 hours, High 5 hours; plus 30 minutes on High
Makes: 8 servings

- 2 to 2½ pounds boneless beef short ribs
- 3 tablespoons all-purpose flour
- 1 tablespoon dried Italian seasoning, crushed

Spicy Beef Stew with Pesto Mashed Potatoes

½ teaspoon crushed red pepper

2 tablespoons cooking oil

1 large onion, cut into wedges

4 carrots, peeled and cut into 1-inch pieces

1 14½-ounce can diced tomatoes with basil, oregano, and garlic, undrained

1 14-ounce can beef broth

1 cup hot-style vegetable juice or vegetable juice

1 medium zucchini, halved lengthwise and cut into ½-inch slices

½ teaspoon finely shredded lemon peel

1 recipe Pesto Mashed Potatoes

1. Trim fat from beef. Cut beef into ¾-inch cubes. In a large bowl stir together flour, Italian seasoning, and crushed red pepper. Add meat; toss to coat with flour mixture. In a large skillet brown meat, half at a time, in hot oil over medium-high heat. Remove meat from skillet and place in a 4- to 5-quart slow cooker. Add onion, carrot, and undrained diced tomatoes to slow cooker. Add beef broth and vegetable juice.

2. Cover and cook on low-heat setting for 10 to 12 hours or on high-heat setting for 5 to 6 hours.

3. If using low-heat setting, turn to high-heat setting. Add zucchini. Cover and cook for 30 minutes more. Stir in lemon peel just before serving. Serve in shallow bowls with Pesto Mashed Potatoes.

Pesto Mashed Potatoes: Peel 3 pounds russet, round white, or yellow baking potatoes; quarter potatoes. In a large covered saucepan cook potato in enough boiling lightly salted water to cover for 20 to 25 minutes or until tender; drain. Mash with a potato masher or beat with an electric mixer on low speed. Add ¼ cup purchased basil pesto and 3 tablespoons butter, cut up and softened. Season to taste with salt and black pepper. Gradually beat in ½ to ⅔ cup half-and-half, light cream, or milk to make mixture light and fluffy.

Per serving: 417 cal., 24 g total fat (8 g sat. fat), 82 mg chol., 807 mg sodium, 24 g carbo., 3 g fiber, 27 g pro.

Hot and Spicy Sloppy Joes

Pop the meat mixture into the slow cooker in the morning, then spend the rest of the day catching up on Christmas shopping or baking. The extra-special slow-cooked sloppy joe mixture will be ready to go at dinnertime. For a quick and easy side dish, serve with purchased deli potato salad or coleslaw.

Prep: 25 minutes Cook: Low 8 hours, High 4 hours
Makes: 12 to 14 sandwiches

2 pounds ground beef

4 medium onions, cut into bite-size strips

4 medium green sweet peppers, cut into bite-size strips

2 medium red sweet peppers, cut into bite-size strips

1 cup ketchup

¼ cup cider vinegar

1 fresh Scotch bonnet chile pepper, seeded and finely chopped (see note, page 11), or ¼ teaspoon cayenne pepper

1 tablespoon chili powder

½ teaspoon salt

½ teaspoon ground black pepper

12 to 14 hoagie rolls or hot dog buns, split and toasted

1. In a very large skillet cook ground beef and onion until meat is brown and onion is tender. Drain fat from meat; discard.

2. In a 5- to 6-quart slow cooker combine ground beef mixture, sweet pepper strips, ketchup, vinegar, chile pepper, chili powder, salt, and black pepper.

3. Cover and cook on low-heat setting for 8 to 10 hours or on high-heat setting for 4 to 5 hours. Serve in toasted rolls or buns.

Per sandwich: 592 cal., 18 g total fat (6 g sat. fat), 48 mg chol., 1,051 mg sodium, 83 g carbo., 6 g fiber, 27 g pro.

Cheesy Chicken-Corn Chowder

Give this dress-up-a-can-of-soup recipe a try—it's an all-time favorite! Canned soup makes it quick, and the stir-ins make it delicious. It's the perfect comfort food for a cold winter night.

Prep: 15 minutes **Cook:** 15 minutes
Cool: 15 minutes **Makes:** 4 main-dish servings

- 2 skinless, boneless chicken breast halves (about 8 ounces total)
- 1 cup water
- ¼ cup chopped onion
- ¼ cup chopped celery
- 1 10¾-ounce can condensed cream of chicken soup
- 1 cup loose-pack frozen whole kernel corn
- ½ cup milk
- ½ cup shredded American cheese or cheddar cheese (2 ounces)
- 2 tablespoons chopped pimiento

1. In a medium saucepan combine chicken, the water, onion, and celery. Bring to boiling; reduce heat. Simmer, covered, for 15 to 20 minutes or until chicken is no longer pink. Remove chicken, reserving cooking liquid in saucepan.

2. When cool enough to handle, chop chicken. Return chicken to mixture in saucepan; stir in soup, corn, milk, cheese, and pimiento. Bring just to boiling, stirring until cheese melts.

Per serving: 252 cal., 11 g total fat (5 g sat. fat), 55 mg chol., 816 mg sodium, 19 g carbo., 2 g fiber, 21 g pro.

Onion-Cheese Supper Bread

This quick, flavorful bread makes a delicious and hearty side for a soup supper. Dip thick buttered wedges of it into the Cheesy Chicken-Corn Chowder.

Prep: 15 minutes **Bake:** 20 minutes
Oven: 400°F **Makes:** 8 servings

- 2 tablespoons butter or margarine
- ½ cup chopped onion
- 1 egg
- ½ cup milk
- 1½ cups packaged biscuit mix
- 1 cup shredded American cheese or cheddar cheese (4 ounces)
- 2 teaspoons poppy seeds

1. Preheat oven to 400°F. Grease an 8×1½-inch round baking pan. Set aside. In a small skillet melt 1 tablespoon of the butter over medium heat. Add chopped onion; cook until onion is tender.

2. In a small bowl whisk together egg and milk. Add to biscuit mix; stir just until moistened. Add the chopped onion mixture, half of the cheese, and half of the poppy seeds to biscuit mix mixture. Spoon batter into prepared pan, spreading evenly. Sprinkle with the remaining poppy seeds. Melt remaining 1 tablespoon butter; drizzle over batter in baking pan.

3. Bake for 10 minutes. Sprinkle with remaining cheese. Bake about 10 minutes more or until a toothpick inserted near the center comes out clean.

Per serving: 202 cal., 12 g total fat (6 g sat. fat), 49 mg chol., 528 mg sodium, 16 g carbo., 1 g fiber, 6 g pro.

Solving the Leftover Dilemma

Meals made in the slow cooker often yield enough for leftovers, tapping into the "cook once/eat twice" kitchen philosophy. To store leftovers, immediately after the meal transfer food to freezer-safe containers, dividing larger amounts into smaller containers for quicker cooling in the refrigerator. Label the container and immediately place the leftovers in the refrigerator or freezer. Store in the refrigerator for up to 3 days or the freezer for 2 to 3 months.

When ready to serve, thaw frozen food in the refrigerator. Transfer it to a saucepan; cook and stir over low heat until heated through. Or place the frozen food in a microwave-safe dish and heat, stirring several times. Always reheat leftovers to a safe internal temperature of 165°F. Note: Do not store food in the crockery liner of the slow cooker in the refrigerator because it may not cool quickly enough to be safe to eat as leftovers.

Deep-Dish Chicken Pie

Rich, creamy, and oh-so-delicious—chicken pot pie may be the most satisfying winter casserole of all time! When the temperature dips below zero, this recipe is perfect for warming both heart and soul.

Prep: 50 minutes **Bake:** 30 minutes
Stand: 20 minutes **Oven:** 400°F **Makes:** 6 servings

  1 **recipe Pastry Topper**
  2 **tablespoons butter or margarine**
  3 **medium leeks or 1 large onion, chopped**
  1 **cup sliced fresh mushrooms**
 ¾ **cup sliced celery**
 ½ **cup chopped red sweet pepper**
 ⅓ **cup all-purpose flour**
  1 **teaspoon poultry seasoning**
 ¼ **teaspoon salt**
 ¼ **teaspoon ground black pepper**
1½ **cups chicken broth**
  1 **cup half-and-half, light cream, or milk**
2½ **cups chopped cooked chicken**
  1 **cup loose-pack frozen peas**
  1 **egg, beaten**

1. Prepare Pastry Topper; set aside.

2. Preheat oven to 400°F. In a large saucepan melt butter over medium heat. Add leek, mushrooms, celery, and sweet pepper; cook for 4 to 5 minutes or until tender. Stir in the flour, poultry seasoning, salt, and the black pepper. Add broth and half-and-half all at once. Cook and stir until thickened and bubbly. Stir in cooked chicken and frozen peas. Pour into a 2-quart rectangular baking dish.

3. Place pastry over the hot chicken mixture in baking dish. Turn edges of pastry under; flute to the edges of dish. Brush with some of the beaten egg. If desired, place reserved pastry shapes on top of pastry. Brush again with egg.

4. Bake for 30 to 35 minutes or until crust is golden. Let stand for 20 minutes before serving.

Pastry Topper: In a medium bowl stir together 1¼ cups all-purpose flour and ¼ teaspoon salt. Using a pastry blender, cut in ⅓ cup shortening until pieces are the size of small peas. Sprinkle 1 tablespoon cold water over part of the mixture; gently toss with a fork. Push moistened dough to side of bowl. Repeat moistening dough, using 1 tablespoon cold water at a time, until all the dough is moistened (4 to 5 tablespoons cold water total). Form dough into a ball. On a lightly floured surface, roll dough into a 13×9-inch rectangle. Using a sharp knife, cut slits in pastry to allow steam to escape. If desired, use a small cookie cutter to cut shapes from pastry.

Per serving: 471 cal., 26 g total fat (10 g sat. fat), 113 mg chol., 543 mg sodium, 33 g carbo., 3 g fiber, 26 g pro.

Deep-Dish Chicken Pie

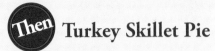

Then Turkey Skillet Pie

This cheese-topped pie, with its luscious "crust" of stuffing, won the Prize Tested Recipe® Contest in the 1970s and endures as one of the most satisfying ways to use leftover turkey.

Prep: 25 minutes **Cook:** 10 minutes
Stand: 5 minutes **Makes:** 6 servings

- ⅓ cup chopped celery
- 6 tablespoons butter or margarine
- ⅔ cup water
- 2 cups herb-seasoned stuffing mix
- 3 eggs, beaten
- 1 5-ounce can evaporated milk (⅔ cup)
- 2 tablespoons finely chopped onion
  Dash ground black pepper
- 3 cups finely chopped or ground
  cooked turkey*
- 1 cup shredded Swiss cheese (4 ounces)
- 2 tablespoons snipped fresh parsley
- 1½ cups leftover turkey gravy or one
  12-ounce jar roasted turkey gravy

1. In a large skillet cook celery in hot butter until tender. Stir in the water. Add stuffing mix; toss to coat. Set aside.

2. In a medium bowl combine the egg, evaporated milk, onion, and pepper. Stir in turkey. Spoon turkey mixture into a well-greased 8-inch skillet; sprinkle with cheese.

3. Top with stuffing mixture; cover. Cook over medium-low heat for 10 to 15 minutes or until an instant-read thermometer inserted in center registers 170°F. Sprinkle with parsley. Let stand for 5 minutes.

4. Meanwhile, in a small saucepan heat gravy until bubbly; ladle over individual servings.

*Note: Do not use deli-style turkey.

Per serving: 528 cal., 33 g total fat (17 g sat. fat), 227 mg chol., 760 mg sodium, 23 g carbo., 2 g fiber, 34 g pro.

Now Individual Turkey Pizzas

This recipe was created as a fun new way to enjoy leftover turkey. It calls on some terrific convenience products—packaged salad mix, peppercorn ranch dressing, bottled minced garlic, Italian bread shells, and bottled roasted red sweet peppers—that weren't available to cooks in earlier generations.

Prep: 20 minutes **Broil:** 4 minutes
Makes: 4 servings

- 4 cups mesclun or other mixed baby greens
- ¼ cup bottled peppercorn ranch
  salad dressing
- 1 tablespoon olive oil
- ½ teaspoon bottled minced garlic or
  bottled roasted minced garlic
- 4 8-inch Italian bread shells or packaged
  prebaked pizza crusts
- 3 cups chopped cooked turkey
- ¾ cup bottled roasted red sweet pepper,
  drained and chopped
- 1½ cups shredded mozzarella cheese
  (6 ounces)
  Bottled peppercorn ranch salad dressing
  (optional)

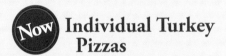

Individual Turkey Pizzas

1. In a large bowl combine greens and the ¼ cup salad dressing; toss to coat. Set aside.

2. In a small bowl combine olive oil and minced garlic. Lightly brush the top side of each bread shell with the oil mixture. Place bread shells, oiled sides up, on a very large baking sheet or two large baking sheets. Broil 4 to 5 inches from the heat for 2 to 3 minutes or until bread shells are light brown (if using two sheets, broil one sheet at a time).

3. Top bread shells with turkey and sweet pepper. Sprinkle with cheese. Broil about 2 minutes more or until cheese melts. Top with greens. If desired, pass additional salad dressing.

Per serving: 827 cal., 36 g total fat (13 g sat. fat), 116 mg chol., 1,287 mg sodium, 70 g carbo., 3 g fiber, 55 g pro.

Savory Ham and Eggs

This recipe was originally published in the 1930s as a special-occasion dish for company. However, these days it would make an incredibly quick and tasty "oops—forgot about dinner!" recipe.

Start to Finish: 30 minutes **Makes:** 5 to 6 servings

8	hard-cooked eggs (see note, page 24)
½	cup finely chopped cooked ham
¼	cup butter, softened
1	tablespoon chopped onion
1	teaspoon snipped fresh parsley
½	teaspoon Worcestershire sauce
¼	teaspoon yellow mustard
3	tablespoons butter
½	cup all-purpose flour
⅛	teaspoon paprika
¼	teaspoon salt
	Dash ground black pepper
1	14-ounce can chicken broth
1	cup milk
1	cup shredded process American cheese (4 ounces)
4	slices toasted bread, each cut diagonally into 4 triangles (16 triangles total)

Savory Ham and Eggs

1. Halve the hard-cooked eggs lengthwise and remove yolks. Set whites aside. Place yolks in a bowl; mash with a fork. Add ham, the ¼ cup butter, the onion, parsley, Worcestershire sauce, and mustard to yolks. Fill egg whites with yolk mixture; set aside.

2. In a large skillet melt the 3 tablespoons butter over medium heat. Stir in flour, paprika, salt, and pepper. Add chicken broth and milk. Cook and stir until thickened and bubbly. Cook and stir for 2 minutes more. Carefully place filled eggs in skillet. Sprinkle with cheese. Cover and cook about 5 minutes more or until cheese is melted. Serve with toast points.

Per serving: 514 cal., 36 g total fat (18 g sat. fat), 416 mg chol., 1,327 mg sodium, 26 g carbo., 1 g fiber, 23 g pro.

131

Butterscotch Pudding

Butterscotch Pudding

This homemade pudding takes only 20 minutes to prepare and uses just seven ingredients—most of which you'll likely have on hand. For kids, scatter broken candies across the top. For company, add spoonfuls of a tangy topper (see Pudding Toppers, below) to the top of the pudding.

Prep: 20 minutes **Chill:** 4 hours **Makes:** 8 servings

   1 **cup packed light brown sugar**
   ¼ **cup cornstarch**
   ¼ **teaspoon salt**
   4 **cups half-and-half or light cream**
   5 **egg yolks, slightly beaten**
   ¼ **cup butter, sliced**
   2 **teaspoons vanilla**
      Pudding Toppers* (optional)

1. In a medium saucepan combine brown sugar, cornstarch, and salt. Whisk in the half-and-half.

2. Cook over medium heat until mixture is thickened and bubbly, whisking constantly. Cook and stir for 2 minutes more. Remove from heat. Gradually whisk about 1 cup of the hot mixture into egg yolks. Add egg yolk mixture to mixture in saucepan. Bring to a gentle boil; reduce heat. Cook and whisk constantly for 2 minutes more. Remove from heat. Whisk in butter and vanilla until combined. Pour pudding into a large bowl. Cover surface of pudding with plastic wrap. Chill for 4 to 5 hours or until well chilled. If desired, garnish individual servings with your choice of topper.

Per serving: 373 cal., 23 g total fat (13 g sat. fat), 189 mg chol., 182 mg sodium, 38 g carbo., 0 g fiber, 5 g pro.

*Pudding Toppers: If desired, choose from one or more of these three topping ideas:
• Top servings with chopped chocolate-covered English toffee.
• Sprinkle servings with a mixture of crumbled soft cookies (such as oatmeal, chocolate chip, or molasses) and dried cherries.
• For a tangy topper, combine ⅓ cup goat cheese, ¼ cup crème fraîche, and 1 tablespoon sugar. Spoon over servings. Dust with freshly grated nutmeg.

Date-Nut Pudding

Dates are a favorite holiday treat, and this 1945 treasure is a wonderfully old-fashioned way to use them. Refrigerate any leftover sauce and reheat it another time to serve over ice cream.

Prep: 20 minutes **Bake:** 30 minutes
Oven: 350°F **Makes:** 12 servings

- 1 cup chopped pitted dates
- ½ cup boiling water
- 1 tablespoon butter
- 1½ cups all-purpose flour
- 1½ teaspoons baking powder
- ½ teaspoon salt
- 1 egg, beaten
- ½ cup granulated sugar
- ½ cup light-colored corn syrup
- 1 teaspoon vanilla
- 1 cup chopped walnuts
- 1 cup packed brown sugar
- ½ cup butter
- 2 tablespoons light-colored corn syrup
- ½ cup whipping cream

1. Preheat oven to 350°F. In a small bowl combine dates, the boiling water, and the 1 tablespoon butter; set aside. In a medium bowl stir together flour, baking powder, and salt; set aside.

2. In a medium bowl stir together egg, granulated sugar, the ½ cup corn syrup, and the vanilla until well mixed. Stir in the date mixture and flour mixture. Stir in the walnuts. Pour into a greased 11×7½×1½-inch baking pan.

3. Bake for 30 to 35 minutes or until a toothpick inserted near the center comes out clean; cool pudding slightly.

4. Meanwhile, for the sauce, in a medium saucepan combine the brown sugar, the ½ cup butter, and the 2 tablespoons corn syrup. Cook and stir over medium heat until mixture comes to a full boil. Stir in the whipping cream. Return to a full boil. Remove from heat. Serve warm sauce with pudding.

Per serving: 428 cal., 19 g total fat (9 g sat. fat), 54 mg chol., 221 mg sodium, 63 g carbo., 2 g fiber, 4 g pro.

Busy-Day Cake

If you don't remember what a made-from-scratch cake tastes like, treat yourself and your family to this easy one-layer treat. Keep the ingredients on hand for a warming, homespun dessert to serve any night during the holidays.

Prep: 25 minutes **Bake:** 30 minutes
Cool: 30 minutes **Oven:** 350°F
Makes: 8 servings

- 1⅓ cups all-purpose flour
- ⅔ cup granulated sugar
- 2 teaspoons baking powder
- ⅔ cup milk
- ¼ cup butter, softened
- 1 egg
- 1 teaspoon vanilla
- ¼ cup packed brown sugar
- 2 tablespoons butter, softened
- 1 tablespoon milk
- ½ cup flaked coconut
- ¼ cup chopped nuts (optional)

1. Preheat oven to 350°F. Grease an 8×1½-inch round cake pan; set aside.

2. In a medium mixing bowl combine flour, granulated sugar, and baking powder. Add the ⅔ cup milk, the ¼ cup butter, the egg, and vanilla. Beat with an electric mixer on low speed until combined. Beat on medium speed for 1 minute. Pour batter into prepared pan.

3. Bake about 30 minutes or until a toothpick inserted near the center comes out clean.

4. While cake is baking, in a small bowl stir together brown sugar and the 2 tablespoons butter until combined. Stir in the 1 tablespoon milk; stir in coconut and, if desired, nuts. Spread topping over warm cake. Broil about 4 inches from heat for 3 to 4 minutes or until golden. Cool in pan on a wire rack for 30 minutes. Serve warm.

Per serving: 295 cal., 13 g total fat (8 g sat. fat), 52 mg chol., 170 mg sodium, 42 g carbo., 1 g fiber, 4 g pro.

New Year's Eve
—Then and Now

For this New Year's Eve, select from two fun and festive menus. Go retro with a mostly '70s-inspired menu that begins with a warm, mellow buttered cranberry drink so popular during that easygoing decade and ends with—what else?—fondue. For something current, choose the second menu. It enjoys a spirited start with a glittering martini and features flavors you might find at a bustling corner bistro. Either menu will be delicious and doable—and a memorable way to toast the New Year.

Crab-Stuffed Chicken, Confetti Rice, and Green Beans
Amandine, pages 138–139

Buttered Cranberry Cocktail

Hot buttered rum was a popular drink in the 1970s. Perhaps you forgot (or were too young to know!) how tasty the smooth hot drink can be! This recipe, also from that decade, features cranberry juice and spices for holiday appeal.

Prep: 15 minutes **Cook:** 15 minutes
Makes: about 17 (6-ounce) servings

- 2 48-ounce bottles cranberry juice (12 cups)
- 1 cup packed brown sugar
- 9 whole cardamom pods, lightly crushed
- 4 inches stick cinnamon
- 1 teaspoon whole allspice
- 1 cup brandy
- ½ cup bourbon
- ⅓ cup butter
    Stick cinnamon (optional)

1. In a Dutch oven combine the cranberry juice and brown sugar; stir until the sugar dissolves. To make a spice bag, cut a double-thick 6-inch square of 100%-cotton cheesecloth; place the cardamom pods, the 4 inches stick cinnamon, and the whole allspice in the center of cheesecloth square. Bring up corners and tie with 100%-cotton kitchen string. Add to cranberry juice mixture. Bring to boiling; reduce heat. Cover and simmer for 15 minutes. Remove from heat. Discard spice bag.

2. Stir in the brandy and bourbon. Serve in small mugs. Add a thin pat of the butter to each serving. If desired, serve with cinnamon stick stirrers.

Per serving: 223 cal., 4 g total fat (2 g sat. fat), 9 mg chol., 34 mg sodium, 36 g carbo., 0 g fiber, 0 g pro.

Rumaki

Those bold chicken livers … that salty bacon … that crunch of chestnuts … that spicy-sweet glaze … yes, everything diners have always loved about Rumaki is right here in this classic recipe.

Prep: 30 minutes **Marinate:** 4 hours
Bake: 15 minutes **Oven:** 425°F
Makes: 24 to 28 appetizers

- 12 ounces chicken livers (about 10 livers)
- 2 tablespoons dry sherry
- 2 tablespoons soy sauce
- 2 tablespoons water
- 1 tablespoon packed brown sugar
- 1 tablespoon cooking oil
- ⅛ teaspoon garlic powder
    Dash ground ginger
- 12 to 14 slices bacon, cut in half crosswise
- 1 8-ounce can sliced water
    chestnuts, drained
    Bottled chutney (optional)

1. Cut livers in half; cut any extra-large livers into thirds. Place liver in a resealable plastic bag set in a deep bowl. For marinade, in a small bowl combine sherry, soy sauce, the water, brown sugar, oil, garlic powder, and ginger; pour over liver. Seal bag; turn to coat livers. Marinate in the refrigerator for 4 to 24 hours, turning bag occasionally.

Rumaki and Buttered Cranberry Cocktail

2. Preheat oven to 425°F. Line a 15×10×1-inch baking pan with foil; set aside. Drain liver, discarding marinade. Wrap a bacon piece around a liver piece and 1 or 2 water chestnut slices. Secure with a wooden toothpick. Place in prepared baking pan. Repeat with remaining bacon, liver, and water chestnuts. Bake about 15 minutes or until bacon is brown and liver is no longer pink, turning once. Serve warm. If desired, serve with chutney.

Per appetizer: 42 cal., 2 g total fat (1 g sat. fat), 53 mg chol., 116 mg sodium, 1 g carbo., 0 g fiber, 4 g pro.

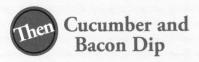 ## Cucumber and Bacon Dip

In recent years, you probably spotted fancy chip-and-dip sets at garage sales and in collectibles shops. When you make this delicious homemade recipe, you'll understand why some dips are worthy of such thoughtful presentations.

Prep: 10 minutes Chill: 30 minutes
Makes: about 2⅔ cups

- 2 cups dairy sour cream
- ½ cup peeled, seeded, and finely chopped cucumber (about ½ of a small cucumber)
- 1 envelope onion soup mix (½ of a 2.2-ounce package)
- 2 tablespoons chopped pimiento (one 2-ounce jar)
- 2 tablespoons lemon juice
- ½ teaspoon Worcestershire sauce
- 4 slices bacon, crisp-cooked and crumbled Assorted vegetable dippers

1. In a medium bowl combine sour cream, cucumber, dry soup mix, pimiento, lemon juice, and Worcestershire sauce. Cover and chill for 30 minutes to 4 hours.

2. Stir in crumbled bacon. Serve with assorted vegetable dippers.

Per 2 tablespoons dip: 55 cal., 5 g total fat (3 g sat. fat), 10 mg chol., 185 mg sodium, 2 g carbo., 0 g fiber, 1 g pro.

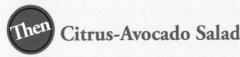 ## Citrus-Avocado Salad

Pomegranate seeds are one of today's happening ingredients, but this gorgeous salad from 1939 proves cooks long ago also appreciated their delightful crunch and jewellike tones. With sparkling dashes of color and bold sparks of citrusy flavor, this salad is a great way to brighten a winter meal.

Start to Finish: 30 minutes Makes: 8 servings

- 4 medium oranges
- 2 ruby red grapefruit
- 4 small ripe avocados, halved, pitted, and peeled
- ¼ cup pomegranate seeds (optional)
- 8 leaves red-leaf lettuce
- 1 recipe Celery Seed Dressing

1. Peel and section oranges and grapefruit, working over a bowl to catch juices; set juices aside. Dice the orange and grapefruit sections.

2. Brush avocado halves with reserved fruit juices. Heap diced orange and grapefruit sections into the avocado halves. If desired, top with pomegranate seeds. Serve each avocado half on a lettuce leaf. Drizzle with Celery Seed Dressing. (Refrigerate any remaining dressing for another use.)

Celery Seed Dressing: In a small bowl, blender, or food processor combine ½ cup sugar, ⅓ cup lemon juice, 1 teaspoon celery seeds, 1 teaspoon dry mustard, 1 teaspoon paprika, and ½ teaspoon salt. With mixer, blender, or food processor running, slowly add ¾ cup salad oil in a thin, steady stream. (This should take 2 to 3 minutes.) Continue mixing, blending, or processing until mixture reaches desired consistency. Makes about 1¼ cups.

Per serving: 335 cal., 27 g total fat (4 g sat. fat), 0 mg chol., 152 mg sodium, 25 g carbo., 5 g fiber, 2 g pro.

 # Crab-Stuffed Chicken

Redolent of crab, laced with a wine-mushroom sauce, and finished with a sheen of rich Swiss cheese, this perennial pleaser was first developed in 1977 and has been starring in elegant "dinner at eight" parties ever since. Serve with Confetti Rice and Green Beans Amadine for a special dinner presentation.

Prep: 45 minutes **Bake:** 35 minutes
Oven: 350°F **Makes:** 8 servings

  8 **skinless, boneless chicken breast halves (about 2½ pounds total)**
  3 **tablespoons butter**
  ¼ **cup all-purpose flour**
  ¾ **cup milk**
  ¾ **cup chicken broth**
  ⅓ **cup dry white wine**
  1 **tablespoon butter**
  1 **cup chopped fresh mushrooms**
  ¼ **cup chopped onion**
  1 **6¼-ounce can crabmeat, drained, flaked, and cartilage removed**
  ½ **cup coarsely crushed saltine crackers (10 crackers)**
  2 **tablespoons snipped fresh parsley**
  ½ **teaspoon salt**
      Dash ground black pepper
  2 **tablespoons butter**
  1 **cup shredded Swiss cheese (4 ounces)**
  ½ **teaspoon paprika**

1. Place each chicken breast half between two pieces of plastic wrap. Using the flat side of a meat mallet and working from the center out, pound chicken to about ⅛-inch thickness. Remove plastic wrap.

2. For the sauce, in a medium saucepan melt the 3 tablespoons butter; stir in flour. Add milk, chicken broth, and wine all at once; cook and stir until thickened and bubbly. Set aside.

3. In a medium skillet melt the 1 tablespoon butter over medium heat. Add mushrooms and onion; cook and stir until tender. Stir in crabmeat, crushed crackers, parsley, salt, and pepper. Stir in 2 tablespoons of the sauce.

4. Preheat oven to 350°F. Top each chicken piece with about ¼ cup of the crab mixture. Fold in sides; roll up. If necessary, secure with wooden toothpicks.

In a large skillet cook the chicken rolls, half at a time, in the 2 tablespoons hot butter until brown on all sides, turning to brown evenly.

5. Place chicken rolls, seam sides down, in a 3-quart rectangular baking dish. Pour remaining sauce over all. Bake, covered, about 35 minutes or until chicken is no longer pink (170°F). Uncover; sprinkle with Swiss cheese and paprika. Bake about 2 minutes more or until cheese melts.

6. Transfer chicken to a platter. Whisk crab mixture in baking dish until smooth; pass with chicken.

Per serving: 368 cal., 16 g total fat (9 g sat. fat), 140 mg chol., 526 mg sodium, 8 g carbo., 0 g fiber, 43 g pro.

 # Confetti Rice

This recipe comes from Best Buffets *cookbook, published in 1974. As its name suggests, this is a festive, colorful way to serve rice.*

Prep: 10 minutes **Cook:** 14 minutes
Stand: 10 minutes **Makes:** 8 side-dish servings

  2 **cups cold water**
  1 **cup uncooked long grain rice**
  1 **teaspoon salt**
  ½ **cup chopped onion**
  ¼ **cup butter or margarine**
  ¾ **cup loose-pack frozen peas**
  ¼ **cup chopped pecans or almonds, toasted**
  8 **cherry tomatoes, quartered**
  ¼ **teaspoon seasoned salt**
  ¼ **teaspoon ground black pepper**

1. In a medium saucepan combine cold water, rice, and the 1 teaspoon salt. Bring to boiling; reduce heat. Simmer, covered, for 14 minutes. Remove from heat. Let stand, covered, for 10 minutes.

2. Meanwhile, in a medium skillet cook onion in hot butter until tender. Add peas and pecans; cook and stir until heated through. Add onion mixture, tomato, seasoned salt, and pepper to hot rice; toss gently to combine.

Per serving: 176 cal., 8 g total fat (4 g sat. fat), 15 mg chol., 398 mg sodium, 23 g carbo., 2 g fiber, 3 g pro.

Green Beans Amandine

This oldie but goodie never really went out of style. Diners have been enjoying its buttery, nutty, lemony flavors for decades.

Start to Finish: 25 minutes
Makes: 8 side-dish servings

20   ounces whole fresh green beans or two
       9-ounce packages frozen cut green beans
 3   tablespoons butter or margarine
 ⅓   cup slivered almonds
 1   tablespoon lemon juice
 ¼   teaspoon salt

1. In a covered large saucepan cook fresh green beans in a small amount of boiling salted water for 10 to 15 minutes or until crisp-tender. (Or cook frozen beans according to package directions.) Drain; keep warm.

2. Meanwhile, in a small saucepan melt butter over medium heat. Add almonds; cook and stir until golden. Remove from heat; stir in lemon juice and salt. Stir almond mixture into beans.

Per serving: 93 cal., 7 g total fat (3 g sat. fat), 11 mg chol., 107 mg sodium, 6 g carbo., 3 g fiber, 3 g pro.

NEW YEAR'S EVE—

Buttered Cranberry Cocktail

Rumaki or Cucumber and Bacon Dip

Citrus-Avocado Salad

Crab-Stuffed Chicken

Confetti Rice

Green Beans Amandine

Chocolate-Butter Mint Fondue

Crab-Stuffed Chicken, Confetti Rice, and Green Beans Amandine

Bourbon-Infused Honey (center)

 **Chocolate-Butter Mint Fondue**

Some like it … sweet! If you're in that crowd, you'll love this dessert fondue direct from Snacks and Appetizers *cookbook published in 1974.*

Start to Finish: 20 minutes **Makes:** 6 to 8 servings

  1 **14-ounce can sweetened condensed milk**
  1 **7-ounce jar marshmallow creme**
  1 **6-ounce package semisweet chocolate pieces (1 cup)**
  ⅓ **cup crushed butter mints**
  ¼ **cup milk**
  2 **tablespoons crème de cacao (optional)**
     Fresh strawberries, pineapple chunks, banana slices, cubed pound cake, cubed angel food cake, pirouette cookies, and/or shortbread cookies

1. In a medium saucepan combine the sweetened condensed milk, marshmallow creme, chocolate pieces, and butter mints. Cook and stir over low heat until chocolate melts. Stir in milk and, if desired, crème de cacao.

2. Transfer to a fondue pot; place over a fondue burner. Spear fruit or cake pieces on fondue forks; dip into fondue mixture, swirling to coat.

Per serving: 481 cal., 13 g total fat (8 g sat. fat), 23 mg chol., 118 mg sodium, 90 g carbo., 2 g fiber, 8 g pro.

 Bourbon-Infused Honey

Great appetizers don't have to be difficult! Set out a jar of this sweet nectar, inviting guests to drizzle a little on top of their cheese and crackers. (It's especially good with blue cheese!) For a little something extra to nibble on, serve with apples, gourmet olives, and a selection of deli meats.

Prep: 5 minutes **Cook:** 5 minutes
Cool: 1 hour **Makes:** 1 cup

  1 **cup honey**
  1 **large bay leaf**
  ¼ **cup bourbon**

1. In a small saucepan combine honey and bay leaf; heat over medium heat just until mixture bubbles around the edges. Reduce heat to low and cook for 5 minutes. Remove from heat. Stir in bourbon. Let stand about 1 hour or until cooled. Discard bay leaf. Transfer honey to a jar. Store in the refrigerator for up to 5 days.

Per tablespoon: 73 cal., 0 g total fat (0 g sat. fat), 0 mg chol., 1 mg sodium, 17 g carbo., 0 g fiber, 0 g pro.

 **Cranberry Cosmopolitan**

Cocktails have definitely made a comeback. You'll want to serve this in a crystal-clear martini glass to show off its color and sparkle. Double, triple, or quadruple the recipe if serving several people.

Start to Finish: 5 minutes **Makes:** 1 serving

   Ice cubes
3 tablespoons vodka
1 tablespoon orange liqueur
2 teaspoons frozen cranberry
   juice concentrate
1 teaspoon lime juice
   Orange peel twist (optional)
   Fresh cranberry (optional)

1. Fill a cocktail shaker with ice cubes; add vodka, orange liqueur, cranberry juice concentrate, and lime juice. Cover and shake vigorously. Strain into a martini glass. If desired, garnish with orange peel twist and a cranberry.

Per serving: 170 cal., 0 g total fat (0 g sat. fat), 0 mg chol., 1 mg sodium, 11 g carbo., 0 g fiber, 0 g pro.

 **Mixed Greens with Cardamom-Curry Dressing**

Make this intriguing, crowd-pleasing dressing your "house dressing" for your parties this winter.

Start to Finish: 10 minutes **Makes:** 12 servings

1 8-ounce carton dairy sour cream
½ cup grapefruit juice or ruby red
   grapefruit juice
1 tablespoon honey
1 teaspoon curry powder
1 teaspoon ground cardamom
½ teaspoon ground cinnamon
¼ to ½ teaspoon ground black pepper
⅓ cup salad oil
20 cups mesclun or other torn mixed
   salad greens
   Freshly ground black pepper (optional)

1. For dressing, in a blender or food processor combine sour cream, grapefruit juice, honey, curry, cardamom, cinnamon, and the ¼ to ½ teaspoon pepper. Cover and blend or process until combined. With blender or processor running, slowly add oil in a steady stream until mixture is thickened. Serve immediately, or cover and chill until ready to serve (up to 3 days).

2. Before serving, stir dressing to combine. Serve with salad greens. If desired, sprinkle with additional freshly ground pepper.

Per serving: 128 cal., 12 g total fat (4 g sat. fat), 10 mg chol., 15 mg sodium, 5 g carbo., 0 g fiber, 1 g pro.

Mixed Greens with Cardamom-Curry Dressing

NEW YEAR'S EVE— **Now**

Cranberry Cosmopolitans

Assorted Cheeses with Bourbon-Infused Honey

Mixed Greens with Cardamom-Curry Dressing

Prosciutto-Stuffed Chicken Breasts with Pears

Parmesan Risotto

Chocolate Crème Brûlée

Prosciutto-Stuffed Chicken Breasts with Pears and Parmesan Risotto

1. Preheat oven to 375°F. Grease a 15×10×1-inch baking pan. Set aside.

2. Using your fingers, gently separate the chicken skin from the meat of the breasts, leaving the skin attached along one side; set aside.

3. For stuffing, in a medium bowl combine semi-soft cheese, fontina cheese, Parmesan cheese, and prosciutto. Divide cheese mixture among chicken breast halves, spreading cheese mixture between the skin and meat of each breast half.

4. Place chicken, bone sides down, in prepared baking pan. Brush chicken with the 2 tablespoons melted butter. Bake for 45 to 55 minutes or until chicken is no longer pink (170°F).

5. Meanwhile, in a very large skillet melt the 1 tablespoon butter over medium heat. Add pear slices; cook and stir for 2 to 3 minutes or just until tender. In a small bowl whisk together apple juice and cornstarch. Add to pear slices in skillet. Cook and stir until thickened and bubbly. Cook and stir for 2 minutes more. Remove from heat. Stir in sage. To serve, spoon pear mixture over chicken breasts.

Per serving: 522 cal., 32 g total fat (14 g sat. fat), 152 mg chol., 356 mg sodium, 18 g carbo., 3 g fiber, 39 g pro.

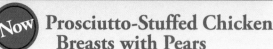

Prosciutto-Stuffed Chicken Breasts with Pears

Here's a totally up-to-date take on stuffed chicken breasts. A little prosciutto adds a lot of flavor, while the combination of cheeses provides richness. The pears complement the cheeses beautifully while adding seasonal appeal.

Prep: 30 minutes **Bake:** 45 minutes
Oven: 375°F **Makes:** 8 servings

- 8 medium chicken breast halves with bone (about 4 pounds total)
- 1 5.2-ounce container semisoft cheese with herbs
- 2 ounces fontina or mozzarella cheese, shredded (½ cup)
- ¼ cup grated Parmesan cheese
- ¼ cup chopped prosciutto (about 1½ ounces)
- 2 tablespoons butter or margarine, melted
- 1 tablespoon butter or margarine
- 4 medium pears, cored and thinly sliced
- 1 cup apple juice or apple cider
- 1 tablespoon cornstarch
- 2 teaspoons snipped fresh sage

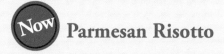

Parmesan Risotto

If you think risotto is high maintenance for a dinner party, try this rendition. Unlike many risottos, this version doesn't require constant stirring. For bigger dinner parties, make two batches of risotto.

Prep: 5 minutes **Cook:** 25 minutes
Stand: 5 minutes **Makes:** 3 or 4 side-dish servings

- ⅓ cup chopped onion
- 1 tablespoon butter or margarine
- ⅔ cup uncooked Arborio or long grain rice
- 2 cups water
- 1 teaspoon instant chicken bouillon granules
- 1 cup loose-pack frozen peas (optional)
- ¼ cup grated Parmesan or Romano cheese

1. In a medium saucepan cook onion in hot butter until tender; add rice. Cook and stir for 2 minutes more. Carefully stir in the water, bouillon granules, and a dash of *ground black pepper*. Bring to boiling; reduce heat. Cover and simmer for 20 minutes (do not lift cover).

2. Remove saucepan from heat. If desired, stir in peas. Let stand, covered, for 5 minutes. Rice should be tender but slightly firm, and the mixture should be creamy. (If necessary, stir in a little water to reach desired consistency.) Stir in Parmesan cheese.

Per serving: 179 cal., 6 g total fat (3 g sat. fat), 10 mg chol., 571 mg sodium, 25 g carbo., 0 g fiber, 6 g pro.

Chocolate Crème Brûlée

Crème brûlée became a favorite bistro dessert in the 1990s, and it wasn't long before some chocolate-loving food editor created a version chock-full of chocolate! Try this for a sophisticated finale to your evening.

Prep: 25 minutes **Bake:** 35 minutes
Cool: 1 hour **Oven:** 325°F **Makes:** 6 servings

2⅔ **cups whipping cream**
  4 **ounces semisweet or bittersweet**
     chocolate, chopped
  6 **egg yolks, slightly beaten**
  ⅓ **cup sugar**
1¼ **teaspoons vanilla**
  ¼ **teaspoon salt**
  3 **tablespoons sugar**

1. Preheat oven to 325°F. In a medium heavy saucepan combine 1 cup of the whipping cream and the chocolate. Heat and stir over low heat until chocolate is melted. Remove from heat. Gradually add the remaining 1⅔ cups whipping cream, whisking until well mixed.

2. In a large bowl whisk together egg yolks, the ⅓ cup sugar, the vanilla, and salt. Gradually whisk the cream mixture into the egg yolk mixture.

3. Place eight 6-ounce ramekins or custard cups into a roasting pan. Set pan on the oven rack. Pour the egg mixture into the ramekins or custard cups. Pour enough boiling water into the roasting pan around the ramekins or custard cups to cover the outside bottom half of the dishes. Bake for 35 to 40 minutes or until set. Transfer dishes from pan with water to a wire rack. Let cool slightly.

4. Place the 3 tablespoons sugar in a small heavy skillet or saucepan. Cook over medium-high heat just until sugar begins to melt, shaking skillet occasionally to heat sugar evenly. Do not stir. Reduce heat to low. Cook until sugar is melted and golden (watch closely; sugar melts quickly). After sugar begins to melt and mixture bubbles, use a wooden spoon to stir as necessary. Drizzle melted sugar in a zigzag pattern over custard in ramekins. Cool for 1 hour before serving.

Per serving: 583 cal., 50 g total fat (30 g sat. fat), 351 mg chol., 146 mg sodium, 31 g carbo., 1 g fiber, 6 g pro.

Chocolate Crème Brûlée

Chalet Cookie Church

Over the years, the editors, food stylists, and Test Kitchen pros from the Better Homes and Gardens® publications have combined their talents to create many kinds of fanciful structures made from gingerbread and other kinds of cookie dough—everything from ornate Victorian homes and cookie villages to humble barnyards, churches, and manger scenes. These projects have garnered many fans! In fact, the editors of *Christmas Cookies*® magazine love hearing from home bakers, many of whom send pictures of their creative ideas. Customize this all-new Chalet Cookie Church—created for this special issue—to your own style of decorating.

Chalet Cookie Church, page 146

Chalet Cookie Church

Rolling and cutting dough pieces: 1 hour
Decorating: 2 hours
Assembly: 1 hour
Drying: 3 hours

Bake: 9 minutes per batch **Oven:** 375°F/300°F
Makes: 1 cookie church

- 2 recipes Sugar Cookie Dough (page 94)
- 30 fruit-flavored rectangular hard candies, unwrapped (about half of a 14-ounce bag)
- 2 recipes Royal Icing (page 94)
   Gel or paste food coloring* in moss green, red, yellow, and brown
   Small fresh thyme sprigs (optional)
   Crisp baked crackers, broken into pieces
   Mixed nuts
   Creme-filled pirouette cookies
   Powdered sugar (optional)
   Small fresh rosemary sprigs (optional)
   Hazelnuts (optional)

Equipment you will need:
   Parchment paper
   Chalet Cookie Church pattern pieces (see page 156), enlarged to 200% and covered with clear adhesive plastic
   Foil
   Pastry bags with couplers and small star, round, and ribbon tips*
   Small clean artist's paintbrushes
   White batting (optional)

1. Rolling, cutting, and baking dough: Prepare dough for Sugar Cookie Star Cutouts as directed. Divide dough into 8 equal portions; chill dough as directed. Preheat oven to 375°F. Transfer one portion of the dough to a sheet of parchment paper cut to fit a baking sheet; roll the dough to ⅛- to ¼-inch thickness. Arrange some of the pattern pieces on top of dough, leaving at least 1 inch of dough between pieces. Cut around the pattern pieces with a sharp knife. Remove excess scraps of dough; set aside for rerolling. When making the wall pieces, cut out the indicated openings for windows and doors, carefully removing each of the window cutouts in one piece. Cut window cutouts in half lengthwise and place on parchment (these will be the window shutters). Roll the remaining dough (and reroll the scraps) to have enough dough to cut additional pieces. When

cookie sheet is full, bake for 9 to 11 minutes or until edges are light brown and centers are firm. If cookie cutouts spread during baking, carefully trim edges as necessary while baked cookies are still hot. Cool on cookie sheet for 1 minute. Transfer cookie pieces and parchment to wire racks; cool completely. Repeat rolling, cutting, and baking until all the pattern pieces are made.

2. Making candy windows: Preheat oven to 300°F. Line a cookie sheet with foil. For candy windowpanes, place fruit-flavored rectangular candies in a heavy resealable plastic bag; seal bag. Using the flat side of a meat mallet or a rolling pin, coarsely crush candies. Spread crushed candies on prepared cookie sheet, mixing colors to create a stained glass appearance and make a 9×7½-inch rectangle. Bake for 5 to 8 minutes or until candies are melted together. Cool on cookie sheet on a wire rack for 5 minutes or just until candy surface is dry to the touch but still soft. Use a long sharp knife to deeply score the candy lengthwise into five 1½-inch-wide rows of windows. Score three of the rows into 4½-inch lengths and score the other two rows into 3-inch lengths. Cool completely. When needed, break windows apart at scored lines and peel from foil.

3. Decorating: Prepare Royal Icing. To decorate church pieces, tint about ¼ cup of the icing with green food coloring. Add water, a few drops at a time, until icing is the consistency of paint. Using a small paintbrush, paint a thin coating of green icing on the church shutters and doors; set aside to dry. Tint about 2 tablespoons of the icing with red food coloring. Add water, a few drops at a time, until icing is the consistency of paint. Using a small paintbrush, paint a 1½×2-inch rectangle in the center of each of the square steeple pieces; set aside to dry. Tint about 1 cup of the icing yellow; place in a pastry bag*** fitted with a coupler and a small round tip. Line work surface with parchment paper; set all of the church pieces out on parchment. To attach candy windowpanes to church, turn church walls over on work surface so the front side is down. Use small lines or dots of piped yellow icing to attach the candy windows to the cookie walls, covering the window openings. Let dry for 15 minutes. Carefully turn the walls over so the front sides face up. To decorate the fronts of the windows, use the small round tip to pipe more yellow icing onto the edges of windows and make crisscross patterns on the windows and on the square steeple pieces.

Fit a ribbon tip on the coupler on the pastry bag of yellow icing; pipe yellow beams across front and back church walls. If desired, attach thyme sprigs to beams while frosting is still wet.** To make little nails on shutters and doors, tint a tiny amount of the icing brown with food coloring. Add water, a few drops at a time, until icing is the consistency of paint. Use a clean artist's paintbrush to make dots of brown icing on the shutters and doors. If desired, paint a brown cross above church door.

4. Assembling walls: Assemble church on a large tray or cutting board. To assemble, have some heavy tumblers or glass measuring cups on hand to support church walls. Fit a pastry bag with a coupler and a small star tip. Place some white icing in pastry bag. Stand up the front of the church and line up with short side of church base. Hold in place with tumblers. Pipe icing onto the bottom of inside edge of the church front. Attach it to the base; stand up a side wall of church on top of the base. Pipe icing onto the edges of side wall that will touch front and base. Attach the side wall, using the tumblers or measuring cups to hold pieces in place. Continue by piping icing onto the edges of the other side wall of the church; hold in place with tumblers or measuring cups. Next stand up the back wall of the church. Pipe some icing onto all inside edges of the back wall. Press back wall against the edges of the side walls and base. Hold the back wall in place with a tumbler or measuring cup. Place doors inside the door openings and pipe a line of frosting to hold in place. Let these four walls dry for 1 hour before attaching roof. Remove the tumblers or measuring cups when dry.

5. Attaching the roof: Pipe plenty of icing along the top edges of one-half of the church. Set one roof piece on top of icing; press down gently to adhere to icing. Prop up lower edge of roof with a tumbler or measuring cup of appropriate height. Repeat with other half of the roof. Pipe a line of icing down center of roof where the two roof pieces join.

6. Attaching the steeple: Assemble the steeple front, sides, and back pieces, one at a time, on top of the roof. Pipe icing at corners and edges where they meet the roof. To assemble steeple roof, pipe a line of icing along edges to join. If needed, place a ball of paper toweling or foil inside the steeple to hold up the center of the roof. Dry for 1 hour.

7. Attaching the shingles: Pipe zigzag lines of icing along the bottom third of a roof side, making sure zigzag lines are close together. Arrange rows of broken cracker pieces on the wet icing, starting with the bottom edge and working toward the top. Continue piping more icing and adding rows of broken crackers until roof side is covered. Repeat on the other side of roof and finally on the steeple roof.

8. Decorating the church: Pipe decorative zigzag edging along all seams and front edges of roof. Attach mixed nuts to bottom edges of walls using some icing. Attach painted shutters to the window edges with more icing. Attach pirouette cookies to front door frame. Use a small serrated knife to gently saw some pirouette cookies into small pieces for a cross. Join them together using icing. Let dry completely before attaching to top of steeple with more icing. Let completed cookie church dry for at least 1 hour.

9. Optional finishing touches: If desired, sift powdered sugar over church for a snowy effect. If desired, place a piece of white batting on the cutting board or tray around the church to resemble snow. If desired, for trees, stand up small sprigs of rosemary in the batting around church.** If desired, make a path to the church with hazelnuts.

*Note: Look for pastry bags, couplers, tips, and gel and paste food coloring in the hobby section of local department stores or the cake decorating section of hobby stores.

**Note: Fresh thyme and rosemary will last only for a short time before wilting. If you choose to use the thyme, it can be added immediately before displaying the church. Attach with a small amount of fresh icing.

***Tip: If you don't own pastry bags, use a heavy-duty resealable plastic bag. Cut a small hole in one corner of the bag and fit with desired decorating tip. Fill bag with icing and pipe as directed.

Terrific Party
and Potluck Dishes

Christmas parties and gatherings are the best time to pull out all the stops with exceptional recipes. This chapter features some of the most beautiful-but-doable dishes that appeared in Better Homes and Gardens® publications over the years, plus a selection of brand-new recipes created just for this busy season. Serve the ever-favorite Coq au Vin Rosettes or Three-Cheese Ziti and Smoked Chicken Casserole when you want to host a stylish party. And thanks to dishes such as Potatoes with Caramelized Onions and Ham Gratin, you'll never be at a loss when friends say, "Please bring a dish."

Potatoes with Caramelized Onions and Ham Gratin, page 152

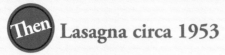

Then Lasagna circa 1953

There's no shortage of lasagna recipes in the food world, but this classic version has been a top-of-the-line favorite for over 50 years. Not many recipes have that kind of staying power!

Prep: 40 minutes **Bake:** 35 minutes
Stand: 10 minutes **Oven:** 375°F
Makes: 12 servings

- 1 **pound bulk Italian sausage**
- 2 **14½-ounce cans diced tomatoes, undrained**
- 1 **12-ounce can tomato paste**
- 1 **tablespoon dried basil, crushed**
- 2 **cloves garlic, minced**
- 1 **teaspoon salt**
- 8 **dried lasagna noodles**
- 3 **cups ricotta cheese**
- ½ **cup grated Parmesan cheese**
- 2 **tablespoons dried parsley flakes**
- 2 **eggs, beaten**
- ¼ **teaspoon salt**
- ¼ **teaspoon black pepper**
- 4 **cups shredded mozzarella cheese (1 pound)**

1. In a large skillet cook sausage until brown; drain off fat. Add undrained tomatoes, tomato paste, basil, garlic, and the 1 teaspoon salt to sausage in skillet. Bring to boiling; reduce heat. Cover and simmer for 5 minutes, stirring once. Meanwhile, cook lasagna noodles according to package directions. Drain; rinse and drain again.

2. In a medium bowl combine ricotta cheese, Parmesan cheese, parsley flakes, eggs, the ¼ teaspoon salt, and the pepper; set aside. Set aside ½ cup of the mozzarella for topping.

3. Preheat oven to 375°F. Place half of the cooked noodles in a 3-quart rectangular baking dish; spread with half of the ricotta cheese mixture. Sprinkle with half of the remaining mozzarella cheese and top with half of the sausage mixture. Repeat layers.

4. Bake about 25 minutes or until heated through. Sprinkle with the ½ cup mozzarella cheese. Bake for 10 minutes. Let stand for 10 minutes before serving.

Per serving: 454 cal., 27 g total fat (14 g sat. fat), 125 mg chol., 932 mg sodium, 23 g carbo., 2 g fiber, 27 g pro.

Lasagna circa 1953

Now Red Pepper Lasagna

While Italian-American styles of lasagna often call on cheese for luscious richness, traditional Italian styles often rely on a creamy white sauce.

Prep: 50 minutes **Bake:** 35 minutes
Stand: 20 minutes **Oven:** 350°F **Makes:** 8 servings

- 1 **tablespoon olive oil**
- 1 **15-ounce jar roasted red sweet pepper, drained and cut into thin strips**
- 1 **28-ounce can crushed tomatoes**
- 2 **tablespoons dried basil, crushed**
- 4 **cloves garlic, minced**
- ¾ **teaspoon ground black pepper**
- ½ **teaspoon salt**
- 8 **ounces Italian sausage, browned and drained (optional)**
- ⅓ **cup butter or margarine**
- ⅓ **cup all-purpose flour**
- ½ **teaspoon ground nutmeg**
- ½ **teaspoon salt**
- 3 **cups milk**
- 12 **no-boil lasagna noodles**
- 1¼ **cups finely shredded Parmesan cheese (5 ounces)**

1. For the sauce, in a large saucepan heat olive oil over medium heat. Add roasted red sweet pepper; cook for 1 minute. Stir in tomatoes, basil, garlic, black pepper, and ½ teaspoon salt. Bring to boiling; reduce heat. Simmer, uncovered, for 20 minutes, stirring often. Set aside to cool. If desired, stir in cooked sausage.

2. For white sauce, in a medium saucepan melt butter over medium heat. Stir in flour, nutmeg, and ½ teaspoon salt until smooth. Add milk all at once. Cook and stir until thickened and bubbly. Set aside.

3. Preheat oven to 350°F. To assemble, grease the bottom of a 3-quart rectangular baking dish. Cover bottom of prepared baking dish with 3 lasagna noodles. Spread about 1 cup of the sweet pepper sauce over the pasta. Top with ¾ cup of the white sauce, spreading evenly; sprinkle with about ¼ cup of the Parmesan cheese. Repeat layers three more times Be sure the top layer of noodles is completely covered with sauce. Sprinkle with the remaining Parmesan cheese.

4. Bake, uncovered, for 35 to 40 minutes or until bubbly and light brown on top. Let stand for 20 minutes before serving. If desired, garnish with tomato wedges and herb sprigs.

Per serving: 321 cal., 15 g total fat (8 g sat. fat), 36 mg chol., 728 mg sodium, 34 g carbo., 3 g fiber, 14 g pro.

Three-Cheese Ziti and Smoked Chicken Casserole

If you don't consider a casserole a high-class dish, take a look at this one.

Prep: 25 minutes **Bake:** 25 minutes
Stand: 10 minutes **Oven:** 375°F **Makes:** 6 servings

Butter
12 **ounces dried cut ziti**
3 **tablespoons butter or margarine**
2 **cloves garlic, minced**
3 **tablespoons all-purpose flour**
¼ **teaspoon salt**
¼ **teaspoon ground white pepper**
3½ **cups milk**
8 **ounces Asiago cheese, finely shredded**
  (1½ cups)
4 **ounces fontina cheese, finely shredded**
  (1 cup)
2 **ounces blue cheese, crumbled (½ cup)**

2 **cups chopped smoked chicken or**
  shredded purchased roasted chicken
⅓ **cup panko (Japanese-style) bread crumbs**
  or fine dry bread crumbs
2 **teaspoons white truffle oil or melted butter**

1. Preheat oven to 375°F. Butter a 2-quart baking dish; set aside. Cook pasta according to package directions. Drain pasta; return to hot saucepan. Cover and keep warm.

2. Meanwhile, in a medium saucepan melt the 3 tablespoons butter over medium heat. Add garlic; cook for 30 seconds. Stir in flour, salt, and white pepper. Add milk all at once. Cook and stir until thickened and bubbly. Add Asiago, fontina, and blue cheeses, stirring until melted. Add chicken, stirring to combine.

3. Pour cheese mixture over cooked ziti; gently toss to coat. Transfer mixture to the prepared baking dish. In a small bowl combine panko crumbs and truffle oil. Sprinkle crumb mixture evenly over mixture in baking dish.

4. Bake about 25 minutes or until bubbly and light brown. Let stand for 10 minutes before serving.

Per serving: 753 cal., 39 g total fat (22 g sat. fat), 141 mg chol., 953 mg sodium, 56 g carbo., 2 g fiber, 43 g pro.

Three-Cheese Ziti and Smoked Chicken Casserole

Potatoes with Caramelized Onions and Ham Gratin

Potatoes with Caramelized Onions and Ham Gratin

Scalloped potatoes are always a welcome addition to the party table. Update the dish with caramelized onions, white cheddar cheese, and just a little ham for flavor.

Prep: 50 minutes **Bake:** 1 hour
Stand: 15 minutes **Oven:** 350°F
Makes: 6 main-dish or 10 to 12 side-dish servings

- 1 tablespoon olive oil
- 1 tablespoon butter
- 2 large yellow onions, peeled and cut into thin wedges
- 1½ cups whipping cream
- ½ cup milk
- 2 tablespoons snipped fresh sage or 1 teaspoon dried sage, crushed
- 3 cloves garlic, minced
- 1 teaspoon salt
- ¼ teaspoon ground black pepper
- 3 pounds Yukon gold or other yellow-flesh potatoes, thinly sliced (about 8 cups)
- 8 ounces thinly sliced cooked ham, cut into bite-size strips (1½ cups)
- 8 ounces aged white cheddar cheese, shredded (2 cups)

1. For caramelized onions, in a large skillet heat oil and butter over medium heat. Stir in onion wedges; cook, uncovered, about 20 minutes or until onion is tender, stirring frequently. (If necessary, reduce heat to medium-low to prevent overbrowning before onion is tender.) Increase heat to medium-high and cook about 5 minutes more or until onion is golden, stirring frequently. Remove from heat. Set aside.

2. In a medium bowl stir together whipping cream, milk, sage, garlic, salt, and pepper. Set aside.

3. Preheat oven to 350°F. Lightly grease a 3-quart rectangular baking dish. Arrange half of the potato in the prepared dish, overlapping as necessary. Sprinkle with ham and caramelized onion. Sprinkle with half of the white cheddar cheese. Layer remaining potato over cheese. Pour cream mixture over potato and top with remaining cheese.

4. Bake for 60 to 65 minutes or until top is golden and potato is tender. Cover and let stand for 15 minutes before serving.

Per main-dish serving: 631 cal., 43 g total fat (25 g sat. fat), 150 mg chol., 1,175 mg sodium, 41 g carbo., 4 g fiber, 22 g pro.

Citrus Corned Beef Sandwiches

If your New Year's Day festivities are more about bowl games than elegant brunches, make these pleasing party sandwiches. Serve with coleslaw, potato salad, and an array of chips and dips. (Cold beer tastes great with these too!)

Prep: 30 minutes **Cook:** Low 8 hours, High 4 hours
Makes: 8 sandwiches

- 1 2- to 3-pound corned beef brisket with spice packet
- 1 cup water
- ¼ cup Dijon-style mustard
- ½ teaspoon finely shredded orange peel
- ⅔ cup orange juice
- 2 tablespoons all-purpose flour
- 8 kaiser rolls, split
- 8 thin slices Muenster cheese (about 6 ounces)

1. Trim fat from meat. Sprinkle contents of spice packet over brisket; rub in with your fingers. Place brisket in a 3½- or 4-quart slow cooker. In a small bowl combine the water and Dijon mustard; pour over brisket. Cover and cook on low-heat setting for 8 to 10 hours or on high-heat setting for 4 to 5 hours. Remove meat; cover to keep warm. Strain juices, reserving liquid; discard any solids.

2. For orange sauce, in a small saucepan whisk together orange peel, orange juice, and flour. Gradually stir ½ cup of the reserved cooking juices into the mixture in the saucepan. Cook and stir until thickened and bubbly. Cook and stir for 1 minute more. Remove from heat.

3. To serve, preheat broiler. Scrape any whole spices from surface of brisket. Thinly slice meat across the grain. Arrange rolls, cut sides up, on a very large baking sheet. Broil 4 inches from heat for 1 to 2 minutes or until toasted. Remove roll tops from baking sheet. Place sliced meat on bottom halves of rolls. Drizzle about 2 tablespoons of the orange sauce over the meat on each roll. Top with cheese. Broil for 1 to 2 minutes more or until cheese melts. Add roll tops.

Per sandwich: 463 cal., 22 g total fat (8 g sat. fat), 78 mg chol., 1,383 mg sodium, 35 g carbo., 1 g fiber, 29 g pro.

Coq au Vin Rosettes

For a delightful one-dish meal, the sophisticated flavors of coq au vin are rolled into pasta rosettes.

Prep: 35 minutes **Bake:** 35 minutes **Oven:** 325°F
Makes: 8 servings (16 rosettes)

- 2 tablespoons butter or margarine
- 3 cups sliced fresh mushrooms (8 ounces)
- ½ cup chopped onion
- 8 skinless, boneless chicken breast halves (2 to 2½ pounds total), cut into 1-inch pieces
- ¾ cup dry white wine
- ½ teaspoon dried tarragon, crushed
- ½ teaspoon ground white pepper
- ⅛ teaspoon salt
- 8 dried lasagna noodles
- 1 8-ounce package cream cheese, cut up
- ½ cup dairy sour cream
- 2 tablespoons all-purpose flour
- ½ cup half-and-half, light cream, or milk
- 1 cup shredded Gruyère cheese (4 ounces)
- 1 cup shredded Muenster cheese (4 ounces)

1. Preheat oven to 325°F. In a large skillet melt butter over medium-high heat. Add mushrooms and onion; cook for 4 to 5 minutes or until tender, stirring occasionally. Add chicken, wine, tarragon, white pepper, and salt. Bring just to boiling; reduce heat. Cover and simmer for 5 minutes, stirring once. Remove from heat.

2. Meanwhile, cook lasagna noodles according to package directions. Halve noodles lengthwise. Curl noodle halves into 2½-inch diameter rings; place noodle rings, cut sides down, in a 3-quart rectangular baking dish. Using a slotted spoon, spoon chicken mixture into center of noodle rings, reserving liquid in skillet. Add cream cheese to reserved liquid; heat and stir just until cream cheese is melted.

3. Stir together sour cream and flour; stir in half-and-half. Add the sour cream mixture and cheeses to the cream cheese mixture in skillet. Cook and stir over medium heat until thickened and bubbly. Spoon cheese mixture over rings in baking dish. Bake, covered, about 35 minutes or until heated through.

Per serving (2 rosettes): 731 cal., 32 g total fat (18 g sat. fat), 249 mg chol., 494 mg sodium, 22 g carbo., 1 g fiber, 83 g pro.

 **Chile-Cheese Enchiladas**

This dish from the 1970s amazed a recent taste panel at the Better Homes and Gardens® Test Kitchen. While the ingredients seem basic, they add up to a surprisingly yummy dish.

Prep: 30 minutes **Bake:** 20 minutes
Stand: 5 minutes **Oven:** 425°F **Makes:** 6 servings

3½ cups shredded Monterey Jack cheese
       (14 ounces)
¾   cup chopped onion
12 6- to 7-inch flour tortillas
¼   cup butter or margarine
¼   cup all-purpose flour
2   cups chicken broth
1   8-ounce carton dairy sour cream
1   4-ounce can diced jalapeño pepper,
       drained
1   recipe Spicy Salsa

1. Preheat oven to 425°F. Place ¼ cup of the cheese and 1 tablespoon of onion on each tortilla; roll up. Place tortillas, seam sides down, in a 3-quart rectangular baking dish or divide between two 1½-quart rectangular baking dishes.

2. In medium saucepan melt butter over medium heat; stir in flour. Add chicken broth all at once; cook and stir until mixture is thickened and bubbly. Remove saucepan from heat. Stir in sour cream and pepper. Pour sour cream sauce over rolled tortillas in baking dish. Bake, covered, for 20 minutes.

3. Sprinkle remaining ½ cup Monterey Jack cheese on top of tortillas; let stand for 5 minutes. Serve with Spicy Salsa.

Spicy Salsa: In a small bowl stir together 1 medium tomato, seeded and finely chopped; ½ cup finely chopped onion; 1 fresh jalapeño chile pepper (see note, page 11), seeded and finely chopped; ¼ cup tomato juice; and ½ teaspoon salt.

Per serving: 516 cal., 31 g total fat (18 g sat. fat), 84 mg chol.,
1,534 mg sodium, 33 g carbo., 2 g fiber, 25 g pro.

 **Verde Chicken Enchiladas**

In the 1970s, when the Cheesy Green Enchiladas dish was created, food lovers had difficulty finding Mexican ingredients. Times sure have changed! This casserole takes advantage of the abundance of terrific Mexican-style products available today.

Prep: 35 minutes **Bake:** 30 minutes
Oven: 350°F **Makes:** 6 servings

1   18-ounce tub refrigerated taco sauce with
       shredded chicken
8   ounces asadero, queso quesadilla, or
       Monterey Jack cheese, shredded (2 cups)
⅓   cup thinly sliced green onion
1   16-ounce jar green salsa
12 6-inch corn tortillas
       Assorted toppers (such as purchased
       salsa, dairy sour cream, guacamole,
       shredded lettuce, chopped tomato,
       and/or sliced ripe olives) (optional)

1. Preheat oven to 350°F. In a large bowl combine chicken, half of the cheese, and the green onion.

2. Spread ¼ cup of the green salsa in the bottom of a 3-quart rectangular baking dish. In a small saucepan heat the remaining green salsa until warm. Pour the warm salsa into a pie plate or shallow bowl. Dip one of the tortillas in warm salsa; fill with about ¼ cup of the chicken mixture, spooning chicken mixture just below the center of tortilla. Roll up tortilla and place, seam side down, in baking dish. Repeat with remaining tortillas and remaining chicken mixture. Pour any remaining warm salsa over enchiladas. Sprinkle with remaining cheese.

3. Tent with foil and bake for 30 to 35 minutes or until heated through. If desired, serve with assorted toppers.

Per serving: 364 cal., 12 g total fat (6 g sat. fat), 71 mg chol.,
1,317 mg sodium, 41 g carbo., 5 g fiber, 21 g pro.

Verde Chicken Enchiladas

Chalet Cookie Church Patterns (continued from page 147)

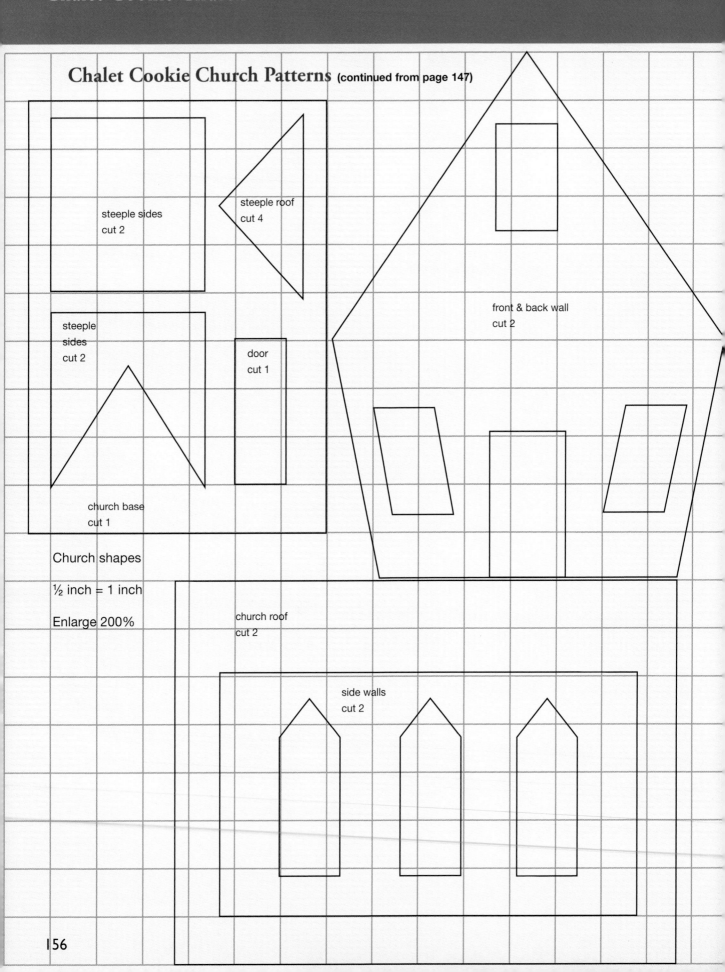

steeple sides
cut 2

steeple roof
cut 4

steeple
sides
cut 2

door
cut 1

church base
cut 1

Church shapes

½ inch = 1 inch

Enlarge 200%

front & back wall
cut 2

church roof
cut 2

side walls
cut 2

A

Almonds
  Almond-Cinnamon Cookies, 98
  Apricot-Almond Crunch Pie, 80
  Green Beans Amandine, 139
  Raspberry-Almond Rolls, 75
  Raspberry-Almond Tassies, 110
  White Christmas Cherry-Almond Fudge, 116
Appetizers. *See also* Dips and Spreads
  Bridge Party Mix, 122
  Calypso Shrimp Skewers, 48
  cheese selections, 35
  crudités, preparing and arranging, 41
  Golden Cheese Wheel, 45
  Herbed Leek Tart, 44
  Holiday Shrimp Rounds, 48
  Party Nachos, 46
  Phyllo-Wrapped Hazelnut and Brie, 46
  Rumaki, 136
  Sausage Bites, 47
  Sesame-Soy Meatballs, 49
  Soy-Sauced Chicken Wings, 51
  Spicy Lime Snack Mix, 38
  Spicy Wings with Avocado Salsa, 51
  Sweet-and-Sour Glazed Chicken
    Sausage Bites, 47
  Toasted Nuts with Rosemary, 38
  Tropical Fruit and Nut Party Mix, 122
Apples
  Apple-Cranberry Deep-Dish Pie, 80
  Apple Frosting, 109
  Apples and Cheese Spoon Bread, 72
  Baked Apples, 91
  Buttery Cider Glazed Turkey, 12
  Molasses-Fig Baked Apples, 91
  Spiced Apple Drops, 109
Apricots
  Apricot-Almond Crunch Pie, 80
  Apricot Icing, 73
  Brandied Apricot Loaves, 73
Au gratin and scalloped dishes, about, 25

B

Bacon
  All-Time Favorite Quiche Lorraine, 64
  Brunch Egg Casserole, 59
  Cucumber and Bacon Dip, 137
  pancetta, about, 9
  Rumaki, 136
  Wilted Greens and Poached Egg Salad, 9
  Wilted Spinach Salad, 8
Beans
  Green Beans Amandine, 139
  Green Beans Parmesan, 26
  Party Nachos, 46
Beef
  Celebration Roast, 16
  Citrus Corned Beef Sandwiches, 153
  Hot and Spicy Sloppy Joes, 127
  Hot Reuben Dip, 41
  Sesame-Soy Meatballs, 49
  Spicy Beef Stew with Pesto Mashed
    Potatoes, 126
  Super-Simple Beef Stew, 126
Beets
  Harvard Beets, 27
  peeling, tip for, 27
  Sweet-Glazed Beets with Crème Fraîche, 27
Biscuits, Cottage Cheese-Chive, 69
Biscuits, Up-and-Down, 77
Bourbon-Infused Honey, 140
Braising foods, 14
Brandied Apricot Loaves, 73
Bread pudding
  Chocolate-Cherry Bread Pudding, 90
  Christmas Morning Strata, 62
Breads. *See also* Coffee Cakes
  Apples and Cheese Spoon Bread, 72

Blue Cheese and Walnut Focaccia, 70
  Brandied Apricot Loaves, 73
  Cheddar Batter Bread, 68
  Classic Cinnamon Rolls, 76
  Cottage Cheese-Chive Biscuits, 69
  Creamy Cinnamon Rolls, 76
  Dill Batter Bread, 69
  Feather Rolls, 71
  Onion and Olive Focaccia, 70
  Onion-Cheese Supper Bread, 128
  Peanut Butter Banana Bread, 119
  Raspberry-Almond Rolls, 75
  Reduced-Fat Stuffed French Toast, 55
  Spoon Bread Soufflé, 72
  Stuffed French Toast, 55
  Up-and-Down Biscuits, 77
Breakfast and Brunch
  All-Time Favorite Quiche Lorraine, 64
  Baked Eggs with Cheese and Basil Sauce, 59
  Baked Italian Omelet, 63
  Brunch Egg Casserole, 59
  Cheese and Mushroom Brunch Eggs, 61
  Chocolate Chip Pancakes with Raspberry
    Syrup, 57
  Christmas Morning Strata, 62
  Cinnamon Breakfast Muffins, 58
  Citrus-Mint Kiss, 55
  Cream Cheese-Raspberry Coffee Cake, 58
  Double-Batch Brunch Eggs, 61
  Easy Cheese and Mushroom Brunch Eggs, 61
  Mushroom, Spinach, and Havarti Quiche, 64
  Peanut Waffles with Butterscotch Sauce, 56
  Puffed Oven Pancake, 56
  Reduced-Fat Stuffed French Toast, 55
  Sausage, Broccoli, and Eggs Brunch
    Casserole, 62
  Stuffed French Toast, 55
  Turkey Benedict, 60
  Warm Citrus Fruit with Brown Sugar, 54
Brownies
  Marmalade-Nut Brownies, 111
  Trilevel Brownies, 110
  Triple-Chocolate Coffee Brownies, 111
Butternut Squash Gratin with Creamed
  Spinach, 23
Butterscotch Pudding, 132
Butterscotch Sauce, 56

C

Cakes
  Best-Ever Chocolate Cake, 90
  Busy-Day Cake, 133
  Chocolate-Mousse Torte, 88
  Christmas Pound Cake, 118
  Cocoa Ripple Ring, 74
  Cowboy Coffee Cake, 74
  Cream Cheese-Raspberry Coffee Cake, 58
  Grapefruit Chiffon Cake, 86
  Mocha and Cherry Cake, 88
  Peppermint Swirl Chiffon Cake, 86
Candies
  Buttery Cashew Brittle, 118
  Chocolaty Candy Cane Drops, 114
  Hazelnut Toffee, 117
  Mocha Fudge, 114
  Snowy White Truffles, 116
  Toasted Nutty White Fudge, 115
  White Christmas Cherry-Almond Fudge, 116
  White Coconut Fudge, 115
Celery Seed Dressing, 137
Chalet Cookie Church, 146
Cheddar cheese
  Apples and Cheese Spoon Bread, 72
  Brunch Egg Casserole, 59
  Cheddar Batter Bread, 68
  Cheesy Chicken-Corn Chowder, 128
  Christmas Morning Strata, 62
  Curried Chutney and Cheddar Cheese
    Logs, 42

Goldilocks Potatoes, 16
  Leeks au Gratin, 24
  Onion-Cheese Supper Bread, 128
  Party Nachos, 46
  Potatoes with Caramelized Onions and
    Ham Gratin, 152
  Smoky Cheese Ball, 42
Cheese. *See also* Cheddar cheese; Cream cheese
  All-Time Favorite Quiche Lorraine, 64
  Baked Eggs with Cheese and Basil Sauce, 59
  Baked Italian Omelet, 63
  Belgian Creamed Potatoes, 19
  Blue Cheese and Walnut Focaccia, 70
  Butternut Squash Gratin with Creamed
    Spinach, 23
  Cheese and Mushroom Brunch Eggs, 61
  Chile-Cheese Enchiladas, 154
  Citrus Corned Beef Sandwiches, 153
  Coq au Vin Rosettes, 153
  Cottage Cheese-Chive Biscuits, 69
  Crab and Poblano Soup, 11
  Creamed Onions, 25
  Double-Batch Brunch Eggs, 61
  Easy Cheese and Mushroom Brunch Eggs, 61
  Golden Cheese Wheel, 45
  Gouda Pecan Spread, 44
  Green Beans Parmesan, 26
  Hot Reuben Dip, 41
  Individual Turkey Pizzas, 130
  Lasagna circa 1953, 150
  Mushroom, Spinach, and Havarti Quiche, 64
  Olive Cheese Ball, 42
  Parmesan, buying, 26
  Parmesan Risotto, 142
  Phyllo-Wrapped Hazelnut and Brie, 46
  Red Pepper Lasagna, 150
  Sausage, Broccoli, and Eggs Brunch
    Casserole, 62
  Savory Ham and Eggs, 131
  Scalloped Spinach, 25
  selecting, for appetizers, 35
  Swiss Corn Bake, 26
  Three-Cheese Scalloped Potatoes, 19
  Three-Cheese Ziti and Smoked Chicken
    Casserole, 151
  Turkey Skillet Pie, 130
  Twice-Baked Jarlsberg Potatoes, 20
  Verde Chicken Enchiladas, 154
Cheesecake, Maple-Pumpkin, 85
Cherry Glazed Pork, 14
Cherry-Nut Rum Balls, 102
Cherry Winks, 106
Chicken
  Cheesy Chicken-Corn Chowder, 128
  Coq au Vin Rosettes, 153
  Crab-Stuffed Chicken, 138
  Deep-Dish Chicken Pie, 129
  Prosciutto-Stuffed Chicken Breasts with
    Pears, 142
  Rumaki, 136
  Soy-Sauced Chicken Wings, 51
  Spicy Wings with Avocado Salsa, 51
  Sweet-and-Sour Glazed Chicken Sausage
    Bites, 47
  Three-Cheese Ziti and Smoked Chicken
    Casserole, 151
  Verde Chicken Enchiladas, 154
Chiles
  Chile-Cheese Enchiladas, 154
  Crab and Poblano Soup, 11
  Hot and Spicy Sloppy Joes, 127
  Party Nachos, 46
  Spicy Salsa, 154
  working with, 11, 60
Chocolate
  Best-Ever Chocolate Cake, 90
  Brownie Meringues, 104
  Chocolate-Butter Mint Fondue, 140
  Chocolaty Candy Cane Drops, 114

Chocolate-Cherry Bread Pudding, 90
Chocolate Chip Pancakes with Raspberry
   Syrup, 57
Chocolate Crème Brûlée, 143
Chocolate Ganache Glaze, 87
Chocolate Glaze, 74
Chocolate-Mint Creams, 101
Chocolate-Mousse Torte, 88
Chocolate-Peanut Blowouts, 106
Chocolate-Peanut Mousse Pie, 82
Chocolate Rum and Butter Cookies, 97
Chocolate-Sour Cream Frosting, 90
Chocolate Truffle Winks, 107
Chocolaty Bourbon and Nut Pie, 81
Chocolaty Candy Cane Drops, 114
Cocoa Ripple Ring, 74
French Pistachio Buttercreams, 103
Fudge Ribbon Pie, 83
Hazelnut Toffee, 117
Macaroon Brownie Pie, 82
Marmalade-Nut Brownies, 111
Mocha and Cherry Cake, 88
Mocha Frosting, 88
Mocha Fudge, 114
Orange-Chocolate Rounds, 98
Orange-Mocha Cream Liqueur, 121
Peanut Butter Banana Bread, 119
Peanut Butter Blossoms, 100
Peanut Butter Munchies, 99
Ricotta Filling (for cake), 88
Trilevel Brownies, 110
Triple-Chocolate Coffee Brownies, 111
Ultimate Nut and Chocolate Chip Tart, 84
Chowder, Cheesy Chicken-Corn, 128
Church, Chalet Cookie, 146
Chutney, Pear-Cherry, 120
Chutney and Cheddar Cheese Logs, Curried, 42
Coconut
Busy-Day Cake, 133
Calypso Shrimp Skewers, 48
Curried Chutney and Cheddar Cheese
   Logs, 42
Golden Macaroons, 105
Macaroon Brownie Pie, 82
Snowdrift Coconut Cream Pie, 84
Snowy White Truffles, 116
Toasted Nutty White Fudge, 115
White Coconut Fudge, 115
Coffee
Dublin Eggnog, 34
Mocha and Cherry Cake, 88
Mocha Frosting, 88
Mocha Fudge, 114
Orange-Mocha Cream Liqueur, 121
Triple-Chocolate Coffee Brownies, 111
Coffee cakes
Cocoa Ripple Ring, 74
Cowboy Coffee Cake, 74
Cream Cheese-Raspberry Coffee Cake, 58
Cookies and Bars
Almond-Cinnamon Cookies, 98
Brownie Meringues, 104
Chalet Cookie Church, 146
Cherry-Nut Rum Balls, 102
Cherry Winks, 106
Chocolate-Mint Creams, 101
Chocolate-Peanut Blowouts, 106
Chocolate Rum and Butter Cookies, 97
Chocolate Truffle Winks, 107
Coffeehouse Crisps, 109
dough, freezing, 96
dough, making ahead, 96
drop cookies, about, 107
French Pistachio Buttercreams, 103
Golden Macaroons, 105
Hickory Nut Macaroons, 105
Key Lime Snowballs, 102
Marmalade-Nut Brownies, 111
Orange-Chocolate Rounds, 98

Patterns, Chalet Cookie Church, 156
Peanut Butter Blossoms, 100
Peanut Butter Munchies, 99
Pecan Crispies, 108
Pink Peppermint Twists, 104
Rainbow Cookies in a Jar, 120
Raspberry-Almond Tassies, 110
Spiced Apple Drops, 109
Sugar Cookie Dough, 94
Sugar Cookie Star Cutouts, 96
Toy Cookie Bouquet, 94
Trilevel Brownies, 110
Triple-Chocolate Coffee Brownies, 111
White Chocolate Kisses, 100
Corn Bake, Swiss, 26
Cornmeal Pastry, 65
Crab and Poblano Soup, 11
Crab Bisque, 10
Crab-Stuffed Chicken, 138
Cranberries
Apple-Cranberry Deep-Dish Pie, 80
Berry-Burgundy Glazed Ham, 13
Citrus Cranberry Ice Ring, 36
Cranberry Cosmopolitan, 141
Cranberry Fluff, 30
Cranberry-Ginger Relish, 13
Cranberry-Pineapple Punch, 36
Cream Cheese
Cream Cheese Icing, 76
Cream Cheese-Raspberry Coffee Cake, 58
Grapefruit-Cream Cheese Frosting, 86
Maple-Pumpkin Cheesecake, 85
Olive Cheese Ball, 42
Reduced-Fat Stuffed French Toast, 55
Smoky Cheese Ball, 42
Stuffed French Toast, 55
Crème Brûlée, Chocolate, 143
Crumb Topping, 81
Cucumber and Bacon Dip, 137
Curried Chutney and Cheddar Cheese Logs, 42

D
Date-Nut Pudding, 133
Decorations, food, 27
Desserts. *See also* Cakes; Candies; Cookies and
   Bars; Pies
Baked Apples, 91
Butterscotch Pudding, 132
Chocolate-Butter Mint Fondue, 140
Chocolate-Cherry Bread Pudding, 90
Chocolate Crème Brûlée, 143
Cranberry Fluff, 30
Date-Nut Pudding, 133
Maple-Pumpkin Cheesecake, 85
Molasses-Fig Baked Apples, 91
Raspberry Sauce, 119
Ultimate Nut and Chocolate Chip Tart, 84
Dill Batter Bread, 69
Dips and Spreads
Bourbon-Infused Honey, 140
Chocolate-Butter Mint Fondue, 140
Cucumber and Bacon Dip, 137
Curried Chutney and Cheddar Cheese
   Logs, 42
Four-Onion Dip, 41
Gouda Pecan Spread, 44
Green Goddess Dip, 39
Hot Reuben Dip, 41
Olive Cheese Ball, 42
Smoky Cheese Ball, 42
Drinks. *See also* Punch
Almond Cream Liqueur, 121
Buttered Cranberry Cocktail, 136
Citrus-Mint Kiss, 55
Cranberry Cosmopolitan, 141
Dublin Eggnog, 34
Orange-Mocha Cream Liqueur, 121
Very Berry Martinis, 121
White Strawberry Sangria, 34

E
Eggnog, Dublin, 34
Eggnog Punch, Orange-, 34
Eggs
Baked Eggs with Cheese and Basil Sauce, 59
Baked Italian Omelet, 63
Brunch Egg Casserole, 59
Cheese and Mushroom Brunch Eggs, 61
Double-Batch Brunch Eggs, 61
Easy Cheese and Mushroom Brunch Eggs, 61
hard-cooked eggs, preparing, 24
Leeks au Gratin, 24
poached eggs, preparing, 60
Sausage, Broccoli, and Eggs Brunch
   Casserole, 62
Savory Ham and Eggs, 131
Turkey Benedict, 60
Wilted Greens and Poached Egg Salad, 9
Wilted Spinach Salad, 8
Enchiladas, Chile-Cheese, 154
Enchiladas, Verde Chicken, 154

F
First courses
Citrus-Avocado Salad, 137
Crab and Poblano Soup, 11
Crab Bisque, 10
Mixed Greens with Cardamom-Curry
   Dressing, 141
Orange-Fennel Autumn Salad, 8
Wilted Greens and Poached Egg Salad, 9
Wilted Spinach Salad, 8
Focaccia, Blue Cheese and Walnut, 70
Focaccia, Onion and Olive, 70
Fondue, Chocolate-Butter Mint, 140
French Toast, Reduced-Fat Stuffed, 55
French Toast, Stuffed, 55
Frostings
Apple Frosting, 109
Chocolate-Sour Cream Frosting, 90
Grapefruit-Cream Cheese Frosting, 86
Mocha Frosting, 88
Fruits. *See also* specific fruits
Fruited Ice Ring, 35
Fruit Salade Flan, 31
Ginger Marinated Fruit, 30
Pork Roast with Harvest Fruits, 14
Puffed Oven Pancake, 56
Spiced Fruit Punch, 36
Tropical Fruit and Nut Party Mix, 122
Warm Citrus Fruit with Brown Sugar, 54
Fudge
Mocha Fudge, 114
Toasted Nutty White Fudge, 115
White Christmas Cherry-Almond Fudge, 116
White Coconut Fudge, 115

G
Gift Foods. *See also* Candies
Almond Cream Liqueur, 121
Bridge Party Mix, 122
Buttery Cashew Brittle, 118
Chocolaty Candy Cane Drops, 114
Christmas Pound Cake, 118
Hazelnut Toffee, 117
Mocha Fudge, 114
Orange-Mocha Cream Liqueur, 121
Peanut Butter Banana Bread, 119
Peanut Butter Glaze, 119
Pear-Cherry Chutney, 120
Rainbow Cookies in a Jar, 120
Raspberry Sauce, 119
Snowy White Truffles, 116
Toasted Nutty White Fudge, 115
Tropical Fruit and Nut Party Mix, 122
Very Berry Martinis, 121
White Christmas Cherry-Almond Fudge, 116
White Coconut Fudge, 115